JOHN

JOHN

Storyteller, Interpreter, Evangelist

WARREN CARTER

 HENDRICKSON PUBLISHERS

John: Storyteller, Interpreter, Evangelist
© 2006 by Hendrickson Publishers, Inc.
P. O. Box 3473
Peabody, Massachusetts 01961-3473

ISBN-13: 978-1-56563-523-4
ISBN-10: 1-56563-523-X

Except where otherwise noted, Scripture quotations are from the New Revised Standard Version of the Bible, copyright © 1989 by the Division of Christian Education of the National Council of the Churches of Christ in the United States of America. Used by permission. All rights reserved.

Printed in the United States of America

First Printing — June 2006

Cover Art: Makoto Fujimura. "Zero Summer." Mineral Pigments and Gold on Kumohada Paper. Photograph by Ed Gorn.

"*Zero Summer* imagines the unimaginable horror of Hiroshima and Nagasaki, and yet points to epiphanic awakening that transcends human imagination at the same time. T. S. Eliot, who coined this term in his 'Four Quartets,' longed for that eternal summer, birthed out of the 'still point,' where imagination is met with grace and truth." —Makoto Fujimura

Library of Congress Cataloging-in-Publication Data

Carter, Warren, 1955–
    John : storyteller, interpreter, evangelist / Warren Carter.
        p. cm.
    Includes bibliographical references (p.   ) and indexes.
    ISBN-13: 978-1-56563-523-4 (alk. paper)
    ISBN-10: 1-56563-523-X (alk. paper)
    1. Bible. N.T. John—Criticism, interpretation, etc. I. Title.
    BS2615.52.C37 2006
    226.5'06—dc22
                    2006003268

Contents

John: Interpreter

John: Evangelist

Preface

This book is an introduction to the fourth gospel in the New Testament, the Gospel of John. It examines three aspects of John's gospel: its story of Jesus (chs. 1–6; genre, plot, characters, language, style), its interpretation of existing materials about Jesus for changing circumstances (chs. 7–8; sources, use of Scripture, historical context), and its formulation of the good news of Jesus (chs. 9–10; who John is, Johannine theology). That is, chapters 1–6 examine the work of John the storyteller, chapters 7–8 explore the work of John the interpreter, and chapters 9–10 discuss the work of John the evangelist. A postscript explores some implications of reading John's gospel in our contemporary, multireligious world.

The book is written for college and seminary students who are beginning New Testament studies or taking an elective after doing an introductory course. It is also written for clergy seeking resources for preaching and teaching, and for laity, especially Bible study groups who like to engage a topic in some depth. In addition to providing familiarity with central matters related to the gospel, it also engages the two dominant methods used in current interpretive work, namely, narrative and historical approaches to John's gospel. It thus includes both the synchronic[1] and the diachronic[2] approaches to the gospel, which pervade contemporary Johannine scholarship. Although the book treats narrative or literary matters first (chs. 1–6), readers could begin with the historical matters of chapters 7–8. I have sought to be both clear and as comprehensive as possible in covering significant issues in contemporary interpretation, though complete coverage is impossible.

1 – linguistics: facts of a language system as it exist at a point in time without reference to its history

2 – study of changes in a language system over a period of time

In addition to its synthesis of existing material, the book introduces readers to a neglected element in Johannine interpretation, John's negotiation of the Roman imperial world. To engage the "spiritual gospel" in the context of the Roman imperial world will seem strange to some readers, especially those who are convinced that religion has nothing to do with politics and that any interpretation suggesting such a link must have an agenda foreign to John's gospel (as though nonpolitical, "spiritual" readings do not have an agenda!). This element, though important, nevertheless constitutes a minor part of this volume. *John and Empire* (Harrisburg, Pa.: Trinity Press International, forthcoming) will elaborate this dimension in a more sustained discussion.

Limits of space have prevented offering a detailed history of scholarship,[1] and I am very aware that every part of this book could be expanded at great length. But in the interests of providing an accessible introduction, I have sought to provide manageable discussion that names at least some of the key issues. The interpretive literature on John's gospel is wonderfully extensive, diverse, and insightful. Regrettably, only partial bibliography is possible, but I have endeavored to provide enough resources, especially English-language ones, in endnotes to enable readers to pursue issues profitably. I do not, of course, pretend that this discussion, given limits of space, is comprehensive or representative of all voices and perspectives.

I wish to thank three people in particular for their contribution to this book. Professors Sharon Ringe, Frank Moloney, and Bob Kysar graciously read an early version of the manuscript and provided me with valuable and insightful feedback and encouragement. I am very grateful for their input, time, energy, wisdom, and expertise. Together they have made immense contributions to contemporary Johannine scholarship, as these pages attest. The book's remaining inadequacies, of course, are my responsibility.

I also wish to thank Lee Franklin, Ashkea Herron, and Ashley Cheung for their insightful and generous contribution to the manuscript. Likewise, Shirley Decker-Lucke has been a skilled and patient editor. I am grateful for the opportunity to contribute another volume to Hendrickson's quartet of books on the Gospels: W. Carter, *Matthew: Storyteller, Interpreter, Evangelist* (rev. ed., 2004); F. Moloney, *Mark: Storyteller, Interpreter, Evangelist* (2004); and M. Parsons, *Luke: Storyteller, Interpreter, Evangelist* (forthcoming).

Warren Carter

Notes

1. For maps of contemporary scholarship, see R. Kysar, *The Fourth Evangelist and His Gospel: An Examination of Contemporary Scholarship* (Minneapolis: Augsburg, 1975); R. Kysar, "The Fourth Gospel: A Report on Recent Research," *ANRW* 25.3:2389–480; G. Sloyan, *What Are They Saying about John?* (New York: Paulist, 1991); H. K. Nelson, "Johannine Research," in *New Readings in John: Literary and Theological Perspectives from the Scandinavian Conference on the Fourth Gospel, Arhus, 1997* (ed. J. Nissen and S. Pedersen; JSNTSup 182; Sheffield, Eng.: Sheffield Academic Press, 1999), 11–30; D. M. Smith, "Johannine Studies since Bultmann," *WW* 21 (2001): 343–51; U. Schnelle, "Recent Views of John's Gospel," *WW* 21 (2001): 352–59; R. Brown, *An Introduction to the Gospel of John* (ed. F. Moloney; New York: Doubleday, 2003), 26–39 and passim.

Abbreviations

General

B.C.E.	before the Common Era
ca.	circa
C.E.	Common Era
cf.	*confer*, compare
ch(s).	chapter(s)
diss.	dissertation
ed(s).	editor(s), edited by
e.g.	*exempli gratia*, for example
esp.	especially
et al.	*et alii*, and others
etc.	*et cetera*, and the rest
i.e.	*id est*, that is
ibid.	*ibidem*, in the same place
lit.	literally
n(n).	note(s)
NRSV	New Revised Standard Version
p(p).	page(s)
repr.	reprinted
rev.	revised (by)
RSV	Revised Standard Version
v(v).	verse(s)
vol(s).	volume(s)

Hebrew Bible/Old Testament

Gen	Genesis
Exod	Exodus
Lev	Leviticus
Num	Numbers
Deut	Deuteronomy
Josh	Joshua
1–2 Sam	1–2 Samuel
1–2 Kgs	1–2 Kings
1–2 Chr	1–2 Chronicles
Neh	Nehemiah
Ps	Psalms
Prov	Proverbs
Isa	Isaiah
Jer	Jeremiah
Ezek	Ezekiel
Dan	Daniel
Hos	Hosea
Mic	Micah
Zeph	Zephaniah
Zech	Zechariah

New Testament

Matt	Matthew
Rom	Romans
1–2 Cor	1–2 Corinthians
Gal	Galatians
Eph	Ephesians
1–2 Tim	1–2 Timothy
1–2 Pet	1–2 Peter
Rev	Revelation

Apocrypha and Septuagint

Bar	Baruch
Sir	Sirach/Ecclesiasticus
Wis	Wisdom of Solomon

Old Testament Pseudepigrapha

2 Bar.	*2 Baruch (Syriac Apocalypse)*
1 En.	*1 Enoch (Ethiopic Apocalypse)*

Josephus

Life	*The Life*
Ant.	*Jewish Antiquities*
J.W.	*Jewish War*

Ancient Christian and Non-Christian Writers

Aristotle
Poet.	*Poetica*
	Poetics

Eusebius
Hist. eccl.	*Historia ecclesiastica*
	Ecclesiastical History

Irenaeus
Haer.	*Adversus haereses*
	Against Heresies

Virgil
Aen.	*Aeneid*

Secondary Sources

ABD	Anchor Bible Dictionary. Edited by D. N. Freedman. 6 vols. New York, 1992
ANRW	*Aufstieg und Niedergang der römischen Welt: Geschichte und Kultur Roms im Spiegel der neueren Forschung.* Edited by H. Temporini and W. Haase Berlin, 1972–
BETL	Bibliotheca ephemeridum theologicarum lovaniensium
BSac	*Bibliotheca sacra*
CBQ	*Catholic Biblical Quarterly*
ExpTim	*Expository Times*
JBL	*Journal of Biblical Literature*

JSNT	*Journal for the Study of the New Testament*
JSNTSup	Journal for the Study of the New Testament: Supplement Series
Neot	*Neotestamentica*
NovT	*Novum Testamentum*
NTS	*New Testament Studies*
SBLDS	Society of Biblical Literature Dissertation Series
SBLMS	Society of Biblical Literature Monograph Series
SBLSymS	Society of Biblical Literature Symposium Series
TDNT	*Theological Dictionary of the New Testament.* Edited by G. Kittel and G. Friedrich. Translated by G. W. Bromiley. 10 vols. Grand Rapids, 1964–1976
WW	*Word and World*

PART ONE

JOHN: STORYTELLER

CHAPTER 1

The Genre of John's Gospel

"These are written so that ... through believing you may have life in his name" (20:31). This statement of the gospel's purpose appears near its end. Such a claim invites us to explore the text in order to learn more about what has been written and about the "life" that this gospel offers its readers. In part 1 we will investigate these issues: What sort of writing is the gospel (its genre; ch. 1)? How does it present the story of Jesus (its plot; ch. 2)? Who are its characters (chs. 3–4)? What sort of language does it use (ch. 5)? What sort of style does it employ (ch. 6)? In exploring these issues related to "these [things that] are written," we will also build our understanding of the "life" that the gospel presents. What constitutes this life? Is it individual or communal, spiritual or physical? What relationship does it have to existing societal structures and norms?

This chapter begins to answer these questions by examining one aspect of the "these [things that] are written." What sort of literature are we reading when we read John's gospel? What is its genre?[1]

Genre

John's gospel explicitly identifies itself in very general terms as a "book" (20:30). This term, located near the end of the document, can refer to all sorts of writings, and so it is not a very helpful indicator of what we are reading. Rather, we will need to look for other clues in the document to identify what sort of book this is.

As readers, we determine a communication's genre—whether written or oral—from the various literary conventions or traits that a speaker or author employs in creating the work's form and content.[2] We observe these conventions or features from the beginning of a work (for a written work, its cover, title, a contents page if it has one, chapter headings, layout, etc.) and confirm or modify our recognition of its genre from subsequent features, such as the settings for events, the types of events, the characters, conflicts, and so forth. These literary conventions or clusters of features signal the sort of work we are engaging. From the cluster of features and from our experience of other literature, we decide what sort of work we are encountering, what we can reasonably expect from it, and what sort of "work" or roles we might have to perform as readers.

Discerning the genre of a piece of literature matters because it offers us clues on how to read appropriately. Getting the genre wrong will inevitably mean little chance of our making satisfactory sense of what we're reading. If I think I am reading a romance, for example, when in fact I am reading a mystery thriller, I have misunderstood the conventions of the mystery novel that the author uses, and my expectations for the story will be sadly disappointed. I will misinterpret the conventions and so miss what they are signaling. In the romance, declarations of love might be heartwarming; in the mystery thriller they might be deadly. In a romance we are likely to find them comforting and pleasing, especially since the two lovers have usually had to overcome various obstacles to their love. But in a mystery thriller, when we know that nothing is quite as it seems, we might find such declarations suspenseful, frightening, false, and, finally, fatal. A book might deliberately combine features of both mysteries and romances to create uncertainty and tension. James Bond movies combine characteristics from several genres to create suspense, romance, and comedy.

Determining a work's genre thus involves recognizing the various literary conventions and traits that are employed. Identifying the work's traits or conventions guides us in our efforts to make appropriate sense of what we are reading.

The Genre of John's Gospel

What, then, is the genre or genres of John's gospel?[3] The question might seem unnecessary, since we have been referring to the work as a "gospel." But this simply takes us in a circle back to the starting point: what is a gospel?

The term "gospel" has two meanings in relation to the early Christian writings. First, "gospel" can refer to certain beliefs and experiences about God's saving work encountered in Jesus. In some instances, these affirmations are not immediately specified, presumably because they are known to the audience, elaborated elsewhere in the writing, and/or not relevant to the immediate point the writer is making (see Rom 15:16; Gal 1:6–7; Eph 1:13; 2 Tim 2:8–9). But sometimes the writer immediately explains the term, as Paul does in Rom 1:16–17: "I am not ashamed of the gospel; it is the power of God for salvation to everyone who has faith, to the Jew first and also to the Greek."

Second, "gospel" can refer to written texts, such as John. By one count, thirty-four such writings survive from the early centuries of the Christian movement, but only four of them are included in the Christian New Testament—the gospels according to Matthew, Mark, Luke, and John.[4] None of these New Testament documents calls itself a gospel.[5] Later Christian readers applied the term to them because they saw the four documents doing something similar: telling the story of Jesus from the perspective of faith and for an audience (or congregation) of believers. According to one definition, "a Gospel is a narrative of the public career of Jesus, his passion and death, told in order to affirm or confirm the faith of Christian believers in the Risen Lord."[6]

If later readers designate the genre of John to be a gospel, what genre might its first readers, late in the first century, have assigned to it to guide their engagement with it? What sorts of literature did it resemble?

Not Primarily History

Some people have viewed John as providing an eyewitness account of Jesus' life, a historical record of what he said and did. But such expectations for the gospel are not sustainable for a number of reasons. Most obviously, John 20:31 confirms that the gospel's author is not primarily writing history. Rather, it writes about Jesus from the perspective of faith and for believers.

> These are written so that you may come to believe that Jesus is the Messiah, the Son of God, and that through believing you may have life in his name.

As we will see in chapters 7–9, below, probably about fifty or sixty years separate the time of Jesus from the time of the gospel's writing; this makes the survival of eyewitnesses unlikely. There are also telltale signs that our version of the gospel has been expanded and elaborated; this suggests that the gospel has developed through multiple editions and/or employed multiple sources.[7] We will also have to think about the relationship between John's gospel and the very different presentations of Jesus in the gospels of Matthew, Mark, and Luke, which are called the Synoptic Gospels. Claims, then, of an eyewitness account are not convincing.

Still, scholars agree that although John is not an eyewitness account, it certainly contains historical information about the life and ministry of Jesus. They have debated how much historical information can be demonstrated, the criteria by which to identify it, and the implications of its presence in (or absence from) the narrative. There are essentially three views.

1. Scholars who emphasize considerable historical authenticity[8] appeal to such factors as the significant similarities between John's contents and the Synoptic Gospels,[9] compatibility with the language and themes in the Dead Sea Scrolls,[10] and the gospel's "astonishingly accurate geographical, historical, and religious details" about Jerusalem and Judaism.[11] These details include references to places in Jerusalem, such as the pool of Siloam (9:7), the Kidron Valley (18:1), the archaeologically verified pool in 5:2, and the pavement in 19:13.[12]

2. At the other end of the spectrum, the Jesus Seminar, which applies a range of criteria to the sayings and actions attributed to Jesus in John's gospel, finds only 4:44b to be probably spoken by Jesus ("A prophet gets no respect on his own turf"). In addition, the Seminar decided that John's gospel includes only a few other pieces of "historically reliable information" that is "virtually certain" or "probably reliable." This information includes Jesus as a former follower of John the Baptist who attracted some of John's followers (1:35–51), that Jesus was arrested (18:12b), and taken to Pilate (18:28) who had him beaten (19:1) and crucified (19:16, 18).[13]

3. Scholars occupying the middle ground recognize considerably greater continuities between Jesus and John's presentation, in both what Jesus says and what Jesus does.[14] For instance, C. H. Dodd finds "mini" or kernel parables that derive from Jesus at the heart of some of Jesus' sayings and discourses in John, such as the good shepherd (10:1–5) and the grain of wheat (12:24).[15] Many scholars see other actions (at least in some [unrecoverable?] form) as likely being authentic to the historical Jesus. One scholar offers a list, acknowledged as incomplete, that includes traditions about Jesus and about Jesus' followers: gathering dis-

ciples, a number of whom are known by name (John 1); conflict or competition with John the Baptist; challenging the temple (2:13–17); a visit to Samaria; healings; Sabbath disputes; a Nazareth origin and brothers (7:1–10); an awareness of being commissioned or sent from God, who is his Father; numerous visits to Jerusalem; accusations of being demon possessed and/or leading the people astray as a false prophet (7:45–52; 8:48); crucifixion by Pilate.[16]

But although they do not dispute that the gospel employs historical information, most recognize that the gospel is not primarily concerned with the conventional historical tasks of providing accurate and verifiable historical information and of analyzing the causes and effects of historical events. Instead it is much more concerned to present this information in relation to, and as part of, its much larger agenda, namely, to proclaim the significance of Jesus as the one who makes available "life" to those who entrust themselves to him. That is, the gospel is not passing on information about Jesus for its own sake or trying to understand the person of Jesus in a disinterested way. Rather it is deeply invested in the importance of Jesus. It seeks to elicit and sustain the believing response of its readers because it thinks nothing is more important in the whole world—this one and the next. In doing so, the gospel is as much concerned with the present (and future) as with the past, and as much concerned with the response of the reader as with the material it presents. This is more like preaching than historical writing.

Claims, then, of an eyewitness account are not convincing. But even if we were reading an eyewitness account, even if someone had been operating a video camera while Jesus conducted his ministry, we readers would have to recognize the partial nature of John's story and the particular faith perspective that selects its content and shapes its telling. Moreover we would have to recognize the pastoral goals of securing faith and transmitting life to the reader that shape the story. These observations will help us to determine the gospel's genre accurately.

Not a Unique Genre

A long tradition of scholarship has claimed that the gospels form their own genre. Some have argued that the gospels are without parallel in other contemporary literature, that they are "of their own kind" (*sui generis*).[17] This argument appeals primarily to the unique content of the gospels and their proclamation about the identity of Jesus as the risen

Christ and Lord in whom people are to believe in order to know life. This proclamation about Jesus in story form utilizes traditions about Jesus that are theologically and pastorally interpreted. The gospels comprise "tradition remembered and interpreted in the light of faith."[18] Ultimately, so the argument goes, the gospels' content makes them unique.

Such a description helpfully identifies the interconnection between traditions about Jesus and interpretations of his significance evident in the gospels. But such content and technique cannot be the basis for determining their genre or for deciding that they are like no other written document. Many different kinds of writing present material about a historical figure with a particular spin to it. And many kinds of writing want to either persuade readers to their point of view or confirm and strengthen the commitments that readers already have. This is evident in historical studies, biographies, newspaper articles, political propaganda, and sermons, to name a few examples.

Moreover, from a literary point of view, the claim that the gospels form their own genre and are unlike any other makes no sense. If they were unique, no writer could create them and no audience would understand them. Every writer is constrained and shaped by the conventions and genres of his or her literary culture. A writer can, as many great artists have done, creatively extend and stretch existing genres. But inventing a new genre is culturally impossible. Moreover, even if a writer did somehow manage to invent a unique genre, no reader would comprehend it because, as we have seen, genres depend on the ability of readers to recognize the cluster of features that constitute it and to be guided by those features in engaging the work.

Not a Jewish Theodicy Narrative

A further suggestion about the genre of John's gospel comes from Margaret Davies, who thinks that the clue to its genre lies in its relationship to the Jewish Scriptures.[19] She points out that the gospel shares numerous theological assumptions, language, and stylistic features with scriptural narratives, such as those concerning Moses and the exodus, Elijah and Elisha, Israel and its kings, and wisdom's presence in the world. She concludes that the "genre of the Fourth Gospel, therefore, like that of scriptural narratives, is a theodicy, a vindication of divine providence in view of the existence of evil."[20]

Davies is right to draw attention to these connections with the Jewish Scriptures. There is no doubt that John's gospel is deeply indebted to the Scriptures. We will return to this dimension in chapter 7, below. And she is right to underline that God's purposes provide the gospel's central perspective. But Davies is not convincing in claiming theodicy as the genre of the Scriptures she cites and of John's gospel. The term "theodicy" traditionally refers to efforts "to defend divine justice in the face of aberrant phenomena that appear to indicate the deity's indifference or hostility toward virtuous people."[21] In these terms theodicy is not a genre but a theme or topic or part of the content that writings of various genres might engage. Concern with the questions of theodicy does not thereby determine a genre. Matters of theodicy could be included in a comedy, a tragedy, or a philosophical or theological essay.

The inappropriateness of claiming theodicy as a genre is evident in the various scriptural literatures that Davies discusses. In outlining connections with the Moses story, she refers to Exodus, Leviticus, Numbers, and Deuteronomy. In appealing to Wisdom literature, she identifies Job, Proverbs, Sirach, Wisdom of Solomon, and Baruch. Assuming for a moment that these quite different writings may have a common *thematic* concern to understand God's strange and/or apparently indifferent ways in an evil world (and this assumption needs much more consideration), a quick read of Exodus and Proverbs illustrates that they are very different kinds of writing, including narratives, dialogues, and proverbs. And it seems difficult to cast John as a work in which God is "indifferent or hostile" when the gospel repeatedly declares God's sending of Jesus to reveal God's love for the world (3:16).

Ancient Biography

More persuasive than these three claims is the view that in reading John's gospel, we encounter a text that belongs to the genre of ancient biography, or *bios*. The adjective "ancient" has a key role in describing this genre. Ancient biographies differ from modern biographies and kiss-and-tell books in important ways. One crucial difference is that, as pre-Freud, ancient biographies did not focus on a person's internal processes and on the growth and development of their personality.[22] Rather, ancient biographies understood external actions to reveal a person's character or virtue (and vices). This did not rule out any concern with development, but it shifted the focus significantly.

Describing the features of ancient biographies, Richard Burridge notes that it is impossible to isolate this genre from several other types of literature.[23] Features of one genre are mixed with features from another. One genre exists in relationship to, and in some overlap with, neighboring genres. There is, for example, overlap between ancient biographies and moral philosophy, religious teaching, encomia, stories and novels, political beliefs, and histories.

In his discussion of ten ancient biographies, Burridge identifies the cluster of features that readers would have expected to find in works of this genre. He organizes these features under four divisions: opening features, subject, external features, and internal features.[24] Burridge analyzes the four canonical gospels, finds these features present, and concludes that John's gospel, like the other three, belongs to the genre of ancient biography.

Burridge identifies two conventional *opening features* in John:

1. Title: There is no original title for John's gospel, but the title "According to John," added probably in the second century, resembles the titles added to the other gospels. The addition of the same sort of title suggests that John is understood as the same literary genre.

2. Opening formulae/prologue: Like other biographies, John begins with a prologue, in this case a poetic or hymnic celebration of God's revelation through the "Word" (1:1–18). And as in other biographies, the name of the main character, Jesus Christ, is included at the end of the prologue (1:17), identifying him as the subject of the prologue. It also appears at the beginning of the subsequent narrative (1:20, 29–34, 35–37).

Under *subject,* Burridge identifies in John two other features of ancient biography:

1. Analysis of the verb's subjects: Biographies typically focus on the actions and words of their central character. In John, Jesus is the subject for more than 30 percent of the verbs, and more than half of the verbs in the gospel concern his deeds or words. Jesus, in both his deeds and his teaching, is the central focus of the narrative.

2. Allocation of space: More specifically, a number of biographies focus significant attention (about a quarter to a third of the narrative) on events surrounding the end of the subject's life. This is true for John's gospel, in which the last week of Jesus' life occupies about one-third of the narrative.

Burridge discusses seven *external features* typical of ancient biography and present in John:

1. Mode of representation: John is a continuous prose narrative that includes dialogues and extended discourses.

2. Size: John comprises 15,416 words, in the medium range of length for biographies.

3. Structure: John employs a basic chronological order to tell the story of Jesus, with discourse and dialogue material inserted into it.

4. Scale: John employs a narrow focus, with attention focused on the main subject, Jesus.

5. Literary units: Biographies, especially those concerning philosophers and teachers, typically employ three units—stories, dialogues, and speeches or discourses. John follows this pattern.

6. Use of sources: John probably employs some oral and/or written sources in making its presentation of Jesus. (Chapters 7–9, below, will discuss the sources that the gospel's author [or authors] may have interpreted and the editions through which the gospel may have developed.)

7. Methods of characterization: John presents Jesus' character through the narration of his words and actions. Occasionally it offers some insight into his inner thought world (e.g., 6:15).

Burridge identifies seven typical *internal features* in John:

1. Setting: The gospel's focus on its central character, Jesus, determines where things happen. Burridge notes that Jesus is absent from only 9 percent of the gospel's verses, and in most of these he is the subject of the conversation (e.g., 1:19–28; 7:45–52; 11:45–53, 55–57; 20:24–25).

2. Topics: Ancient biographies conventionally discuss five topics related to the central character: ancestry; birth and upbringing; great deeds; virtues; death and consequences. John covers the same range of topics, though with very minimal attention to the second, Jesus' birth and upbringing (cf. 1:46; 7:40–42, 52). The opening of the prologue traces his ancestry back to "the beginning . . . with God" (1:1–3). The gospel narrates at least seven or eight great deeds or signs: changing water to wine (2:1–11), healing the official's son (4:46–54) and the paralyzed man (5:2–15), feeding the crowd (6:1–14), walking on water (6:16–21), giving sight to the blind man (ch. 9), raising Lazarus (ch. 11), and miraculously catching many fish (21:1–14). Jesus' extensive teaching is a further notable act (chs. 3, 5, 6, 13–17). Jesus' virtues emerge through his actions and words. And as we have noted, about one-third of the narrative concerns Jesus' death and resurrection, along with his

teaching (chs. 13–17) to the disciples on how they should live, with the Spirit's help, once he has ascended to heaven.

3. Style: John's style is not elevated. It is straightforward, often joining sentences with "and" (parataxis) or supplying no connection (asyndeton). The vocabulary is limited, with certain key words (e.g., "life") frequently repeated (for discussion, see ch. 5, below).

4. Atmosphere: John employs a serious, steady, reverent atmosphere.

5. Quality of characterization: Ancient biographies frequently combine the stereotypical with the real in presenting characters. John likewise mixes both elements. Jesus appears very much in control and almost superhuman as he unwaveringly does God's will, yet he is capable of very human responses: tired and thirsty (4:6–7), disappointed with the disciples (6:67), grieving and angry at the death of his friend Lazarus (11:33, 35, 38), and troubled at the close of his ministry and in the face of death (12:27).

6. Social setting and occasion: John's gospel tells the story of Jesus in such a way as to address the issues of its time and the community of his followers. (Chapter 9, below, will return to this complicated question.)

7. Authorial intention and purpose: Ancient biographies have diverse purposes: to praise the central character; to provide examples for readers to follow; to offer information; to entertain; to preserve the memory of the central character; to teach; to engage in debate by defending or correcting opinions about the character (an apologetic purpose) and/or by attacking opponents (a polemic purpose). Several of these purposes clearly apply to John's gospel. As we have seen from 20:31, the focus is on Jesus and on sustaining believers in a way of life. So the gospel informs and teaches. But the story's extensive attention to Jesus' opponents also suggests an apologetic and polemic purpose; an engagement in debates about the significance of Jesus secures the identity of the gospel's readers as a distinctive community.

Inclusion of the Features of Other Genres

Identifying the genre of John's gospel as an ancient biography provides a starting point for further discussion of various aspects of the gospel. But it is not the final word on its genre. As noted above, genres are not rigidly fixed categories, and a work can include features of other genres that add important dimensions. Davies's emphasis (discussed above) on the gospel's use of the Scriptures provides a good example. This feature contributes significantly to locating the story of Jesus in a larger context, that of God's ongoing purposes to save the world from its death-bringing activities and commitments and to offer it a different sort of life, lived in relation to God's good purposes.

We will note briefly two other discussions of John's genre that, while unconvincing in identifying the main genre of the gospel, highlight important aspects of John's story of Jesus. For, if identifying the gospel's genre as that of ancient biography helps to establish an expectation that the work will focus on telling the story of Jesus, it nevertheless leaves unanswered further questions about aspects of the story to be told.

Mark Stibbe agrees that John's gospel is a form of biography, but he argues that the gospel's employment of other genres' features assists in telling the story of Jesus.[25] The gospel evidences "generic depths" that account for the "abiding appeal of the fourth gospel." Stibbe turns to Northrop Frye's notion of archetypal patterns of storytelling to elaborate these generic depths.[26] Frye argues that world literature uses four basic modes of storytelling: romance, tragedy, satire and irony (anti-romance), and comedy. Stibbe argues that John is none of these genres in total; rather, elements of all four modes are evident at key points, creatively rendering the story compelling and appealing.

Frye argues that at the heart of what he identifies as romance is a successful quest in three stages: a journey and some initial minor adventures, a struggle in which the hero and/or his opponent die, and the exaltation of the hero.[27] According to Stibbe, the same three elements of conflict, death, and recognition are present in John. Jesus, sent from God, is not recognized by most people despite his signs and teaching. He comes into conflict with the authorities. The conflict leads to his death, although it is not the opponents' victory, since Jesus gives himself to die. Recognition comes from his disciples and in his vindication by his Father, God, through his resurrection and ascension to God.

But features of tragedy are also present. For Frye, the tragic hero is central to tragedy.[28] The hero appears divine but is very human and behaves in ways that provoke revenge. The carrying out of this revenge produces sacrificial suffering. Likewise in John, Jesus, who existed "in the beginning" and comes from God, reveals God's purposes for human life in a way that challenges the power and societal vision of the Jerusalem-based elite. They repel his challenge by putting him to death, a sacrificial death on the cross.[29]

Moreover, features of satire and irony (anti-romance) are present.[30] Both are important for the gospel. In places the gospel satirizes Jesus' opponents. John 3 mocks the elite leader Nicodemus, who does not understand Jesus, by having him ask a very silly question (3:4, "Can one enter a second time into the mother's womb and be born?"). In chapter 9, Jesus' opponents object to Jesus' giving sight (both physical and spiritual) to a blind man, while they themselves remain (unknowingly) blind to his identity. Basic to irony is an inequity of knowledge or recognition. From the outset of the gospel, readers know answers to the crucial questions about Jesus, namely, his origin, identity and mission. But throughout the gospel, especially the first twelve chapters, the readers watch (and learn more) as characters in the story fail to recognize these crucial dimensions about Jesus.

Stibbe also finds Frye's concept of comedy to be important for John's story of Jesus.[31] Comedy is not primarily about laughter and triviality. Rather it denotes action that descends through numerous obstacles until it rises to a successful resolution. John's Jesus descends from heaven and confronts numerous obstacles from those who do not accept his revelation or believe his claims to be God's commissioned agent, the Christ or Son of God. Even those who say they believe, the disciples, prove unreliable. Yet at the end, after his crucifixion, Jesus is raised in resurrection and ascension, is recognized by his disciples, and returns to God. But absent from this comedic-like ending is any reconciliation or successful resolution with the opponents.

As Stibbe points out, none of Frye's four genres adequately fits the whole of the gospel. Rather, the gospel creatively employs aspects of these genres at particular points as it presents the story of Jesus.

John as Revelation

The notion of revelation or disclosure is central to John's gospel.[32] The gospel claims that God sends Jesus to reveal God's life-giving purposes (1:18; 14:7–10). These purposes include saving people from the current sinful and unjust world so that they might know a different sort of life in relationship to God and each other, a life untouched by sin and death.

John's concern with revealing God's purposes is not unique. A long tradition of Jewish revelatory or apocalyptic literature exists. The adjective "apocalyptic" and its related noun "apocalypse" come from a Greek word that means "revelation." This revelatory literature was written before, contemporary with, and after the Gospel of John. One of the earliest examples, dating from the second century B.C.E., is Dan 7–12. Another notable example, *1 Enoch (Ethiopic Apocalypse)*, comprising five sections, collects material from about the second century B.C.E. to about the time of Jesus and Paul in the first century C.E. Two other works, *4 Ezra* and *2 Baruch (Syriac Apocalypse)*, probably originated at the same time as John, late in the first century C.E. The best-known example of such literature for Christian readers is the New Testament book called (significantly) Revelation, also written late in the first century.

Understanding this literature—often replete with strange symbols, animal-like creatures, and mystifying numbers—is difficult. So too is defining it. One useful definition understands apocalyptic literature as

> a genre of revelatory literature with a narrative framework, in which the revelation is mediated by an otherworldly being to a human recipient, disclosing a transcendental reality which is both temporal, insofar as it envisages eschatological salvation, and spatial insofar as it involves another supernatural world.[33]

There are some limitations to this definition. It does not, for example, identify the circumstances of perceived unrest or crisis (political, social, religious) and powerlessness in the face of great injustice that often produce this literature. Nevertheless it draws attention to important features of revelatory literature.

At first glance it seems to strain all credulity to link John's gospel with such strange writings as Dan 7–12 and Revelation, and many scholars have not done so. Certainly John is not an "apocalypse" like Dan 7–12 and Revelation. But John does share some literary and thematic features of apocalyptic literature. Apocalyptic literature typically employs a "two-age" scheme to denote the present time as unjust, oppressive, and contrary to God's will, and the new age of justice and salvation that God will bring about. John employs such a scheme in anticipating a new age marked by resurrection (6:35) and the return of Jesus (14:1–3) as God's life-giving purposes are established in full. But John also modifies the scheme to emphasize that this life is manifested now through Jesus (17:3).

John Ashton points out further connections between John and features at home in apocalyptic literature.[34] The most obvious connection, apart from that of narrative, is the notion of revelation. John presents the story of Jesus as an account of one who comes from heaven to reveal God's purposes concerning life. The parallels are not exact, since Jesus, being the revelation himself, combines the features

of both the otherworldly agent (often an angel in apocalyptic literature) and the human recipient, features that apocalyptic literature
usually employs (see Rev 1). And somewhat unusual is that John emphasizes that God's life is experienced in the present as well as in the
future. But despite these differences, the gospel's concern with revelation is very clear. It appears at the outset: "No one has ever seen God. It
is God the only Son, who is close to the Father's heart, who has made
him known" (1:18). And it is continually reiterated through references
to Jesus' origin as being from God and to his purpose: to reveal God's
purposes in his words and works (5:36; 14:7–10). For Ashton, this
focus on revelation is an essential feature of apocalyptic traditions, one
expressed often in the term "mystery," to denote "a secret once hidden
and now revealed."[35] Disclosure of God's purposes follows a time of
concealment. John presents Jesus as the one who makes the revelation.

But John employs another apocalyptic feature. In some apocalyptic
texts, such as Daniel (9:23; 10:21; 11:2), the revealer's revelation is obscure and needs further interpretation and elucidation by another figure. Jesus' revelation is certainly obscure for many in John's gospel, both
his opponents and at times his disciples. John employs this motif—the
need for subsequent elaboration of the revealer's revelation—in presenting the role of the Spirit, also called the Spirit of Truth or the Coun-
selor. The Spirit comes to disciples in Jesus' absence to "guide you into
all the truth; for he will not speak on his own, but he will speak whatever
he hears, and he will declare to you the things that are to come" (16:13).
Jesus' revelation continues to be elaborated by the Spirit for the disciples' ongoing existence long after Jesus has returned to heaven.

Although some understand the revelation, others do not (1:10–12).
One of the perplexing features of John's story of Jesus is that Jesus' revelation, paradoxically, often remains a riddle for many people. As is typical of much revelatory literature, insiders or believers or disciples
understand his "riddling discourse" (at least to some extent), but outsiders do not. The more Jesus speaks, the more his words seem to confuse rather than enlighten his hearers even though Jesus claims that he
has spoken plainly (18:20; cf. 10:24–26), something only disciples can
perceive (16:29). Often these outsiders are ridiculed for stupidly not understanding. Nicodemus, for example, in 3:4 is made to ask how a grown
person can enter into his or her mother's womb to be born again. Commonly in apocalyptic literature, the "wise," often a minority, receive the
revelation while the "fools," the majority, cannot understand.

John's presentation of Jesus' revelation employs a further common
apocalyptic feature, that of "correspondence" or similarity between
heaven and earth. Jesus reveals on earth the oneness that he and the

Father enjoyed "from the beginning." He reenacts and displays the heavenly reality of God's will on earth among people. This reality, this knowing God, is the plan and life that Jesus offers to people.

One further dimension that Ashton does not pursue concerns the content of John's revelation. Apocalyptic literature often reveals a new world that is free of injustice and oppression and marked by fertility and wholeness as God's purposes are established in the place of exploitative empires. The revelation of "life" made by John's Jesus incorporates the same features. Jesus' signs or miracles, which point to God's saving purposes, include healings (4:46–54; 5:1–9; ch. 9), feedings (ch. 6), and the raising of Lazarus bodily from death (ch. 11). These signs, like Jesus' corporeal existence, indicate God's faithfulness to redeem God's creation from Rome's oppressive rule. The gospel identifies this tyranny as part of what it calls sin and death (including sickness and want), that which is contrary to God's purposes. Jesus' signs anticipate the reestablishment of an Edenic existence marked by justice, abundance, and wholeness. Life in relation to God entails right relationships and structures among people so that all have access to the resources they need to sustain life.

Implications of John as an Ancient Revelatory Biography

More will be said later about many of the features mentioned in this chapter. What are the implications of this discussion of genre? We have seen that John should be understood as an ancient biography and that the gospel's author incorporates (as do many authors) features of other genres, especially literary and thematic features of revelatory writings. These features assist in the telling of the story of Jesus.

The identification of John's genre as an ancient revelatory biography is important because it provides guidelines that help us engage the gospel. We would expect the gospel, like other ancient biographies, to do the following:

1. Organize its account of Jesus in basically a chronological sequence of important scenes, with the insertion of dialogue and discourse material. (See ch. 2, below, about the gospel's plot.)

2. Focus its attention on Jesus as the main character. (We have noted numerous ways in which biographies create and maintain this focus. Chapter 3 will examine both the content and the means of John's presentation of Jesus and God; chapter 4, his

presentation of other characters in relation to Jesus; and chapters 5–6, other aspects of the gospel—John's language and style. Chapters 2–6 thus focus on aspects of *John as a storyteller.*)

3. Employ sources and address the circumstances of its readers. John's gospel interprets traditions and sources to address its readers' circumstances, to teach them about the life entailed in believing in Jesus, and to engage in both apologetics and polemic against opponents. (Chapters 7–8, which will examine this process, focus on *John as interpreter.*)

4. Promote certain perspectives on, or understandings about, human existence lived in relation to God. (The last two chapters and the Postscript, which discuss John's "good news" or understanding of the gospel as a proclamation of God's life-giving purposes, will explore both the identity of the proclaimer [who is John?] and the content of his proclamation, which centers on "life." Chapters 9–10 thus focus on *John as evangelist.*)

Notes

1. Contemporary Johannine scholarship has not devoted much attention to John's genre. There is no discussion in the groundbreaking study of R. A. Culpepper, *Anatomy of the Fourth Gospel: A Study in Literary Design* (Philadelphia: Fortress, 1983) or in several recent collections of essays on the gospel, such as R. A. Culpepper and C. C. Black, eds., *Exploring the Gospel of John: In Honor of D. Moody Smith* (Louisville: Westminster John Knox, 1996); R. T. Fortna and T. Thatcher, eds., *Jesus in Johannine Tradition* (Louisville: Westminster John Knox, 2001).

2. See the fine discussion by R. A. Burridge, *What Are the Gospels? A Comparison with Graeco-Roman Biography* (Society for New Testament Studies Monograph Series 70; Cambridge: Cambridge University Press, 1992), 26–54; D. Aune, "Gospels, Literary Genre of," in *The Westminster Dictionary of New Testament and Early Christian Literature and Rhetoric* (Louisville: Westminster John Knox, 2003), 204–6.

3. Burridge (*What Are the Gospels?* 3–25) outlines a history of scholarship. H. Attridge ("Genre Bending in the Fourth Gospel," *JBL* 121 [2002]: 3–21) focuses on diverse genres within the gospel but pays little attention to the gospel genre itself (though see p. 18).

4. C. Hedrick, "The Four/Thirty-Four Gospels: Diversity and Division among the Earliest Christians," *Bible Review* 18 (June 2002): 20–31, 46–47.

5. The term appears in Mark 1:1, but there it is unclear whether the term refers to the document or its message and claims.

6. J. A. Ashton, *Understanding the Fourth Gospel* (Oxford: Clarendon, 1991), 409.

7. For example, at 14:30 Jesus seems to end his instructions to disciples, but he then continues to speak for another three chapters. Likewise, 20:30–31 seems to end the gospel on an appropriate note, but another chapter follows. See chs. 7–8, below.

8. E.g., D. Wenham, "A Historical View of John's Gospel," *Themelios* 23 (1998): 5–21; F. Moloney, "The Fourth Gospel and the Jesus of History," *NTS* 46 (2000): 42–58; C. L. Blomberg, *The Historical Reliability of John's Gospel: Issues and Commentary* (Downers Grove, Ill.: InterVarsity, 2001).

9. For example, similarities in narratives (the feeding of the five thousand in 6:1–14), the passion narrative, sayings (compare Mark 6:4 with John 4:44; Matt 11:25–27/Lk 10:21–22 with John 3:35; 13:3). See ch. 7, below.

10. For an early discussion, see W. F. Albright, "Recent Discoveries in Palestine and the Gospel of St. John," in *The Background of the New Testament and Its Eschatology* (ed. W. D. Davies and D. Daube; Cambridge: Cambridge University Press, 1956), 153–71.

11. M. Hengel, *The Johannine Question* (Philadelphia: Trinity Press International, 1989), 110.

12. J. Jeremias, *The Rediscovery of Bethesda* (Louisville: John Knox, 1966); for a more recent, nuanced evaluation, see I. Broer, "Knowledge of Palestine in the Fourth Gospel?" in *Jesus in Johannine Tradition* (ed. R. T. Fortna and T. Thatcher; Louisville: Westminster John Knox, 2001), 83–90.

13. R. Funk, *The Five Gospels: What Did Jesus Really Say?* (New York: Polebridge, 1993), 401–70, esp. 413; *The Acts of Jesus: The Search for the Authentic Deeds of Jesus* (San Francisco: HarperSanFrancisco, 1998), 36, 365–440, esp. 369, 431–35.

14. Brown, *Introduction to the Gospel,* 90–114.

15. C. H. Dodd, *Historical Tradition in the Fourth Gospel* (Cambridge: Cambridge University Press, 1963), 366–87. In his influential commentary, R. Brown (*The Gospel according to John* [2 vols.; Anchor Bible 29, 29A; New York: Doubleday, 1966–1970]) regularly engages this question and often finds some core of authenticity behind the discourses and narratives (see, e.g., 1:275–89 for the sayings material in John 6 and 1:378–79 for a discussion of the John 9 miracle).

16. J. Staley, "What Can a Postmodern Approach to the Fourth Gospel Add?" in *Jesus in Johannine Tradition* (ed. R. T. Fortna and T. Thatcher; Louisville: Westminster John Knox, 2001), 47–57, esp. 51–52.

17. R. Bultmann, "The Gospels (Form)," in *Twentieth Century Theology in the Making* (ed. J. Pelikan; 3 vols.; London: Collins/Fontana, 1969–1970), 1:86–92; see the survey in Burridge, *What Are the Gospels?* 7–13.

18. Ashton, *Understanding,* 433.

19. M. Davies, *Rhetoric and Reference in the Fourth Gospel* (JSNTSup 69; Sheffield, Eng.: JSOT Press, 1992), 67–109.

20. Ibid., 89.

21. J. L. Crenshaw, "Theodicy," *ABD* 6:444–47.

22. E. R. Pelling, ed., *Character and Individuality in Greek Literature* (Oxford: Oxford University Press, 1990), esp. the article by C. Gill, "The Character-Personality Distinction," 1–31.

23. Burridge, *What Are the Gospels?* 55–69; also D. Aune, *The New Testament in Its Literary Environment* (Philadelphia: Westminster, 1987), 17–76.

24. Burridge, *What Are the Gospels?* 109–27, 220–39. I am summarizing Burridge's excellent work.

25. M. W. G. Stibbe, *John's Gospel* (London: Routledge, 1994), 62–72.

26. N. Frye, *Anatomy of Criticism* (Princeton, N.J.: Princeton University Press, 1971), 131–239.

27. Ibid., 187.

28. Ibid., 206–23, esp. 206–8.

29. B. H. Grigsby ("The Cross as an Expiatory Sacrifice in the Fourth Gospel," *JSNT* 15 [1982]: 51–80) sees three emphases elaborating the sacrificial dimension of Jesus' death: the casting of Jesus as the paschal victim (1:29; 19:14; 19:29; 19:36), Christ as the Isaac figure (1:29; 3:16; 19:17), and Christ the cleansing fountain (19:34).

30. Frye, *Anatomy,* 223–39. Chapter 6, below, will return to irony.

31. Ibid., 163–86; also C. Koester, "Comedy, Humor, and the Gospel of John," in *Word, Theology, and Community in John* (ed. J. Painter, R. A. Culpepper, and F. F. Segovia; St. Louis: Chalice, 2002), 123–41.

32. E.g., G. O'Day, *Revelation in the Fourth Gospel: Narrative Mode and Theological Claim* (Philadelphia: Fortress, 1986).

33. J. J. Collins, *The Apocalyptic Imagination: An Introduction to the Jewish Matrix of Christianity* (New York: Crossroad, 1984), 4. Ashton (*Understanding,* 383–87) expresses some reservations and offers his own revised definition.

34. Ashton, *Understanding,* 383–406; also J. Painter, *The Quest for the Messiah: The History, Literature, and Theology of the Johannine Community* (Nashville: Abingdon, 1993), 249–50.

35. Ashton, *Understanding,* 387.

CHAPTER 2

The Plot of John's Gospel

In chapter 1, identifying the genre of John's gospel, we noted that ancient biographies usually organize their accounts of the significant person in a chronological sequence covering ancestry, birth and upbringing, virtues, death, and consequences. John includes these elements (although it pays little attention to Jesus' birth and upbringing). We also noted that matters of genre and types of plot (comedy, tragedy) are closely related. This chapter pursues the question of how the gospel constructs its account of Jesus' life to form the gospel's plot. It examines what constitutes a plot, identifies some of the elements that make up John's plot, and outlines the plot of John's gospel.

> Note to reader: In the following pages I will refer to lots of verses in John's gospel. Unfortunately there is not space to print them all here. It will help your reading if you check out these references in John's gospel.

What Is a Plot?

Interpreters have noted that John consists of two sections, each marked by some thematic unity, with a major break between chapters 12 and 13: chapters 1–12, the book of signs; chapters 13–21, the book of glory.[1] More detailed approaches identify a greater number of sections and discern some unity for each section's content by concentrating either on events or, more often, on themes. For example:[2]

1:1–51	The prelude to Jesus' ministry
2:1–5:47	The "greater things": Jesus' words and works
6:1–10:42	Jesus' words and works: conflict and opposition grow
11:1–12:50	The prelude to Jesus' hour
13:1–17:26	The farewell meal and discourse
18:1–19:42	"The hour has come": Jesus' arrest, trial, and death
20:1–31	The first resurrection appearances
21:1–25	Jesus' resurrection appearances at the Sea of Tiberius

Fernando Segovia proposes a biographical outline (the three major sections) with the second section subdivided in terms of journeys to Jerusalem:[3]

1:1–18	Narrative of the origins
1:19–17:26	Narrative of the public life or career
1:19–3:36	First Galilee/Jerusalem cycle
4:1–5:47	Second Galilee/Jerusalem cycle
6:1–10:42	Third Galilee/Jerusalem cycle
11:1–17:26	Fourth and final journey to Jerusalem
18:1–21:25	Narrative of the death and lasting significance

Such analyses of the gospel's structure are helpful in identifying main sections of the gospel.[4] But when we think of the plot of a movie or novel, we mean much more than just sections. We also mean the sequence of events, the connections between events, the conflict among characters, and elements of causation, surprise, and discovery (the effect of the plot). Is it fair to expect such features in plots of ancient biographies?

The leading literary theorist in the ancient world, Aristotle, discusses plot in *Poet.* 6–17.[5] Among his emphases are these:

- A plot comprises not just a series of events but an ordered combination of incidents.

- This combination of incidents forms a unity of action, not just from a focus on one man but from the representation of the action.

- The action has a beginning, middle, and end and comprises events that are probable and/or necessary.

- The sequence of events must be necessary and/or usual; causation and consequence guide the sequence. The end is a "necessary or usual consequence" of what goes before it.

- The plot needs amplitude or reasonable length—long enough to be taken notice of, short enough to be held in the memory.

- Reversals (changes from one state to another) and/or recognitions (from ignorance to recognition/discovery that causes love or hate) are especially important in the plot's overall shape.

- Plots have an effect on audiences, moving them, especially awakening fear and pity.

Recent literary critics, often focusing on contemporary novels, short stories, movies, and television shows, have developed aspects of Aristotle's insights. Some emphasize the importance of causality in linking events.[6] Others highlight the unity of the action as determined by the work's end.[7] Yet others focus on the plot's impact on the audience.[8] S. Chatman explores the relationship among events, emphasizing "the logic of hierarchy" whereby key events, called *kernels,* provide major branching points that advance the plot, are consequent on previous actions, and raise questions that lead to subsequent events.[9] These major events provide a plot's unity and causality whereas minor events, called *satellites,* elaborate aspects of the kernels.[10]

These discussions identify important issues to consider in formulating John's plot. What elements does the story of Jesus include? How does it sequence these elements? How does it connect them? Where does it begin? What happens in the middle? How does the action progress? What causes things to happen? How are episodes linked? What characters are involved? How does it end? And what effect does organizing the story in this way have on the gospel's readers or hearers?

What Are Some Typical Plots?

Some literary critics, such as Northrop Frye, A. J. Greimas, and Chatman, have ventured in another direction.[11] They have considered the type of action in which the main character is involved and have attempted to describe general or even universal types of plots that any narrative might employ. Biblical scholars have sought to use some of these models to elucidate the plots of the gospels, sometimes with good success, sometimes unsuccessfully because these ancient biographies are not contemporary novels.

Mark Stibbe, for instance, has attempted to employ Greimas's model of a universal "deep structure" for storytelling to elucidate John's plot.[12] For Greimas, plots comprise three axes and four character types (called actants). The first axis (called communication) concerns a commission or task that a sender gives to a receiver. The second axis (volition) concerns the receiver's carrying out the commission. The third axis (power) centers on the opposition the receiver experiences from opponents. Because of this opposition, the receiver obtains assistance from a helper. The three axes of communication, volition, and power, thus involve four characters, or actants: sender, receiver, opponent, helper.

Stibbe sees John's plot in these terms. God is the sender who gives Jesus (the receiver) a commission to manifest God's life among humans (3:16; 20:31).[13] Jesus carries out this work of doing God's will (cf. 4:34) but is opposed by the devil and its agent, the Jerusalem leadership (whom the gospel names "the Jews"; see ch. 4, below). Jesus has no helper, but he does extend his work by becoming a sender in commissioning the disciples to continue his work (20:21b; 14:12). They have a helper (the Paraclete, or Holy Spirit, 14:15–17, 26; 16:7–15) and opponents (15:18–20; 16:2). The gospel also has a counterplot. The devil is the sender who gives the Jerusalem leadership a commission to oppose and kill Jesus (8:38, 44).[14] Their principal helper is Judas, who, directed by Satan (13:2, 27), betrays Jesus.

Greimas's scheme enables Stibbe to identify an overarching unity in the plot, important lines of action, features of characterization, and theological motifs. The fit, however, is not perfect. Stibbe is not convincing in trying to overcome the absence of a helper for Jesus by highlighting Jesus' resolute and solitary commitment to God's will. Although the scheme clarifies aspects of John at a somewhat generalized or abstract level, it does little to show how the plot is formulated on a chapter-by-chapter basis. It gives little attention to specific episodes, connections, and characters in the gospel. And it does not attend to the intermingling and interweaving of the various plot lines in which repetition, contrast, and cumulative effect play significant roles.

Moreover, it does not express well the element of recognition, which Culpepper, borrowing from Aristotle, highlights as being central to John's plot.[15] Culpepper argues that the plot does not develop around Jesus' unfolding character because Jesus is a static character, defined in terms of his identity as God's agent commissioned to reveal God.

Rather, the plot develops in terms of the struggle of characters to recognize Jesus' identity. Repeatedly in his signs (2:1–12; 4:46–53), discourses (chs. 5–6, 8, 10), conversations with individual characters such as Nicodemus (ch. 3) and the unnamed Samaritan woman (ch. 4), and his use of various symbols and images (light, door, vine, good shepherd, way, life, etc.), Jesus discloses his identity. Each scene or individual episode encapsulates the same challenge as to whether the characters will recognize Jesus.

Culpepper's emphasis on recognizing Jesus' identity is well placed. But his focus is too limited. John's story is not just about Jesus' identity but about Jesus' revelation of God's life-giving purposes. John's gospel is not only about knowing that Jesus is the Christ, the son of God, but about experiencing life as shaped by God's just purposes (20:31), which Jesus reveals. Part of the struggle between Jesus and the Jerusalem leaders concerns the understanding of God's purposes. Jesus' revelation is at odds with their societal vision, which upholds their power and privileges. An understanding of the gospel's plot must incorporate individual scenes and motifs as well as elucidate accurately the contribution of specific episodes.

John's Plot: A Proposal

Aristotle's emphasis on the end of the plot as the "necessary or usual consequence" of the preceding action offers a helpful means of understanding John's plot. John's story of Jesus centers on the assertion of Jesus' claim to be God's chosen agent, authorized by God to make a definitive revelation of God's life-giving purposes. In living out this claim in his words and works, Jesus conflicts with the Jerusalem elite and their Roman ally, Pilate, confronting and challenging their power over, and vision of, an unjust societal order that is contrary to God's life-giving purposes. The Jerusalem elite reject Jesus' claim and revelation of God's purposes of life, ultimately putting him to death. But surprisingly, his death is not the end. God raises him, thereby revealing the limit of their power. Meantime some people discern Jesus' origin, identity, and mission, commit themselves to his revelation, and form a counter-community that, assisted by the Holy Spirit, continues Jesus' mission.

Guided by Aristotle's discussion and recalling that ancient biographies often followed a chronological sequence from birth to death, we will identify seven of the numerous elements that make up John's plot and then consider the unity of action that they combine to create.

Prologue

The gospel's first eighteen verses, called the prologue, have provoked much debate. Considerable attention has focused on the unit's origin. Scholars have debated whether John

- wrote all of the verses himself,[16]

- borrowed and edited a hymn from gnostic-Mandaean-Baptist circles,[17]

- borrowed and edited a hymn from Jewish wisdom traditions,[18] or

- borrowed and edited a hymn from John's own community.[19]

On the basis of the similarities of vocabulary and themes in the prologue and the rest of the gospel, the first or last option seems most probable, with likely influence from Jewish wisdom traditions (the third option). The second option has been widely discredited because the written gnostic material used to support it postdates John's gospel.

More important for the plot is the prologue's content and function in relation to the gospel.[20] As the opening unit, the prologue alerts the audience to four major elements that will be prominent in the gospel:

1. Jesus' origin: Verses 1–5 locate the Word, identified by the context of the gospel as Jesus, "in the beginning . . . with God" (1:1–2), as co-Creator (1:3–5). The gospel will constantly repeat Jesus' origin with God as a major point of conflict between Jesus and his opponents. His origin with God is foundational for his identity as God's son or agent. It guarantees the reliability or truth of his revelation of God and God's purposes.

2. John the Baptist: Verses 6–8 (also v. 15) introduce John the Baptist, who bears witness to Jesus. Some scholars have suggested that the references to John function as polemic against followers of John who claim greater importance for John than for Jesus.

3. Response to Jesus: Verses 9–16 sum up what happens when "the Word became flesh" to reveal God's purposes (1:14). Some receive Jesus, become God's children (1:12–13), and behold his glory (1:14), but others reject him (1:10–11). Verses 10–13 function as a plot summary that will be elaborated through the gospel's accounts of his acceptance and rejection. The latter motif, expressed particularly by the alliance of the Jerusalem leadership

and the Roman governor Pilate, leads to his crucifixion. But their most powerful and destructive action cannot prevent Jesus from returning to God in his resurrection and ascension.

4. Jesus' relation to Moses: Verses 17–18 distinguish and link Jesus and Moses. Both persons reveal God's purposes, but Jesus' revelation takes precedence. Central to this issue is the matter of determining who makes a definitive revelation of God's purposes and how people encounter this revelation. This issue will be debated through the gospel as various characters interact with Jesus. Jesus' origin with and return to God guarantee the reliability of Jesus' revelation.

Quest Stories

A second aspect of John's plot comprises what John Painter has identified as quest stories.[21] People frequently seek Jesus the Messiah, asking friendly or hostile questions about the Messiah's identity and his allies. They seek his help (often overcoming obstacles to do so) or try to harm him. Sometimes they fulfill their quest; sometimes they reject Jesus. These quest stories elaborate the prologue's claim that some received him while others rejected him (1:10–13). Such stories cluster in chapters 1–4, 11–12, and 18–20:

- Jerusalem agents interrogate John the Baptist (1:19–28).

- Would-be disciples seek the Messiah, who calls them to discipleship (1:35–42, 43–51).

- Jesus' mother seeks his help at the Cana wedding when the wine runs out (2:1–12).

- Nicodemus seeks God's kingdom (3:1–15).

- The Samaritan woman seeks the Messiah and his water of life (4:1–42).

- The royal official seeks life for his son (4:46–54).

- The crowd looks for Jesus (6:1–40).

- Mary and Martha look for Jesus' help after Lazarus dies (ch. 11).

- Judeans seek to kill Jesus and Lazarus (11:7, 46–57; 12:9–11).

- Greeks seek Jesus (12:20–36).

- Judeans seek to arrest and kill Jesus (chs. 18–19).

- Women seek Jesus' body and find the risen Jesus (20:1–18).

Throughout, Jesus is also on a quest to find those who receive or believe him, as he seeks true worshippers (2:13–22; ch. 4) and disciples (1:35–51; 20:19–21:23). At times Jesus is elusive, difficult to locate (6:15, 25; 7:1, 10–11, 32–36; 8:59; 9:12; 11:21, 54; 12:36) and difficult to understand (3:3–9; 8:21–22; 11:23–25).

This game of hide-and-seek throughout the first twelve chapters underlines the significance of encountering Jesus. Such encounters are elusive: they provide access to life, they require openness to God's purposes, but they can provoke great hostility. His hiding from opponents who want to kill him reinforces the notion that despite their apparent power, he is in control, even of the timing of his death (7:8; 10:17–18). These quest scenes keep the gospel's audience focused on who Jesus is and what he is about.

Signs

A third element of John's plot comprises eight stories in which Jesus works deeds of power:

- Jesus changes water into wine (2:1–11).

- Jesus heals the royal official's son (4:46–54).

- Jesus heals the crippled man (5:1–18).

- Jesus feeds the large crowd (6:1–14).

- Jesus walks on water (6:16–21).

- Jesus heals the man born blind (9:1–7).

- Jesus raises Lazarus from death (11:1–46).

- At the command of the risen Jesus, the disciples catch 153 fish (21:1–14).

The gospel does not identify these actions as "miracles" or "works of power." In fact, the word *dynamis* (δύναμις), used in the Synoptic Gospels for Jesus' miracles, does not appear in John. Rather the gospel signals their significance by labeling them "signs" (*sēmeia*, σημεῖα).[22] Instead of emphasizing these actions as displays of power, the term "signs" indicates that these powerful actions point beyond themselves to a greater significance. They are signs in that they provide those who experience the miraculous action an opportunity to discern Jesus' identity as the definitive revealer of God's purposes, to understand what God's purposes entail, and to commit themselves to Jesus.

It is significant that most of these miraculous signs concern giving life, especially in healing and supplying nourishment. Both wholeness and nourishment were in short supply in Rome's imperial world, where the elite removed the food supply and resources from much of the population through taxation and rents.[23] The resultant inadequate diets, variable food supply, anxiety, and overwork caused poor health and a short life span for many. These realities are reflected in the crowd's demand of 6:34, "Give us this bread always." Physical brokenness and deficient resources were typical of empires such as Rome; prophetic (Isa 25:6–10; 35:5–6) and apocalyptic traditions (2 Bar. 72–74) expected God to end such injustice and transform the world with the establishment of God's purposes. Jesus' actions of healing and supplying nourishment draw on these visions of life as God intends it to be. They are signs that God's purposes for human life include wholeness, fertility, and abundance. The Jerusalem-based, Rome-allied leadership with whom Jesus conflicts are not able to accomplish these purposes because they structure a hierarchical society for their own benefit.

Monologues and Dialogues

Jesus' frequent and lengthy speech contributes a fourth important element to the plot.[24] This speaking is not surprising given the prologue's claim that the "Word became flesh" (1:14). Jesus' words manifest what the Word saw and heard from God (3:32, 34; 8:38a, 40). Response to Jesus' words show who are disciples and who are opponents of God's purposes revealed in Jesus. His verbal revelations, then, and the responses they elicit are integral parts of the gospel's plot.

In the Synoptic Gospels, Jesus' speech often occurs in cryptic exchanges containing pithy one-liners or sound bites. He also tells a number of parables. In John, by contrast, Jesus does not tell parables, and although there are some exceptions (1:35–51; 4:46–54), much of his speech contains lengthy monologues. John 3 begins with a brief dialogue between Jesus and Nicodemus (3:3–10), which is followed by ten continuous verses of Jesus speaking. In chapter 4, in the midst of some dialogue, Jesus speaks for twelve of the first twenty-six verses. In chapter 5, after healing the paralyzed man, Jesus speaks continuously from verse 19 to verse 47. In this section of the gospel, in which Jesus' conflict with the elite intensifies (chs. 5–10), further long monologues appear in chapters 6, 8, and 10, and their content contributes significantly to the unfolding conflict.[25] The longest monologue appears in chapters 14–16 as Jesus instructs the disciples. He appears to stop in 14:31 but carries on for two more chapters before praying continuously in chapter 17.

Jesus presents his words or teaching as originating with God, who sent Jesus (7:16; 8:25–26; 14:10, 24). In speaking, he recognizes God's authority and follows God's instruction (12:49). His words carry out God's purposes to reveal the world's evil (7:7; 15:22), to reveal life (6:63), to save from sin and death (5:34; 8:51), and to draw disciples into ongoing, obedient relation with Jesus (10:27) and loving relation with each other (13:34–35). Jesus' words have continuing value; the Spirit, the Paraclete, is charged with the task of reminding disciples of Jesus' words when Jesus returns to God (14:26). By recalling Jesus' words, the Paraclete continues the work of revealing God's life-giving purposes.

Geography: Galilee/Jerusalem

In the plots of the Synoptic Gospels, Jesus carries out his ministry in Galilee and then travels to Jerusalem for the last week of his life, which ends with his crucifixion (Matt 19:1–21:11; Mark 10:1; 11:1; Luke 9:51–53; 19:28–40). In John's plot, Jesus conducts ministry in the villages and countryside of Judea (e.g., the village of Bethany),[26] Galilee (e.g., the villages of Cana and Capernaum),[27] and Samaria (John 4). But he also travels back and forth to Jerusalem four times and conducts ministry there:

- In 2:13 Jesus travels from Galilee to Jerusalem, enters the temple, and disrupts its means for celebrating Passover (also 2:23; 4:45).

- In 5:1 Jesus again travels from Galilee to Jerusalem.

- In 7:1 Jesus is in Galilee. In 7:10, after saying he is not going to Jerusalem for a festival (7:8–9), he goes there "in secret" and teaches (7:14). In 10:22–23, Jesus is still in Jerusalem.

- In 12:12 Jesus reenters Jerusalem after leaving Judea (10:40) and being in the vicinity of Bethany (cf. 1:28; 11:1, 18; 12:1), where he raised Lazarus. Jerusalem is the location for the rest of the story, which centers on Jesus' crucifixion and resurrection.

This back-and-forth movement fulfills several functions in John's plot. One effect is to keep Jerusalem to the fore, thereby emphasizing the city's importance. A second effect is to underline the conflict between Jesus and the ruling authorities in Jerusalem, who are centered on the temple. Jerusalem is first mentioned in 1:19 when the Jerusalem leaders send priests and Levites to interrogate John the Baptist, who bears witness to Jesus (1:6–8). This scene creates the impression that the Jerusalem leaders exercise constant surveillance, that they spy on, and are antagonistic toward, figures whom they have not authorized. These ominous overtones are intensified in 2:13–22 when Jesus attacks the Jerusalem temple, the basis of their power (cf. 4:20–21). Jesus challenges their power, denouncing their exploitative economic-political leadership. In his second excursion into Jerusalem, they plan to kill him (5:18). In 7:1 he is reluctant to go to Jerusalem because they want to arrest and kill him. These motifs continue through chapters 7–12 (7:19–20, 25, 30, 32, 44; 8:20, 37, 40, 44; 10:31, 39; 11:50, 57; 12:9–11). In chapters 18–19, in Jerusalem, these leaders, along with their ally, the Roman governor Pilate, crucify Jesus. Jerusalem and its leaders are consistently presented as opponents of Jesus and his revelation of God's purposes. But their hostility is thwarted in Jesus' resurrection.

Festivals

A sixth element of John's plot includes festivals that often provide the context for Jesus' frequent journeys to Jerusalem.[28] Along with some other Jews (those who can afford time away from daily work), he travels to Jerusalem to join in temple-led celebrations of God's saving acts and to anticipate the completion of God's saving purposes:

1. Twice Jesus is in Jerusalem for the festival of Passover (2:13–25; 12:1, 12, 20; chs. 13–17), celebrated in March/April. Another Passover is mentioned in 6:4 while Jesus is in Galilee. Passover celebrates liberation from slavery in Egypt as God's act of saving the people from the tyrannical pharaoh (Exod 11–15). This victory included the exodus journey to the promised land, during which God supplied the people with manna and water (Exod 16–17), revealed God's will in giving the Torah ("teaching") with the Ten Commandments (Exod 19–24; Deut 8:2–3; Neh 9:13–15, 20), and made a covenant with the people (Exod 24).

2. In chapter 5 Jesus is in Jerusalem for an unnamed festival (5:1).

3. In chapter 7 Jesus travels secretly to Jerusalem for Tabernacles, or Booths (Sukkoth), an eight-day festival celebrated in September/October. This festival provides the context for chapters 7–8 and possibly for 9:1–10:21. Originally an agricultural festival marking harvest, it also celebrated God's provision for the people during their sojourn in the wilderness (Lev 23:42–43), and it

anticipated the time when all the nations would journey to Jerusalem to honor Israel's God (Zech 14).

4. In 10:22 Jesus is in Jerusalem for the festival of Dedication, or Hanukkah, which celebrated God's saving of the people from the Seleucid tyrant Antiochus IV Epiphanes. Observed in November/ December, it commemorates the Maccabean-led struggle against, and defiance of, Antiochus and the rededication of the altar and temple in 164 B.C.E. (see 1 and 2 Maccabees).

5. The Sabbath appears regularly in John (5:1–47; 7:14–24; 9:1–41). The Sabbath celebrated God's deliverance of the people from Egypt (Deut 5:12–15), God's covenant with Israel (Exod 31:16), and God's creative work and rest from it (Gen 2:2–3). These events were extended in Israel's traditions to observance of Sabbath and Jubilee years, which emphasized God's justice in renewing the land, supplying the poor with food, canceling debt, returning land, and liberating slaves (Exod 23:10–11; Deut 15:1–18; Lev 25). In chapters 5 and 9, Jesus' healings on a Sabbath provoke conflict over how the Sabbath is to be honored.

The constant references to festivals locate Jesus' actions in the midst of Jewish life. The festivals carry the memory and social vision of a different and just way of life ordered by God. By associating Jesus' actions with these festivals of liberation, the gospel interprets his actions and teaching as manifestations of God's ongoing work in saving the people from what is contrary to God's purposes, including Rome's oppressive rule, and as anticipations of the completion of God's salvific work in giving people life.

The Powerful and the Marginalized

A seventh important element in John's plot is the characters. The gospel contains scenes that include a wide spectrum of people, from the powerful to the powerless. (Chapters 3–4, below, consider the characters in more detail.)

We have already noted Jesus' conflict with the Rome-allied Jerusalem leaders based in the temple. These leaders, the Pharisees and chief priests, whom Josephus identifies as the leaders of Judea (*Ant.* 20.251), are allies of Rome. They used the temple to oversee a very hierarchical societal-economic order marked by great privilege, wealth, status, and power for a small elite (perhaps 2–3 percent) at the expense of the rest.[29] Along with the chief priests and Pharisees, the ruling elite include "the

Jews" (see ch. 4, below), Nicodemus (John 3), the royal official or retainer of Herod Antipas (4:46–54),[30] and the Roman governor Pilate
(18:28–19:16).[31] The ruling elite are generally hostile to Jesus. The royal
official in John 4 is an exception, as is Joseph of Arimathea, who seems
to be a secret believer in Jesus, bravely providing a burial for Jesus
(19:38; see 12:42–43).

Most of the scenes, however, concern those who belong to the rest
of society, the 97 percent who make up the non-elite. They are marginal
to the center of power in Jerusalem for reasons of low status, poverty,
disabling disease, geographical and ethnic prejudice, and gender. They
bear the cost of the exploitative, elite-dominated social structure.[32]

1. Low status: Frequently a crowd engages Jesus (6:2, 5; 7:20, 40).
   The wealthy and powerful elite frequently exhibit derision toward those of low status—the poor, weak, and provincial. The
   Jerusalem-based Pharisees despise Galilean people of the land as
   ignorant and accursed (7:49). They dismiss the man born blind
   as incapable of teaching them anything (9:34). Pilate exhibits
   conventional Roman elite prejudice and scorn for the lowly, provincial Jesus and derision for his upper-status Judean allies in Jerusalem (18:28–19:16).[33]

2. Poverty: Poverty (and degrees thereof) was pervasive in the
   Roman imperial world, as Jesus recognizes (12:8). The gospel refers several times to relief for the poorest poor (12:5–6; 13:29)
   and mentions a beggar (9:8).

3. Disease: Disease was pervasive in the ancient world, often the result of a poor food supply and poor nutrition (diseases of deficiency); health was also adversely affected by the payment of
   taxes and rents in kind, overwork, anxiety, and medical ignorance (diseases of contagion).[34] The gospel features a sick child
   who is "weakened," or "incapacitated" ("ill," NRSV), near death
   with a burning fever (4:46–54);[35] a paralyzed man (possibly suffering from rickets developed from infant swaddling and con-
   finement and/or vitamin D and mineral deficiency, 5:1–9);[36] and
   a man blind from birth (ch. 9).[37] Often disease meant societal
   marginalization and isolation from one's household, as evidenced by the paralyzed (5:3–7) and blind (9:8, 18–21) men.
   Both men probably survived by begging (9:8).

4. Geographical and ethnic prejudice: The gospel includes deroga-
   tory comments about the territory and people of Galilee (1:46;
   7:52) and of Samaria (4:9). In contrast to these perspectives, the

gospel presents the Galilean royal official as a model of insightful faith (4:46–54) and the Samaritan woman as a model of faith and mission activity (4:39).[38]

5. Gender: Although there were exceptions, the first-century world was generally patriarchal and androcentric, frequently relegating women to subordinate roles. Women play a significant, though not numerically dominant, role in the gospel. They participate in theological discussion with Jesus and are prominent in bearing witness and proclamation: Jesus' mother (2:1–11; 19:25–27), the Samaritan woman (ch. 4), Mary and Martha (11:1–12:8), and Mary Magdalene (20:1–18).[39]

Jesus consistently dwells among the marginalized and poor and benefits them by offering a transformative life that manifests God's purposes of wholeness and abundance.

John's Plot

How does the gospel's author combine these and numerous other elements to form the gospel's plot? We will take our cues from Aristotle's emphasis on the plot's end as the "necessary and/or usual" consequence of the previous events. Recognition and, in the end, reversal play important roles in producing John's ending. What are the events that lead to the gospel's surprising conclusion?

The Beginning (1:1–18; 1:19–4:54)

The gospel has a double beginning. The plot itself, containing the ordered combination of events that lead through challenge and conflict to Jesus' death, resurrection, and ascension, begins at 1:19. The first eighteen verses—the prologue—offer a big-picture narrative and thematic preview of the gospel's general movement. The main character begins with God and is active in creation (1:1–5), is witnessed to by John (1:6–8), comes into the world especially to his own people, is received by some and rejected by others, and carries out the task of revealing God and God's purposes (1:9–18). These verses alert the gospel's audience to important emphases in the story and frame all that follows.

Although the eighteen verses orient the reader, they also raise questions that require answers, make affirmations that require elaboration, and conceal what will require revelation. Of these verses, only verse 17 names the main character. How does he do his revealing work? What does he reveal? What difference does it make and to whom? What are "life," "light," and "grace and truth"? Why do some reject him? Who are these rejecting people? What interaction do they have with Jesus? What causes their rejection of him? How do they express it? Are they effective? Who receives him? How do some "see his glory"? How do "children of God" live? What happens to Jesus after he has made God known? These questions render the rest of the plot necessary as it works out the consequences of these declarations. The only way of answering these questions is to read the gospel's story.

The story takes as its starting point in 1:19–34 the development of one of these necessities, the role of John the Baptist. Two scenes focus on John, first introduced in verses 6–8, and 15 as a witness to Jesus the light. In his first scene, John testifies that he is not the light (v. 8a) but prepares the way for him (vv. 19–28). In the second scene (vv. 29–34), John testifies to Jesus (v. 8b) as the lamb[40] who takes away the world's sin (v. 29) and who bears the Spirit as God's agent or son (vv. 32–34).

Equally important is the context in which John makes this testimony. His testimony is framed by an inquiry from the Jerusalem-based elite officials into his identity (vv. 19, 21) and baptizing activity (v. 25). The inquirers' lack of interest in joining John's movement casts their inquiries in a suspicious light. Why are they checking up on him? Who are they that John seems to threaten their control?

As John bears witness to Jesus (vv. 35–36), Jesus appears. There is no account of his birth or upbringing. The prologue has emphasized his origin with God and his mission to be in the world. The plot narrates this mission, beginning with positive response to his ministry (cf. v. 10). He begins to gather followers in Judea (Andrew, Simon Peter, vv. 35–42) and Galilee (Philip, Nathanael, vv. 43–51). In both instances, the first disciple bears witness to the second. With a series of titles (Messiah, v. 41; Son of God, v. 49; King of Israel, v. 9), they recognize Jesus as one commissioned by God to reveal and accomplish God's purposes.

Two incidents in John 2 reveal God's purposes. At the wedding in Cana in Galilee, the wine runs out (vv. 1–12). Jesus performs his first sign, changing water into abundant and high-quality wine. Weddings and wine both figure prominently in Israel's traditions about the future establishment of God's good and just purposes, in which God blesses all people with abundant fertility (Isa 25:6–10). The scene in John reveals God's purposes, which contrast with and reverse the present exploitative world, where many lack resources to sustain life. The disciples discern God's power and presence with Jesus (his "glory," John 2:11) and commit themselves to him ("believe in" him, v. 11).

The next scene presents the revelation of God's purposes as a challenge to the ruling elite's way of structuring business as usual (vv. 13–23). Jesus attacks the leaders of the Jerusalem temple, their power base, who maintained and benefited from its unjust structures.[41] Observing the sale of animals to pilgrims in Jerusalem for Passover offerings and the changing of money for the collection of the temple tax (v. 14), Jesus denounces the sellers of doves for making "my Father's house a marketplace [house of trade]" (v. 16). His attack on this trade challenges an activity crucial for the administration of temple worship and for the wealth, political power, and status of the Jerusalem leaders.

Two Scripture citations interpret the action. The echoes of Zech 14:21 in Jesus' denunciation (John 2:16) locate Jesus' action in relation to God's anticipated intervention on behalf of God's people to establish God's just and life-giving purposes over God's enemies. This echo of Zechariah presents the temple leadership as God's opponents, signals their inevitable downfall, and foreshadows the vindication of Jesus. The citation of Ps 69:9 in John 2:17 ("Zeal for your house will consume me") signals the inevitable outcome of Jesus' challenge: it is a fatal challenge; he will die at their hands. But as the Zechariah citation indicates, they will not have the last word.

The leaders respond to Jesus' action by confronting his authority to do such things (v. 18). Jesus' response intensifies the hostility by charging them with destroying the temple (v. 19a) and by mysteriously claiming its replacement in his risen body (vv. 19b–22). The reference anticipates Jesus' death, links the temple leaders to it, and suggests an intensification of the conflict, which will develop through subsequent exchanges in the context of temple-based festivals (Nicodemus, ch. 3; 5:1–18; Tabernacles, ch. 7; Dedication, 10:22; Lazarus, chs. 11–12). It also raises the question of how this death will come about, and signals that their attempts to remove him will not finally be successful but will be thwarted by the resurrection. Moreover, the reference points to the end of the temple with the risen Jesus the locus of God's presence.

The temple scene is thus of great importance for the plot.[42] It introduces the conflict between Jesus and the Jerusalem authorities that will intensify through the gospel in Jesus' repeated trips to Jerusalem and the temple. With its reference to resurrection, it signals the limits of the leaders' power, the vindication of Jesus, the special relationship between Jesus and God, and the inevitable triumph of God's life-giving purposes. The scene introduces and anticipates these developments.

Jesus' relationship with these leaders deteriorates further in 3:1–21 as Jesus exposes the limits of one of them, Nicodemus, who is unable to understand Jesus' explanation of how God works (3:1–10). Nicodemus is like others in Jerusalem whom Jesus does not trust; with apparently superhuman powers, Jesus is able to see through them (2:23–25). Jesus' explanation of God's working centers on his own role as the revealer of God who descended from heaven (1:18, 51) and dies (3:13–14). This is the second reference to Jesus' death (2:18–22). Jesus also emphasizes God's love (3:16a); eternal life as the benefit derived from receiving him by believing or entrusting oneself to him and to his revelation of God's purposes (3:16b–17); judgment (3:18); and the importance of how one lives (3:19–20). Two short scenes follow, restating John's significance as subordinate but witnessing to Jesus (3:22–30), and Jesus' significance as sent from God to reveal God's purposes (3:31–35).

The negative response to Jesus of one of the power elite, Nicodemus, is followed by a contrasting response. The lengthy dialogue of chapter 4 thus introduces another character, the Samaritan woman. She contrasts with Nicodemus in significant ways:

- Nicodemus is named; she is not.

- He is a man; she is a woman.

- He lives in the powerful city of Jerusalem; she lives in the small and powerless city or village of Sychar (perhaps Shechem)[43] in Samaria.

- He is a Jew; she is a despised Samaritan (4:9). Jesus' mission includes Jews and Gentiles.

- He is wealthy, powerful, and of high social status (3:1); she is poor, powerless, and of low social status (4:7).

- He is unable to understand Jesus' theological talk (3:3–10); she persistently questions Jesus and gains understanding from him (4:11–12, 15).

- He recognizes Jesus as "a teacher who has come from God" (3:2, although he cannot learn from Jesus); she recognizes Jesus as a prophet (4:19, 29, 39) and hears him identify himself as the revealer-Messiah (4:26) in response to her confession that she is waiting for such a one (4:25)—a possibility to which she seems open (4:29, 39).

- Nicodemus appears not to believe (ch. 3); the woman believes and, like a good disciple and missionary, bears witness to many others in the city, who commit themselves to Jesus' revelation (4:39–42). They understand Jesus to be the Savior of the world, a title commonly claimed for Rome's emperors.[44]

Jesus returns to Galilee, where he is welcomed (4:43–45; contrast Jerusalem, 2:13–23). There another positive interaction occurs. In the village of Cana (cf. 2:1–12), he heals the son of a royal official, one of the elite, who is probably a retainer (and perhaps a Gentile) in the service of Herod Antipas (4:46–54). Jesus' second sign enacts God's purposes for wholeness. Disease was rife in the world ruled by imperial Rome. Health and wholeness demonstrate the establishment of God's reign (Isa 35:5–6).

The plot has begun with Jesus carrying out his task of revealing God's purposes in his gathering of disciples, in his words, and in his actions. Some have received or entrusted themselves to his revelation and encountered God's purposes. But the plot has also put in play another response. Suspicion from the ruling elite attends John's task of bearing witness to Jesus. Jesus has directly challenged their center of power in the Jerusalem temple. Jesus has shown one of their leaders to be incapable of understanding God's purposes at work in Jesus. Several references to Jesus' death indicate the high stakes at play in this negative response.

The Middle (5:1–17:26)

These negative and positive responses continue in the middle part of the story. Jesus' challenge to the elite necessarily intensifies toward his death at the hands of the Jerusalem elite (chs. 5–12); chapters 13–17 address the consequences for those who have responded positively to Jesus' mission.

Jesus' challenge to the power group in chapters 2–3 inevitably leads to further conflict. In Jerusalem for an unidentified festival (5:1), he again manifests God's purposes for wholeness and health by enabling a man paralyzed for thirty-eight years to walk again (5:1–15). But this action provokes a hostile response from the Jerusalem leaders because it violates their understanding of Sabbath as a day of rest and because Jesus claims God as his Father and the authority to act on God's behalf and do God's will. They decide that such behavior is highhanded and an affront to God (Num 15:30–31)—in a word, blasphemy that deserves death (Lev 24:13–16). It is, of course, an affront to their authority also. Jesus interprets the Sabbath traditions to permit life-giving action that transforms the world they control. And he claims to be God's agent in declaring such purposes. They do not think he has any such right or role.

Jesus elaborates these claims about his identity and authority in the long monologue that follows (5:19–47). His authority is based in his loving yet dependent relationship as Son with God his Father. Jesus carries out God's purposes in giving life (vv. 21–22) and passing judgment (vv. 26–27). But this relationship and these activities reveal not only his identity but also that of his hearers, either as those who, by committing themselves to Jesus, share in God's life (vv. 24–25, 28–29) or as those who, by rejecting Jesus, miss out on that life (v. 29). In verses 31–47 Jesus provides five witnesses to these claims: John the Baptist (vv. 32–35), Jesus' own works (v. 36), God (vv. 37–38), the Scriptures (vv. 39–44), and Moses (vv. 45–47).

Jesus' discourse in chapter 5 has emphasized his authority and relationship to God, his role as agent of God's purposes in giving life and judging, and the consequences of belief and unbelief. Chapters 6–10 develop these themes by employing essentially the same pattern as chapter 5. Jesus performs a sign, and dialogue follows that develops into a discourse delivered by Jesus. Throughout, a few believe while the opposition and hostility between Jesus and the Jerusalem leadership intensify. Their intentions to put Jesus to death figure prominently:

Chapter 6: In Galilee around Passover, Jesus further demonstrates his God-given authority by performing two signs that evoke the exodus story: he feeds five thousand people and walks on water to ensure that the disciples reach the shore safely (vv. 1–21). Both scenes employ themes of the Hebrew Bible to manifest God's life-giving purposes, power, and presence. The dialogue centers on the feeding story as a display of God's purposes (vv. 25–34). Jesus goes on to claim that he is the bread of life that has "come down from heaven" or has been sent from God into the world to reveal these purposes (vv. 35–59). But the leaders find these claims difficult to understand, as do some disciples (vv. 60–71).

Chapter 7: Jesus avoids Jerusalem because of increasing danger but then elusively returns to Jerusalem for the festival of Booths/Tabernacles (Sukkoth). He continues to assert his origin from God along with the life-giving benefit of accepting/believing and obeying his teaching. The leaders' threat to Jesus' life figures prominently, as do the people's divided responses to, and speculation about, Jesus' identity.

Chapter 8: The same themes continue as Jesus dominates a series of increasingly bitter dialogues with the elite. Jesus speaks about his own death and emphasizes the destructive consequences for those who reject his claims and revelation (vv. 12–30). He and the leaders debate what it means to be a descendant of Abraham and child of God (vv. 31–59) and the truth of Jesus' revelation (vv. 32, 45–47). Jesus charges the leaders with being false and descended from, and loyal to, the devil (vv. 42–45).

They charge him with being a despised Samaritan and being controlled by a demon (vv. 45–55), and they try to stone him to death (v. 59).

Chapter 9: Despite the danger, Jesus continues his life-giving mission, restoring sight to a man born blind (vv. 1–7). The rest of the chapter focuses on responses to the healing—from the man's neighbors (vv. 8–10), parents (vv. 18–23), the Jerusalem leaders (vv. 13–41), and the man himself. Whereas the leaders continue their opposition and disparage Jesus as not from God but a sinner (vv. 16, 24), their hostile interrogations of the man who has gained his sight assist that man in gaining insight into Jesus' identity. He identifies Jesus first as the man Jesus (v. 11), then as a prophet (v. 17), then as one from God (v. 33), and finally as Son of Man and Lord (vv. 37–38).

Chapter 10: The tension increases, and the dialogue continues to unfold as a monologue in which Jesus condemns the leaders, contrasting himself as the true shepherd. This image signifies a leader or ruler, one who represents God's rule and purposes (Ps 23; Ezek 34). He claims a close and caring relationship with the sheep, so much so that he is willing to lay down his life for them. He attacks the Jerusalem leaders, however, as "thieves and bandits" who steal resources from the people and threaten their well-being (10:1–21). Around the festival of Dedication, Jesus further claims to be God's agent and one with God in doing God's will. These claims sound like blasphemy to the leaders (10:22–38; cf. 5:16–18). They attempt to stone him and arrest him, but Jesus withdraws and many entrust themselves to him.

After the escalating animosity of chapters 5–10, Jesus' intensifying challenge to the integrity, identity, legitimacy, authority, and societal vision of the Jerusalem leaders, and his repeated claims to be the definitive revealer of God's purposes, only one outcome seems possible. Jesus' challenge cannot go unanswered. He will die at their hands. Chapters 11–12 play out these consequences.

Jesus' raising of Lazarus from death provokes the elite to kill him (11:1–44). Ironically, Jesus' act of giving life becomes the catalyst for the leaders' act of death. Fearing Jesus' popularity, their own loss of power, and Roman retaliation, the leaders plot to arrest and kill Jesus (11:45–57). The death theme increases as Mary, Lazarus's sister, lovingly anoints Jesus for burial (12:1–8) and Jerusalem enthusiastically welcomes Jesus (12:12–19), as do Gentiles (12:20–22). Jesus speaks of the arrival of his "hour," the time of his death, and rehearses his claims of God-given authority, his role as agent of God's purposes in giving life and judging, and the consequences of belief and unbelief (12:23–50).

Although the movement to Jesus' inevitable death slows in chapters 13–17, the reality of his death pervades these chapters.[45] Facing this imminent event, Jesus gathers his disciples to prepare them for life in his absence. During a farewell meal, in an act of loving service and hospitality, Jesus washes their feet (ch. 13). He challenges them to lives marked by loving service (13:12–20, 31–35) and predicts that Judas and Peter will betray him as his death approaches (13:21–30, 36–38). He then instructs them at length about their discipleship after his death (chs. 14–16). Prominent in his teaching are repeated assurances of his continuing presence with them after his death; the necessity of his return to the Father so that he can send the Spirit to assist them until he returns to earth; exhortations to continue in love; and the expectation of continuing opposition as they faithfully live out God's purposes in a rejecting world. Jesus closes the instruction session with a lengthy prayer that God display God's purposes in Jesus' death (17:1–8), in the community of disciples (17:9–19), and in the ongoing life of the church (17:20–26).

The End (Chapters 18–21)

Chapters 18–19 narrate the "necessary and/or usual" consequences of what has happened in the beginning (chs. 1–4) and middle (chs. 5–17) sections of the plot. The movement to Jesus' death proceeds through Jesus' betrayal by Judas, denial by Peter, and arrest by Roman soldiers and police from the Jerusalem leadership (18:1–18, 25–27); his appearance before the high priest (18:12–14, 19–24) and Pilate, who condemns him to be crucified as a kingly pretender (18:28–19:16a); his crucifixion as king of the Jews (a treasonous claim), and death (19:16b–30); the confirmation of his death (19:31–37), and his burial by Joseph and Nicodemus (19:38–42). By the end of chapter 19, the story has finished, as far as the elite are concerned. Jesus' death silences his critique, claims, and challenge. The elite seem to have prevailed, reducing his claims to naught.

But to use Aristotle's terms, a surprising reversal takes place in the last two chapters. Early on the morning of the third day, Jesus appears alive to Mary Magdalene (20:1–18). That evening he passes through locked doors and appears to the disciples (20:19–23). A week later he appears to Thomas and the disciples (20:24–29). Sometime thereafter, at the Sea of Tiberias or in Galilee, Jesus appears again to the disciples (21:1–14). In the resulting breakfast (21:15–24), Jesus speaks to two of the disciples, Peter (21:15–19) and the beloved disciple (21:20–24), about their future roles as part of the church that continues Jesus' work. Peter faces persecution and martyrdom; the beloved disciple is entrusted with mission work.

This last scene raises several questions about the "end" of the gospel plot. The plot, of course, ends in chapter 21; there is no chapter 22. But what happens to Jesus? Several earlier references indicate that he returns to God his Father (13:1; 14:3), although the gospel does not narrate how this happens. The end of the gospel and the departure of Jesus, however, do not mean the end of Jesus' mission. The final commissioning scene with the two disciples elaborates Jesus' previous sending of the disciples (20:21b) to continue his task of manifesting God's life-giving purposes.

Conclusion

John's plot is best understood by attending to its end as the "necessary and/or usual consequence" of the preceding action. John's story of Jesus centers on the assertion of Jesus' claim to be God's chosen agent, authorized by God to make a definitive revelation of God's life-giving purposes. In living out this claim in his words and works, Jesus conflicts with the Jerusalem elite and their Roman ally, Pilate, confronting and challenging their power over, and vision of, an unjust social order that is contrary to God's purposes. The Jerusalem elite reject Jesus' claim and revelation of God's purposes, ultimately putting him to death. But surprisingly, his death is not the end. God raises him, thereby revealing the limit of their power. Some people discern Jesus' origin, identity, and mission, commit themselves to his revelation, and form a counter-community that, assisted by the Holy Spirit, continues Jesus' mission.

Notes

1. E.g., Brown, *Gospel according to John; Introduction to the Gospel,* 298–316; F. Moloney, *The Gospel of John* (Sacra pagina 4; Collegeville, Minn.: Liturgical, 1998).

2. G. O'Day, "The Gospel of John," in *The New Interpreter's Bible* (ed. L. Keck; 12 vols.; Nashville: Abingdon, 1995), 9:491–865, here 512–14.

3. F. F. Segovia, "The Journey(s) of the Word of God: A Reading of the Plot of the Fourth Gospel," *Semeia* 53 (1991): 23–54.

4. For my fourfold structure, see W. Carter, *Pontius Pilate: Portraits of a Roman Governor* (Collegeville, Minn.: Liturgical, 2003), 130.

5. Aristotle, *On the Art of Poetry,* in T. S. Dorsch, *Classical Literary Criticism: Aristotle, Horace, Longinus* (Baltimore: Penguin, 1965), 29–75.

6. E. M. Foster, *Aspects of the Novel* (New York: Penguin Books, 1962), 87.

7. S. Crane, "The Concept of Plot," in *Approaches to the Novel* (ed. R. Scholes; rev. ed.; San Francisco: Chandler, 1966), 233–43, here 241.

8. M. H. Abrams, *A Glossary of Literary Terms* (3d ed.; New York: Holt, Reinhart & Winston, 1971), 127. Also K. Egan, "What Is a Plot?" *New Literary History* 9 (1978): 455–73, here 470.

9. S. Chatman, *Story and Discourse: Narrative Structure in Narrative and Film* (Ithaca, N.Y.: Cornell University Press, 1978), 53–56.

10. This approach works well for Matthew's plot. See W. Carter, *Matthew: Storyteller, Interpreter, Evangelist* (rev. ed.; Peabody, Mass.: Hendrickson, 2004), 149–75. But there are difficulties in applying it to John. Although we could identify some of John's key scenes or kernels, such as the calling of disciples (1:35–51), Jesus' protest in the temple (2:13–22), and the raising of Lazarus (ch. 11), John's gospel is very repetitive with a number of parallel scenes that emphasize important thematic dimensions but do not particularly advance the plot. Moreover, Chatman's formulation focuses attention on actions rather than words (dialogues/monologues), which contribute so much to John's plot. Key themes or strands woven throughout the gospel play an important role.

11. Frye, *Anatomy,* 33–67, 162, 163–71, 186–203; A. J. Greimas, *Semantique structurale* (Paris: Larousse, 1966); Chatman, *Story and Discourse,* 85.

12. Stibbe, *John's Gospel,* 38–53.

13. "Life" includes the experience of God's love (3:16), salvation (3:17–18), and judgment (5:26–27; 3:16; 10:10).

14. NRSV note has "do what you have heard from your father."

15. Culpepper, *Anatomy,* 77–98, esp. 84, 88–89; also R. A. Culpepper, *The Gospel and Letters of John* (Interpreting Biblical Texts; Nashville: Abingdon, 1998), 67–86.

16. C. K. Barrett, *The Gospel according to St. John* (London: SPCK, 1955), 126; O'Day, "Gospel of John," 518.

17. R. Bultmann, "The History of Religions Background of the Prologue to the Gospel of John," in *The Interpretation of John* (ed. J. A. Ashton; Philadelphia: Fortress, 1986), 18–35.

18. C. H. Dodd, *The Interpretation of the Fourth Gospel* (Cambridge: Cambridge University Press, 1953), 272–85; T. H. Tobin, "The Prologue of John and the Hellenistic Jewish Speculation," *CBQ* 52 (1990): 253–69.

19. Brown, *Gospel according to John,* 1:20–23; R. Kysar, *John* (Minneapolis: Augsburg, 1986), 28.

20. W. Carter, "The Prologue and John's Gospel: Function, Symbol, and the Definitive Word," *JSNT* 39 (1990): 35–58; Moloney, *John,* 33–48; F. F. Segovia, "John 1:1–18 as Entrée into Johannine Reality: Representation and Ramifications," in *Word, Theology, and Community in John* (ed. J. Painter, R. A. Culpepper, and F. F. Segovia; St. Louis: Chalice, 2002), 33–64.

21. Painter, *Quest for the Messiah.*

22. See 2:11, 18, 23; 3:2; 4:48, 54; 6:2, 14, 26, 30; 7:31; 9:16; 10:41; 11:47; 12:18, 37. Just once, at 4:48, it calls them "wonders" (*terata,* τέρατα); the phrase "signs and wonders" appears in Exod 7:3–4 and Deut 29:3; 34:11 in reference to the liberation from Egypt; also Wis 10:16.

23. P. Garnsey, *Food and Society in Classical Antiquity* (Cambridge: Cambridge University Press, 1999). Johannine scholarship has paid relatively little attention to the gospel's interaction with the Roman imperial world. For some exceptions, see D. Rensberger, *Johannine Faith and Liberating Community* (Philadelphia: Westminster, 1988), esp. 87–106; C. Koester, "'The Savior of the World' (John 4:42)," *JBL* 109 (1990): 665–80; R. J. Cassidy, *John's Gospel in New Perspective: Christology and the Realities of Roman Power* (Maryknoll, N.Y.: Orbis, 1992); S.-J. Kim, "Johannine Jesus and Its Sociopolitical Context," *Yonsei Review of Theology and Culture* 6 (2001): 209–21; G. Van den Heever, "Finding

Data in Unexpected Places (or: From Text Linguistics to Socio-rhetoric): Towards a Socio-rhetorical Reading of John's Gospel," *Neot* 33 (1999): 343–64.

24. This section is informed by G. O'Day, "'I Have Said These Things to You . . .': The Unsettled Place of Jesus' Discourses in Literary Approaches to the Fourth Gospel," in *Word, Theology, and Community in John* (ed. J. Painter, R. A. Culpepper, and F. F. Segovia; St. Louis: Chalice, 2002), 143–54.

25. Note, e.g., 5:17–18, Sabbath breaking and calling God Father; 6:41–44, Jesus' origin; 8:12–58, Jesus' origin and destiny, descent from Abraham, and his opponents' descent from the devil; ch. 10, the illegitimacy of the Jerusalem leadership as false leaders/shepherds (cf. Ezek 34).

26. Bethany, John 1:28; 11:1; Judea, 3:22.

27. John 1:43; 2:1–12; 4:46–54 (Cana); 4:3, 43–45; 6:1 (the other side of the sea of Galilee); 2:12; 6:17, 24–59 (Capernaum); 7:1–9.

28. G. Yee, *Jewish Feasts and the Gospel of John* (Wilmington, Del.: Michael Glazier, 1989).

29. See G. Lenski, *Power and Privilege: A Theory of Social Stratification* (Chapel Hill: University of North Carolina Press, 1984), 189–296; R. MacMullen, *Roman Social Relations* (New Haven, Conn.: Yale University Press, 1974); on the temple economy, K. C. Hanson and E. E. Oakman, *Palestine in the Time of Jesus* (Minneapolis: Fortress, 1998), 99–159; for John's presentation of the Pharisees and chief priests (John does not mention scribes, Sadducees, or elders), A. J. Saldarini, *Pharisees, Scribes, and Sadducees in Palestinian Society* (Wilmington, Del.: Michael Glazier, 1988), 35–49, 187–98.

30. Although his social status is clear, his occupational identity and ethnicity are ambiguous. Josephus (*Life* 399–406) uses *basilikos* to refer to troops in the service of King Herod Agrippa II; we might expect such troops to be Judeans, but there is evidence for Roman soldiers serving the Herods; so A. H. Mead, "The *basilikos* in John 4:46–54," *JSNT* 23 (1985): 69–72. The term can also denote a (Jewish) "royal official/functionary" in the service of Herod Antipas who is not a soldier (Josephus, *J.W.* 2.595–597). See R. J. Karris, *Jesus and the Marginalized in John's Gospel* (Collegeville, Minn.: Liturgical, 1990), 57–65, who supports the latter option. Significantly, this upper-status person seeks help from the lowly ranked Jesus.

31. Carter, *Pontius Pilate*, 35–54, 127–52.

32. Karris, *Jesus;* C. R. Whittaker, "The Poor," in *The Romans* (ed. A. Giardini; Chicago: University of Chicago Press, 1993), 272–99.

33. MacMullen, *Roman Social Relations;* Karris, *Jesus,* 33–41; Carter, *Pontius Pilate,* 127–52.

34. Garnsey, *Food and Society,* 43–61.

35. In Acts 28:8 fever accompanies dysentery, an infectious disease, and in Josephus, *Life* 402–404, broken bones. Seneca (*Apolocyntosis* 6) has the emperor Claudius die of fever. See K. Weiss, "πυρέσσω, πυρετός," *TDNT* 6:956–58.

36. Garnsey, *Food and Society,* 47–48.

37. Karris, *Jesus,* 42–53.

38. On geographical marginalization, ibid., 54–72.

39. Ibid., 73–95; G. O'Day, "John," in *Women's Bible Commentary: Expanded Edition with Apocrypha* (ed. C. Newsom and S. Ringe; Louisville: Westminster John Knox, 1998), 381–93.

40. Commentators suggest that this image may evoke the Passover lamb, who symbolizes Israel's deliverance from Egyptian captivity (Exod 12:1–13);

and/or the servant in Isa 53:7, who absorbs imperial violence and delivers God's people; and/or an apocalyptic figure who destroys all sin (cf. Rev 17:14).

41. For a good description of the temple's involvement in economic exploitation through landed estates, the requisitioning of supplies for its rituals and personnel (tithes), and the collection of the temple tax, see Hanson and Oakman, *Palestine,* 131–59.

42. M. Matson, "The Temple Incident: An Integral Element in the Fourth Gospel's Narrative," in *Jesus in Johannine Tradition* (ed. R. Fortna and T. Thatcher; Louisville: Westminster John Knox, 2001), 145–53.

43. So Brown, *Gospel according to John,* vol. 1; R. Schnackenburg (*The Gospel according to St. John* [3 vols.; New York: Seabury, 1980–1982]), 1:422–23) disagrees, claiming no good reason for Sychar to displace Shechem and favoring the site of Askar. If Shechem is in view, it was a small village in the first century, but it had a distinguished history. In Josh 24, it was the scene for a covenant ceremony celebrating God's deliverance of the people from Egypt and the gift of the land and requiring the people to serve God faithfully. The Samaritan woman and many from her city are now included in that covenant.

44. Koester, "'Savior.'"

45. F. F. Segovia, *The Farewell of the Word: The Johannine Call to Abide* (Minneapolis: Fortress, 1991); J. C. Thomas, *Footwashing in John 13 and the Johannine Community* (JSNTSup 61; Sheffield, Eng.: JSOT Press, 1991).

CHAPTER 3

Characters: God and Jesus

The discussion of John's plot leads us inevitably to the gospel's characters. This chapter presents a few brief observations about the presentation of characters, especially in ancient biographies, and then examines the characterization of God and Jesus in John's gospel. The next chapter will consider other characters in the gospel.

Building Characters

Without characters there is no plot; without plot there are no characters.[1] What the characters do and say, how they interact with other characters, what conflicts they experience, and with whom and over what, are fundamental elements of most plots. Plots and characters "are inseparably bound up in the reading experience, if not always in critical thought. Each works to produce the other. Characters are defined in and through the plot, by what they do and by what they say. The plot in turn comes into view as characters act and interact."[2]

Characters usually are not fully formed from the outset in a movie or novel. This is especially true of main characters and less so of one-dimensional, or "flat," characters with bit parts and stereotypical roles. Main characters generally emerge gradually as the plot progresses. Various aspects or "character-istics," called traits, appear in their actions, their interactions with other characters and circumstances, and through changes, growth, and inconsistencies. These traits are a character's customary ways of being and doing ("Phoebe is ditzy . . .") and distinguish one character from another (" . . . whereas Monica is obsessive").[3] The cluster of traits combines to form a character with consistent patterns of behavior; we might describe an unusual action as out of character or "un-character-istic." Movies and novels use both direct means, such as naming a characteristic or trait ("God is true," John 3:33),[4] and indirect means that display the character trait.

While a text or movie is making this progressive presentation, readers or viewers have important work to do. We must notice the traits displayed in the ongoing actions and interactions. In John, we must elaborate the cultural (usually biblical) traditions or memories that words or phrases evoke. As we read a novel or view a movie, we must also evaluate the reliability of what we notice. If we are told directly, for example, that a character is a liar, we must assess the accuracy of this declaration in terms of what we know about the one making the statement and in terms of the character's other actions and interactions. We also must make sense of the various and disparate traits that we observe, by combining them to build a character. We build the character tentatively and progressively, waiting for and accessing more data to confirm, elaborate, or overturn earlier impressions. We do much the same sort of work in our daily relationships and interactions with people.

Characters act, speak, interact, and conflict. Moreover, by various means, characters depict points of view or values that we as readers or viewers observe (whether we agree or disagree with them) and by which we evaluate the actions, words, interactions, and conflicts of other characters in the story. Observing and employing these ideological perspectives is sometimes an easy task, especially in classic "good guy/bad guy" situations. Sometimes, however, the perspectives are much more complex and ambiguous. John's gospel uses characters such as God and Jesus to create a particular ideological or theological perspective. All actions, words, interactions, and conflicts—that is, all characters in the gospel and beyond—are assessed in relation to this point of view.

A work's genre—love story, poem, science fiction novel—creates expectations for the types of characters we are likely to encounter. The genre of ancient biography creates three important expectations about the characters in John's gospel:[5]

1. As readers of modern biographies and novels, we expect to gain insight into a character's inner world, especially their motivations and their psychological growth or development. Ancient biographies, by contrast, rarely explore a character's inner world or their development and only occasionally impute motivation or attribute thoughts or attitudes to a character. This is generally true for John's gospel. Jesus does not change or develop through

the story. We do, however, on a few occasions obtain glimpses of Jesus' inner world.[6]

2. Ancient biographies, as we observed in chapter 1, above, are often didactic in purpose. They present and evaluate characters in moral terms, highlighting good or bad qualities for praise (and imitation) or scorn. Aristotle urged the presentation of "morally good," "suitable," "life-like" and "consistent" characters (*Poet.* 1454a). Ancient biographies have some interest in showing how upbringing, education, and experiences shaped these characteristics, although they hold characters responsible for their qualities. They recognize that characters can change, although they tend to see a person's character and career as fairly stable, centered on a key trait or core of features evident in their major contributions to society. For John, Jesus' central characteristic is his faithful revelation of God's purposes even as he challenges and conflicts with the ruling powers who put him to death.

3. Ancient biographies commonly portray characters through indirect means, such as actions, words, interactions, and conflicts. Anecdotes, representative scenes, and comparisons with other characters also make important contributions. These biographies can also provide direct analysis by naming the trait or motivation to be admired or rejected. The ideological agenda that shapes the characterization and emphasizes traits for imitation or censure often produces ideal or stereotypical characters with exaggerated positive or negative qualities. We will see this in John's gospel, for example, in the harshly negative presentation of the Jerusalem leaders (often called "the Jews" [see ch. 4, below]).

God

It might seem strange to begin our discussion of John's characters with God or even to conceive of God as a character in the story. After all, God does not appear and speaks only once (12:28). Surely Jesus is the central character, since the story narrates his actions and words, his interactions and conflicts, which lead to his death.

There is no denying the centrality of Jesus' role. But as the gospel repeatedly makes clear, he is of no significance apart from his relationship with, and role received from, God.[7] Without God's action in sending

Jesus, there would be no plot. Within the context of the intimate relationship between God and Jesus, God authorizes and guarantees Jesus' mission, actions, words, and interactions, all of which reveal God's life-giving purposes (20:30–31).[8] Likewise, this sending action and Jesus' statements about God provoke much conflict, and both action and conflict are crucial elements of characterization and plot, as we have seen. Moreover, God provides the definitive point of view, or perspective, on Jesus.

As the previous section established, what matters in characterization is the presentation or building of particular figures. How are they portrayed? How do they appear in this work? Characterization concerns actions, words, interactions, and conflicts. To study a character—in this instance, God—is to observe the characteristics or traits associated with God that emerge through the narrative and that, when connected, contribute to a particular presentation of God.

> Note to Reader: As I said in chapter 2, in the following pages, I will refer to lots of texts from John's gospel. Unfortunately, there is not space to print out these verses here. It will help your reading to check out these references in John's gospel.

God and the Prologue (1:1–18)

We learn much about God from the opening prologue (1:1–18). God does not change through the narrative, and so the prologue indicates character traits that provide crucial perspectives for the rest of the gospel. God is presented with the following traits:

1. Prior to all else (1:1): God exists "in the beginning." If priority in time also means priority in status (as it often did in John's world) and if longevity is highly valued (as it was in John's world), God is superior to all.

2. Creator (1:1, 3, 10): The opening phrase, "in the beginning" (1:1), evokes the Genesis account of creation: "In the beginning when God created heaven and earth" (Gen 1:1).[9] Commonly the gospel evokes narratives in the Hebrew Bible to present aspects of characters. It assumes that we the readers know these cultural (biblical) traditions and can interpret their significance.[10] To evoke God's creative activity (also John 1:3, 10) is to recognize

God's ownership of or sovereignty over creation and to be receptive to God's way of ordering it.

3. Relational (1:1, 12–14): God exists before creation in relationship with another heavenly being, "the Word" (cf. 17:24). Likewise, when the Word becomes flesh (1:14), relationship continues to be emphasized by denoting God as Father and Jesus as Son, central categories for the gospel (also 1:18). Through Jesus' ministry, God creates relationship with people as children (1:12–13). Relationship is fundamental to God's way of being.

4. Life-giving (1:3–4): God's creative activity gives life to all people. What this life looks like, how it is lived daily in the societal structures and priorities where the Jerusalem leadership, allied with Rome, dominates, is a major issue in the gospel.

5. Opposed but not defeated: John 1:5 ominously refers to darkness that has not been able to overcome God's life-giving activity. The reference frames God's activity in a context of struggle and (futile) resistance from humans (1:10–11) and from cosmic powers ("the ruler of this world," 12:31; 16:11).

6. Intervening and commissioning (1:6–8, 15): God sends John. With this act God intervenes (as God continues to do, 5:17) in the human realm that God has created and to which God has given life. More particularly, God commissions John to a particular role of bearing witness (as 1:19–36 will elaborate).

7. Bearing children/Father (1:12–13): In 1:9–13 those who "received" or "believed" Jesus gain a new identity in becoming "children of God." The "of" construction, common in the gospel, denotes their origin (from the life-giving God) as well as their possession and legitimation by God.[11] The image of being God's children recalls the use of the same designation for God's covenant people, Israel (Exod 4:32; Jer 31:9), an identity that denotes both privileged relationship and the responsibility of enacting God's purposes. These children in 1:12, then, are not the first to be "born . . . of God" (1:13). That God begets children indicates God is a Father, an image used in both 1:14 and 1:18. Thereafter it will become the central image for God.

8. Powerful: The above traits—Creator, life-giving, not defeated by opposition, intervening, commissioning John, begetting children—denote God's powerful activity.

9. Hidden and revealed (1:9–18): The ministry of Jesus (not named until 1:17) emphasizes his special role, to reveal God. Jesus "enlightens" (1:9) and enables others to see the Father's "glory" (1:14, God's power, presence, and purposes) and to receive "grace and truth" (1:16–17). Jesus makes God known (1:18). This revelatory role is necessary because God is elusive and hidden, not seen by any human (1:18; 6:46).

10. Faithful (1:17): Although the gospel emphasizes Jesus' special revelation, we should not conclude that God has been unknown and unknowable previously. Several times the prologue evokes the covenant at Sinai between God and Israel. The covenant term "children of God" appears in 1:12, along with "his own" in 1:11. The verb "lived" (or "tabernacled") in 1:14 recalls God speaking to Moses (Exod 33:9) and God's promise to dwell with God's people (Ezek 37:27). The references to "truth" in 1:14–17 also emphasize God's faithfulness to this covenant relationship (see ch. 5, below). The description of Jesus as "full of grace and truth" (1:14) echoes the covenant pairing often translated, "steadfast love and faithfulness" (Exod 34:6). There is no indication that God has revoked this covenant.

11. Justice-seeking: In John 1:17 God gives the law (or teaching guidelines) through Moses. How and by whom this revelation of God's purposes through Moses is to be interpreted is a major issue in Jesus' ministry (5:45; 9:28–29). Jesus claims Moses' writings point to him (1:45; 5:46), a claim with which his opponents clearly disagree. An important element of God's purposes manifested in Moses' teaching is God's commitment to justice (Exod 20; Ps 33:5; 37:2). Jesus continues this revelation in his attack on the temple, in his conflicts with the Jerusalem leaders who, as Rome's allies, preside over an unjust social structure contrary to God's purposes, and in his miracles/signs of healing and feeding.

God in the Beginning, Middle, and End of Jesus' Ministry (1:19–21:25)

The prologue ends with an emphasis on God's intimate relationship with Jesus and God's revealing activity through Jesus. Jesus "has made him known" (1:18). The rest of the gospel continues this focus on God's revealing activity. The following are some central emphases.

God's revealing activity centers in Jesus. This is possible because God has revealed Godself to Jesus (5:20; 8:38, 40; 12:50; 14:8–9). God's revealing activity in Jesus is expressed fundamentally by two key verbs: "send" and "give." The narrative uses the verb "send"[12] more than forty times to describe God as the sender of Jesus. This sending expresses God's sealing (6:27) and consecrating (10:36) of Jesus. God initiates, authorizes, and guarantees the revelation of God and God's life-giving purposes in Jesus' ministry.

God is the sender, but God is also the giver. As the authorizer and guarantor of Jesus' ministry, God's sending of Jesus means "giving"[13] Jesus (3:16), the true bread from heaven (6:32). God also gives or entrusts to Jesus "all things" (3:35; 13:3; 17:7), including judgment (5:22, 26–27), life (4:10, 14; 5:26; 6:27, 33; 10:28; 17:2), actions/works (5:36; 17:4; cf. 14:10), words (12:49; 17:8), God's name (17:11, 12), and the cup of Jesus' suffering (18:11). God also "gives" insight to various people (3:27), "gives" people to Jesus (6:37, 39, 65; 10:29; 17:2, 6, 9, 24), draws them (6:44; 12:32), and answers prayer (15:16; 16:23). God continues this work (5:17), giving the Paraclete, or Spirit, in Jesus' absence to believers (14:26), seeking worshippers (4:23), and raising dead believers (5:21).

God's sending and giving activity depicts God as revelatory and interventionist, actively working to restore human existence.

1. Motivation: God's sending of Jesus is rooted in and reveals God's active love for the world (3:16). This love expresses God's covenant commitment to a caring relationship with Israel (Hos 3:1; 11:1) and to providing good and just life for Israel and the world (Ps 33:5; 37:28; Jer 31:3).

2. Agent: God lovingly sends Jesus as God's agent to reveal God's presence and purposes in Jesus' words, works, interactions, and conflicts. Jesus descends from heaven, God's abode, accomplishes his revelatory mission, and ascends to God.[14] The gospel particularly, though not exclusively, designates this interaction between God and Jesus with the familial relational terms "Father" and "Son." "Father" is the gospel's most common term for God (used about 120 times whereas "God" is used about 108 times) and is an image used in the Hebrew scriptures to denote God's creative activity, covenant relationship with the people, and redemptive activity on their behalf (Deut 32:6; Isa 63:16; Jer 3:19–20). "Father" is the subject of various verbs denoting interaction with Jesus the Son: loves (3:35; 10:17; 15:9; 17:24), makes things known to (5:20), sends (5:37), bears witness to (5:37;

8:18), instructs (8:28), glorifies (8:54), commands what Jesus is to say (12:49–50). The Son imitates the Father's actions (5:19). This intimate reciprocal relationship is marked by unity in function and purpose: they are one (10:30); the Father is in the Son and the Son is in the Father (10:38; 14:10–11; 17:21); they share life-giving and judging tasks (5:21–22; 8:16); there is mutual knowing (10:15). The Father is with the Son (3:2; 8:29; 16:32).

3. Content and scope: The content of God's revealing work concerns God and God's purposes. To know God and understand God's purposes, people must discern Jesus' identity as God's agent, the one sent from God and thereby authorized to reveal God. Hence, to see Jesus is to see the Father (12:45; 14:9). To know Jesus is to know the Father (8:19; 14:7). The Son's words and works come from the Father (5:36; 8:28; 12:50). What does Jesus reveal? Jesus' declares, "I came that they may have life, and have it abundantly" (10:10; cf. 20:31, the gospel's purpose statement). Life means to "know God" in intimate relationship and encounter with God (17:3). This life is social, lived in relationship with God's children (1:12–13); countercultural in that it is marked by love and service, not domination as in Roman imperial society (13:13–17, 34–35); and material and physical, since it participates in God's life-giving and just purposes of salvation, which include material wholeness and abundant fertility (2:1–12; 3:16–18; 4:46–54; 5:1–18; 6:1–15; and the rest of Jesus' signs; see the discussion of "signs" and "life" in chapter 5 below).

4. Effect: God's revealing activity in Jesus is divisive. Some "believe" or "receive" him, entering into a transformed relationship with God as Father (1:12). That is, they actively commit or entrust themselves to Jesus, accepting his identity as the one sent from God to reveal God's purposes, loving him, and living accordingly with other believers (3:16–21; 6:29; 13:34–35; 14:12, 15, 21; 15:10; 16:27).[15] To believe is to encounter God's love (14:21, 23) and to enter into intimate relationship with God (17:3, 21). Others do not receive Jesus or know him as God's authorized agent and revealer (1:10–11). Not to honor the Son is not to honor the Father (5:23). To hate Jesus is to hate the Father (15:23–24). Not to believe is to encounter condemnation (3:18; 12:48).

5. Context: Often this revelation of God's presence and purposes occurs in contexts of polemic. Throughout the gospel, how or

where God is revealed (e.g., in Jesus or in Moses' teaching, 5:45; 9:28–29) and the sort of society God desires are central issues (5:1–18; ch. 9). Jesus accuses the Jerusalem leaders of not loving God (5:42)—indeed, of not knowing God (7:28–29)—and of not having God as their Father (8:19, 54–55) because they do not understand Jesus to be God's revealer and live in the light of his revelation. Their not "loving" or "hearing" Jesus is, so Jesus claims, proof of their not knowing God as their Father (8:42–43, 47). Jesus, not these leaders, keeps or observes God's word and will (8:55). Their claim to know God is false and reflects their real father, the devil (8:41–47). They accuse Jesus of calling "God his own Father, thereby making himself equal to God" (5:18). Also, the world that rejects Jesus' disciples does not know God (15:18–25, esp. 21; 16:3; 17:25). This context of ignorance requires revelation. Chapter 8, below, will elaborate the historical circumstances of this unfortunate and dangerous polemic.

6. Its completion: When Jesus dies, he announces, "It is finished" (19:30). Raised from death (3:14; 8:28; 12:32), he ascends to God (20:17), returning to the Father who sent him (13:1–3; 14:12, 28; 16:17; 20:17).[16] God's power triumphs over sin, death, and elite opposition to Jesus and his revelation of God's purposes. Jesus' death, however, is not the end of his work. He will return to take disciples to be with God and himself (14:1–3). God's revelatory activity continues, in the meantime, through the Paraclete, or Holy Spirit, whom the Father sends to reveal even greater things to disciples (14:26; 16:13).

Two final aspects of John's image of God as Father deserve comment. Gail O'Day notes that for many women, the image of God as Father has often been painful, evoking patriarchal power and systems of authoritative domination while silencing other biblical images for God.[17] O'Day argues that the solution for this issue is not to eliminate the image from John but to understand the dimensions of John's rich use of the image. It denotes not patriarchy but relationships of intimacy and love as well as birth into a new family or household (1:12–13; 3:3–10; 14:18).

Second, Mary Rose D'Angelo has examined the use of the image of "Father" for God in first-century Judaism.[18] There is considerable overlap with John's use in that it was used as a form of personal address, often evoking God's power, authority, sovereignty, and providence and seeking assurance of forgiveness and help for the afflicted and persecuted. D'Angelo also notes the use of the term "Father" to denote the

Roman emperor's considerable power over his subjects (as children), divinely guaranteed by Father Zeus/Jupiter. Although, surprisingly, she does not discuss John's gospel, this Roman context provides a further edge to the gospel's use of the image. In identifying God as Father and disciples/followers as "children," John both imitates this imperial way of thinking and challenges Rome's claims by asserting God's sovereignty and loving, saving purposes for a transformed way of life, known among a countergroup in the empire.

Jesus

From the discussion of God, it is apparent that we cannot talk about God in John's gospel without talking about Jesus. Some of the main traits in John's presentation of Jesus are sketched here.[19]

John's Christology

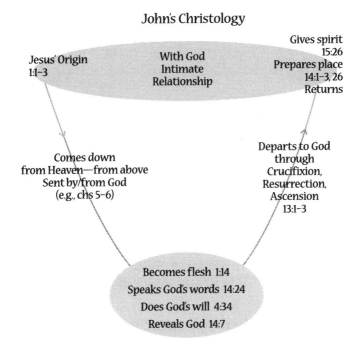

Jesus' Origin
1:1–3

With God
Intimate
Relationship

Gives spirit
15:26
Prepares place
14:1–3, 26
Returns

Comes down
from Heaven—from above
Sent by/from God
(e.g., chs 5–6)

Departs to God
through
Crucifixion,
Resurrection,
Ascension
13:1–3

Becomes flesh 1:14
Speaks God's words 14:24
Does God's will 4:34
Reveals God 14:7

Jesus' Origin and Destiny

The prologue, as we have seen, tells us much about both Jesus and God. The opening verses locate "the Word" with God before creation.

Though never explicitly identified with Jesus, readers come to understand, from the prologue's content (including 1:17) and context at the outset of the gospel, that this Word that "became flesh" (1:14) is Jesus.

Scholars have suggested various philosophical and theological traditions to inform and clarify this notion of the Word. The works of Stoic philosophers, the Hellenistic Jewish writer Philo, gnostics, and Mandaeans have been investigated, as have Jewish notions of the "word of the Lord," Lady Wisdom, and Torah.[20] Although this effort is important and John may evoke several of them, we should not miss the very simple but important observation that a word includes communication or making something known. The term "Word" emphasizes Jesus' identity and function as revealer of God's life-giving purposes.

The gospel emphasizes Jesus' origin in the beginning, in face-to-face relationship with God, as the foundation for claiming the absolute reliability and trustworthiness of Jesus' revelation of God in Jesus' words and works. This claim was made in a historical context of great uncertainty about God's purposes (see ch. 8, below) and in which various traditions claimed to reveal those purposes by means of a revealer figure who had traveled from earth into heaven for a brief visit.[21] In this context of competing claims, John trumps all other contenders by locating the Word with God in the beginning. The Word does not begin on earth and pay a brief visit to the heavens like these other figures. He is with God already in the beginning, sharing in face-to-face interaction with God and in God's work of creation (1:1–3). "What God was the Word also was" (1:1).[22] Such a figure who comes down from God to communicate God's presence and purposes offers reliable revelation.

The gospel constantly reiterates this claim of Jesus' origin from God to guarantee his revelation:

- God has revealed himself to Jesus (5:20; 8:38, 40; 12:50; 14:8–9; 15:15). Jesus is the only one to see God (1:18; 6:46).

- Jesus imitates what he sees the Father doing (5:19). Jesus' words and works come from the Father (5:36; 12:50).

- Two little English prepositions, "of"[23] (often meaning "from") and "from"[24] (often used with "God," the "Father," and "heaven"), express the origin of Jesus and of his revelation in words and actions.

- In addition to the verbs of "sending" and "giving," discussed above, verbs such as "descends from"/"comes down from" (3:13; 6:33, 38, 41–42, 50, 51, 58) and "comes from" (8:42; 13:3; 16:27–28, 30; 17:8) maintain the emphasis on Jesus' origin from God.

- People struggle to understand and accept that Jesus originates with and is authorized by God (6:41–43; 7:27–28, 41; 8:21–22). Those who do know Jesus' origin understand that they too have God as their Father and are "from God" (8:42, 47).

- Through his "lifting up" in his death, resurrection, and ascension (3:14–15; 8:28; 12:32), Jesus returns to God. This return attests his acceptability to God, confirming and securing his revelation (13:1–3; 14:12, 28; 16:17; 20:17).

Jesus the Agent of God's Purposes

Originating with God, Jesus "becomes flesh" as the agent of God's purposes. Various titles used throughout the gospel emphasize his identity and tasks as God's agent. The opening chapter of John introduces a number of these titles, requiring that we read on to find out how they are elaborated through the gospel:

1. Lamb of God (1:29, 36): Spoken by John the Baptist, this title identifies Jesus as the one appointed by God to "take away the sin of the world." The image of the lamb might pick up traditions of the lamb who conquers or overcomes all sin (cf. Rev 7:17; 17:14); the Passover lamb, which was not a sacrifice of sin but points to God's liberation of the people from Egyptian oppression (Exod 12:1–13); or the Suffering Servant, who absorbs Babylonian imperial violence to free the people (Isa 52:13–53:12, esp. 53:7). Significantly, each tradition understands sin not just as individual failures but as the activities and orientation of nations and empires whose imperial power is contrary to God's purposes. And resisting and overcoming this sin or evil, instead of sacrificing, are the means of liberation, of "taking away" the sin. Later in the gospel, John will link Jesus' death with Passover. Jesus dies unblemished like a Passover lamb (19:33–36; cf. Exod 12:46) on the day of preparation for Passover, when the lambs are slaughtered (19:14–18). But by placing this title at the beginning of Jesus' ministry, the gospel shows that all of Jesus' life (words and works) undertakes this task of liberating from sin.

2. Son of God (1:34, 49): This designation is discussed in the section "Jesus the Son of God: Unity and Subordination," below.

3. Rabbi, teacher (1:38; also 1:49): The Word, Jesus, uses many words in teaching or revealing God's purposes. "Rabbi," used

regarding Jesus by both disciples (4:31; 9:2; 11:8) and non-disciples (3:2; 6:25; and regarding John the Baptist, 3:26), denotes an important but limited understanding of Jesus' identity and function.

4. Messiah (or its Greek form, Christ; 1:41; see 1:17, 20, 25): This term literally means "anointed"; anointing was an act that denoted commissioning. God anointed or commissioned kings (Ps 2:2), prophets (1 Kgs 19:16), priests (Lev 4:5), even the Gentile Persian ruler Cyrus (Isa 44:28; 45:1) to serve God in particular ways. There was no widespread expectation for the Messiah in first-century Judaism, and among those who did look for a Messiah, there was no agreed-upon job description or tasks that the Messiah would perform.[25] Although the term recognizes Jesus as God's anointed one, it raises a question. What is Jesus commissioned to do? In 1:29 he will take away sin. As king, he will enact God's rule and represent God's purposes. In 3:16–18 he comes to save, not condemn, the world. In 10:10 he comes to give abundant life, life of the new age, which knows only God's just purposes. He is thus commissioned to be God's agent, revealing God's life-giving and transforming salvific purposes.

5. King of Israel (1:49): This is a double-sided term. On the one hand, the king conventionally represents in Israel's traditions God's good and just purposes among all people, as expressed, for instance, in Psalm 72, a "royal psalm." But under Roman rule, the term was coopted. Only Rome could designate such a king, and the title had belonged for about four decades to King Herod, Rome's ally and puppet king. Through the first century, various rebel figures revived a tradition of popular kingship by claiming the title or representing themselves as the people's king. Rome's retribution was swift. It viewed such figures as dangerous insurrectionists and executed them.[26] The giving of this title to Jesus signals not only that he reveals and represents God's purposes and reign in his words and works (3:3, 5; 6:15) but also that, in doing so, he conflicts with the Roman-controlled social order, a role that endangers Jesus' life (12:13–15; 19:12). The title's prominent use in his trial before Pilate (four times; 18:33–39) and in the crucifixion scenes (seven times; 19:3, 14, 15, 19–21) indicates that Jesus is executed as a rebellious kingly pretender.[27] His resurrection reveals the limits of Rome's power, which cannot keep him dead. He also overcomes the power of Satan, who had also brought about his death (13:2, 26–27; 12:31; 16:11).

6. Son of Man (1:51):[28] This is the first of thirteen uses of this term, which is used only by Jesus.[29] "Son of Man" can refer simply to a human being (a "mortal," Ezek 2:1; 3:1), but most scholars hold that John's use was influenced by the presentation, in Dan 7:13–14, of a heavenly agent who makes known God's "everlasting dominion" and "kingship" over "all peoples, nations, and languages." The use of the term for Jesus in 1:51 emphasizes his revelatory role by referring to the heavens being opened (Ezek 1:1) and by evoking the story of Jacob's dream ladder, which connects heaven and earth (Gen 28:12). This revelatory role as Son of Man is also evident in 3:13, which refers to Jesus' descent from heaven; in 5:27, which refers to his role as future, eschatological judge (cf. Dan 7; 1 En 46); and in 6:27, 53, which refers to his revelation of God's life. In 9:35 "Son of Man" seems to point to Jesus' judging and life-giving roles in the present.

A minority scholarly view posits another link with Dan 7, identifying the "one like a son of man" in Dan 7:13 with the holy ones of the Most High who suffer and die at the hands of enemies and thereby experience God's vindication (Dan 7:14, 21–25, 27).[30] This emphasis sees "Son of Man" highlighting aspects of Jesus' earthly ministry (so John 1:14) rather than his heavenly origin and descent. It points not only to his revelatory activity but especially to his death, Jesus' lifting up on the cross (3:14;[31] 8:28; 12:32–34), in which God glorifies Jesus (12:23; 13:31). "Son of Man" is understood here to have a much more restricted referent than "Son of God," which refers to all dimensions of Jesus' existence.

The two options, however, seem to be something of a false antithesis. Jesus' ministry as Son embraces both his revelatory, life-giving activity and his death. Nor is his death the end; it reveals God's presence and power as the means by which he departs to God through his resurrection and ascension.[32] The gospel's emphasis on the descent from and ascent to heaven, the abode of God, frames his revelatory work and crucifixion. The verbs often associated with "Son of Man"—"lifting up" (3:14–15; 8:28; 12:32), "descend" and "ascend" (1:51; 3:13; 6:62), and "glorify" (12:23; 13:31–32)—have multiple levels of meaning and should not be limited to the cross.[33]

Jesus the Son of God: Unity and Subordination

John's central designation for Jesus is "Son" or "Son of God."[34] Christian readers, shaped by the christological and trinitarian debates of the third to fifth centuries and the affirmations of the councils of Nicaea (325 C.E.) and Chalcedon (451 C.E.), immediately understand "Son of God" to affirm Jesus' divine nature and being. But for John's gospel, predating these debates by several centuries, this meaning is anachronistic. The Hebrew Bible's use of the term emphasizes relationship and agency. The people of Israel (Exod 4:22; Hos 11:1), the king (Ps 2:7), angels (Job 38:7), the righteous person who lives faithful to the covenant guidelines (Wis 2:18) are called sons of God. In relationship with God, each is an agent of God's purposes. In the Greco-Roman world, the same term, also denoting relationship and agency, identifies miracle workers, teachers, kings, and emperors. Applied to Jesus, the term indicates Jesus' close relationship with his Father, God (loved by God, 3:35; 5:20; 17:23), and his function as the revealer of God's saving purposes.

John underlines the following elements of Jesus' sonship:

1. The *uniqueness* of this relationship. Jesus is the only or unique Son (μονογενής, *monogenēs*, 1:14, 18; 3:16–18), in unique relationship with God. John uses the term "Son" (υἱός, *huios*) for Jesus but a different term (τέκνα, *tekna*) for those empowered to become "children of God" (1:12–13).

2. The *unity* between Jesus and the Father. They are one (10:30), not in the sense of a shared nature but in the sense of a common will. To see or know Jesus is to see or know the Father (8:19; 12:45; 14:7, 9). On eight occasions, Jesus uses a formula of divine revelation (Exod 3:14; Isa 43:25; 51:12; 52:6, "I am") for himself,[35] and on twelve further occasions,[36] to reveal God's purposes being enacted through him, he uses the phrase "I am" with an image from everyday life that is often used in the Hebrew Bible to describe God's interaction with humans.

3. They are *not the same*. They are separate entities, or more accurately, Jesus is subordinated to the Father. Jesus declares that "the Father is greater than I" (14:28). He carries out the Father's commandment (12:49–50).

4. Jesus' role as *dependent on and derivative of* God, who sent him. Jesus can do nothing of his own account (5:19). He imitates the Father (5:19), doing God's will (4:34), speaking God's words (8:28; 12:50), performing God's works (5:36; 10:37–38; 14:10), sharing in God's functions of giving life and judging (5:21–22).

5. Jesus' *mission*. As Son, Jesus is God's agent revealing God's salvation. This salvation is necessary because humans do not believe

or accept the revelation, now made in Jesus, of God's just purposes for creation (16:8). Humans prefer conformity to, and acceptance or approval by, other humans instead of conformity to God's purposes (5:41–44). God sends the Son, Jesus, to manifest God's salvation, which consists of God's life-giving purposes (3:16–17; 5:34; 12:47). He is Savior of the world (4:42). Humans participate by believing or entrusting themselves to Jesus' revelation and believing God (3:16–18; 12:45). Those who reject the revelation know the condemnation of judgment (3:18). The gospel calls this encounter with God's saving presence "eternal life" (3:16; 6:40).

Jesus' Words and Works

Jesus' words and works reveal the contours of this salvation. Jesus' words in chapters 1–12 continually rehearse these claims about his identity and role as God's revealer. Especially in chapters 5–12, Jesus speaks a great deal and manifests in his healings, feedings, and declarations God's purposes for life. His words intensify the conflict with the elite, place his hearers in a "crisis of decision" whereby they must decide how to respond to the revelation, elaborate the implications for a new identity and way of life for those who believe, and conflict with and condemn those who do not accept Jesus' claims. In chapters 13–17 his words primarily instruct disciples about how to live in his absence (see ch. 4, below).

Jesus' works also reveal God's saving purposes by enacting the transformation and different way of life that God intends for creation. As noted in chapter 2, above, the gospel identifies his works of power not as miracles but as "signs" because, for those with eyes to see, they point to Jesus' identity as God's agent and reveal God's life-giving purposes:

1. Jesus supplies abundant food (2:1–11; 6:1–14; 21:1–14). For most people in Rome's world, the food supply was unpredictable and inadequate; this caused pervasive undernourishment and resulted in diseases from both deficiency and contagion.[37] Prophetic writings (Isa 25:6–10) and eschatological texts (*4 Ezra* 8:52–54; *2 Bar.* 29:5–8; 73) offered visions of abundant food when God's just and life-giving purposes would be established finally and fully on earth. Jesus' feedings reveal and anticipate that establishment.

2. Jesus heals the sick (4:46–54; 5:1–18; 9:1–7) and raises the dead (11:1–46). Disease and deformity were rife in Rome's world. Prophetic writings (Isa 35:5–6) and eschatological texts (4 Ezra 7:112–115; 8:52–54; 2 Bar. 29:5–8; 73) offered visions of wholeness and health upon establishment of God's just and life-giving purposes, revealed and anticipated by Jesus' healings.

3. Jesus confronts the temple, the power base of the Jerusalem leadership group who preside over an exploitative economic and social order in alliance with the dominating power of Rome.[38] In announcing the Jerusalem temple's destruction by those who administer it (2:19), John interprets its destruction by Rome in 70 C.E. as God's judgment on this unjust and faithless social order.

4. Jesus walks on water (6:16–21). With this act, which emulates God's actions (Job 9:8; Ps 77:16–20; Isa 43:2) and recalls God's sovereignty over the water in creation and the exodus from Egypt, Jesus reveals God's sovereignty over creation and God's saving presence for the fearful and threatened disciples.

Jesus' Death and Resurrection

Jesus' death results from a combination of factors: God's will (Jesus' hour, 2:4; 7:30; 8:20; 12:23–27; the cup given him by God, 18:11), Jesus' consent (10:17–18; 18:1–11), Satan's opposition (13:2, 27), Judas' betrayal (13:2, 21–30; 18:1–11), and conflict with and opposition from the alliance of Jerusalem leaders and Pilate (18–19). Jesus' death continues his lifelong mission of revealing God's saving purposes:

1. Jesus willingly lays down his life (10:17–18; 15:13), revealing God's love for all people (3:16) and modeling the way of life required of disciples (13:34–35; 15:12–17).

2. Jesus' death is an enthronement, revealing his identity as the king who represents God's purposes (18:33–37; 19:15).

3. Jesus' death shows that God's life-giving and saving purposes, revealed in Jesus' healings, feedings, and critique of the temple, place him at fundamental odds with the elite social order. The narrative reveals the Jerusalem and Roman leaders' profound opposition to God's purposes and their commitment to the emperor, not to God (19:15). Their opposition means God's judg-

ment on the status quo, which is their rejection of God's order revealed by Jesus, God's agent (12:49).

4. Jesus' death reveals the limits of the power alliance of the Jerusalem and Roman elite. God's resurrecting power shows that their combined efforts (18:12–14, 19–24, 28–19:16) to execute Jesus are ineffective. God's purposes cannot be overcome. In this way, Jesus' death overcomes and takes away "the sin of the world" (1:29), the unbelief or rejection of God's purposes (16:9), by showing that it does not have the final say. The Passover setting, celebrating the liberation from Egyptian tyranny, underlines not sacrifice but God's liberation of people from all that opposes God's purposes.

5. The "lifting up," or exaltation, of Jesus in his crucifixion, resurrection, and ascension displays God's approval for or vindication of his ministry as a faithful revelation (3:13–14; 8:28; 12:32). Jesus' death is a means of departure, a return to the Father, who authorizes and guarantees Jesus' revelation.

6. Jesus' death and resurrection are a glorification (17:1) in that they reveal the power and life-giving purposes of God (see ch. 10, below).

Conclusion

This discussion of the presentation of God and Jesus shows the extensive interaction between the two. Within the context of their intimate relationship as Father and Son, God originates and authorizes Jesus' mission to reveal God's purposes. Jesus is the definitive Word, the divinely commissioned agent of the guaranteed and reliable revelation of God's saving and life-giving purposes.

Notes

1. For helpful discussions of characterization, see Chatman, *Story and Discourse;* Culpepper, *Anatomy,* 99–148; B. Hochman, *Character in Literature* (Ithaca, N.Y.: Cornell University Press, 1985); J. Darr, *On Character Building: The Reader and the Rhetoric of Characterization in Luke-Acts* (Louisville: Westminster John Knox, 1992); W. H. Shepherd, *The Narrative Function of the Holy Spirit as a Character in Luke-Acts* (SBLDS 147; Atlanta: Scholars Press, 1994), 43–98; Stibbe, *John's Gospel,* 5–31; C. Conway, *Men and Women in the Fourth Gospel: Gender and Johannine Characterization* (SBLDS 167; Atlanta: Society of

Biblical Literature, 1999), 1–68; D. Rhoads and K. Syreeni, eds., *Characterization in the Gospels: Reconceiving Narrative Criticism* (JSNTSup 184; Sheffield, Eng.: Sheffield Academic Press, 1999).

2. S. Moore, *Literary Criticism of the Gospels* (New Haven, Conn.: Yale University Press, 1989), 15.

3. Chatman, *Story and Discourse*, 107–38, esp. 121–26.

4. Also light, 3:21; spirit, 4:24; the only true God, 5:44; 17:3.

5. Burridge, *What Are the Gospels?* 121, 143–44, 175–77, 220–39; G. H. Polman, "Chronological Biography and AKME in Plutarch," *Classical Philology* 69 (1974): 169–77; C. Gill, "Character-Development in Plutarch and Tacitus," *Classical Quarterly* 33 (1983): 469–87; Pelling, ed., *Characterization*.

6. John 2:21, 24; 6:6, 15, 61; 7:1, 39; 11:33, 38; 12:33; 13:1, 3, 11, 21; 16:19; 18:4; 19:28; 21:19.

7. C. K. Barrett, "Christocentric or Theocentric? Observations on the Theological Method of the Fourth Gospel," in *New Testament Essays* (Philadelphia: Westminster, 1982), 1–18.

8. P. W. Meyer, "The Presentation of God in the Fourth Gospel," in *Exploring the Gospel of John: In Honor of D. Moody Smith* (ed. R. A. Culpepper and C. C. Black; Louisville: Westminster John Knox, 1996), 255–73, esp. 264–65. Also Culpepper, *Anatomy*, 112–15; D. F. Tolmie, "The Characterization of God in the Fourth Gospel," *JSNT* 69 (1998): 57–75; T. Larsson, *God in the Fourth Gospel: A Hermeneutical Study of the History of Interpretations* (Coniectanea biblica: New Testament Series 35; Stockholm: Almqvist & Wiksell International, 2001); M. M. Thompson, *The God of the Gospel of John* (Grand Rapids: Eerdmans, 2001).

9. J. Painter, "Earth Made Whole: John's Rereading of Genesis," in *Word, Theology, and Community in John* (ed. J. Painter, R. A. Culpepper, and F. F. Segovia; St. Louis: Chalice, 2002), 65–84.

10. See further ch. 7, below.

11. Degrees of origin, possession, and legitimation are evident in various "of God" constructions: lamb (1:29, 36), angels (1:51), kingdom/empire (3:3), words (3:36), gift (4:10), love (5:42), works (6:28; 9:3), bread (6:33), Holy One (6:69), glory (11:40), Son (10:36; 20:31). See Keck, "Derivation as Destiny."

12. Two verbs meaning "send" are used. An (f) indicates God as Father as the subject of the verb: *pempō* (πέμπω), 1:33; 4:34; 5:23 (f), 24, 30, 37 (f); 6:38, 39, 44 (f), 7:16, 18, 28, 33; 8:16, 18 (f), 26, 29; 9:4; 12:44, 45, 49 (f); 13:16, 20; 14:24 (f); 15:21; 16:5; *apostellō* (ἀποστέλλω), 3:17, 34; 5:36 (f), 38; 6:29, 57 (f); 7:29; 8:42 (f); 10:36 (f); 11:42 (f); 17:3, 8, 18, 21 (f), 23, 25 (f); 20:21 (f).

13. The verb is *didōmi* (δίδωμι).

14. P. Borgen, "God's Agent in the Fourth Gospel," in *The Interpretation of John* (ed. J. A. Ashton; Philadelphia: Fortress, 1986), 67–78; W. Meeks, "The Man from Heaven in Johannine Sectarianism," *JBL* 91 (1972): 44–72; repr. in *The Interpretation of John* (ed. J. A. Ashton; Philadelphia: Fortress, 1986), 67–78.

15. The verb *pisteuō* (πιστεύω) occurs ninety-eight times, thirty-one times with the preposition *eis* (εἰς) followed by a reference to Jesus, meaning to "believe in/be faithful to" Jesus, and twenty times with a pronoun or noun in the dative case, often emphasizing "acceptance of a message." So Brown, *Introduction to the Gospel*, 112–13. See further ch. 6, below.

16. G. Nicholson, *Death as Departure: The Johannine Descent-Ascent Schema* (SBLDS 63; Chico, Calif.: Scholars Press, 1983).

17. O'Day, "John," in *Women's Bible Commentary* (ed. Newsom and Ringe), 392–93. Also D. Lee, "Beyond Suspicion? The Fatherhood of God in the Fourth Gospel," *Pacifica* 8 (1995): 140–54.

18. M. D'Angelo, "Abba and 'Father': Imperial Theology and the Jesus Traditions," *JBL* 111 (1992): 611–30, esp. 623–26; also W. Carter, *Matthew and the Margins: A Sociopolitical and Religious Reading* (Maryknoll, N.Y.: Orbis, 2000), 139, 164, 454.

19. Culpepper, *Anatomy*, 106–12; Stibbe, *John's Gospel;* T. Pollard, "The Father-Son and God-Believer Relationships according to St. John: A Brief Study of John's Use of Prepositions," in *L'Évangile de Jean: Sources, Rédaction, Théologie* (ed. M. de Jonge; BETL 44. Gembloux: J. Duiculot, 1977), 363–69.

20. For a useful summary, see Brown, *Gospel according to John,* 1:519–24.

21. Carter, "Prologue."

22. Translation from Moloney, *John,* 33–35, 42.

23. Children, 1:12–13; words, 3:34; gift, 4:10; works, 6:28; 9:3; true bread, 6:33; Holy One, 6:69.

24. From heaven, 3:13, 31; 6:31–33, 38, 41, 50, 51, 58; from the father, 6:45; 8:38; 10:18, 32; 15:15; 16:28; from God, 3:2; 6:46; 7:17; 8:40, 42, 47; 9:33; 13:3; 16:27.

25. In *Psalms of Solomon* 17 the Messiah is an earthly king who non-militarily removes the Romans; in *1 En.* 37–71 the Messiah is a heavenly figure who executes judgment on the day of judgment especially against oppressive kings and exploitative landowners; in *4 Ezra* the Messiah is a descendant of David who overthrows Rome and makes people joyful until the judgment. See M. de Jonge, "The Messiah," *ABD* 4:777–88; J. H. Charlesworth, ed., *The Messiah: Developments in Earliest Judaism and Christianity* (Minneapolis: Fortress, 1992); G. W. E. Nickelsburg, *Ancient Judaism and Christian Origins: Diversity, Continuity, and Transformation* (Minneapolis: Fortress, 2003), 89–117.

26. Josephus, *Ant.* 17.271–285 (Judas son of Ezekias, Simon, Athronges); *J.W.* 2.433–448 (Menachem), 4.503–544, 556–584; 7.153–155 (Simon bar Giora).

27. Carter, *Pontius Pilate,* 127–52.

28. See the classic article by Meeks, "Man from Heaven"; Schnackenburg, *John* 1.529–42; Ashton, *Understanding,* 337–73; F. Moloney, *The Johannine Son of Man* (Rome: Libreria Ateneo Salesiano, 1976). See Brown, *Introduction to the Gospel,* 252–59, and the interesting exchange between Brown's views in the main text (emphasizing Jesus' heavenly and earthly existence) and the quite different views of the editor, F. Moloney (Jesus' earthly existence), in the notes.

29. John 1:51; 3:13, 14; 5:27; 6:27, 53, 62; 8:28; 9:35; 12:23, 34 (two times); 13:31.

30. F. Moloney, "The Johannine Son of Man Revisited," in *The Christology and Theology of the Fourth Gospel: Essays by Members of the New Testament Studies Johannine Writings Seminar* (ed. G. van Belle and J. van der Watt; BETL; Leuven: Peeters, 2005), 177–202.

31. In Num 21:9 Moses places the serpent on a pole, a *sēmeion;* the gospel uses the same Greek word translated as "sign." The Son of Man is the locus of salvation.

32. Nicholson, *Death as Departure.*

33. See the exchange between Brown and Moloney in Brown, *Introduction to the Gospel,* 256–58.

34. "Son," used absolutely eighteen times: 1:18 (?); 3:16, 17, 35, 36a, 36b; 5:19b, 19c, 20, 21, 22, 23a, 23b, 26; 6:40; 8:35, 36; 14:13; 17:1; "Son of God," used nine times: 1:34, 49; 3:18; 5:25; 10:36; 11:4, 27; 19:7; 20:31. On this section, see Schnackenburg, *John* 2.172–86; Ashton, *Understanding*, 292–329; Thompson, *The God*, 57–100, 227–40; C. K. Barrett, "'The Father Is Greater than I,' John 14:28: Subordinationist Christology in the New Testament," in *New Testament Essays* (Philadelphia: Westminster, 1982), 19–36. P. N. Anderson (*The Christology of the Fourth Gospel: Its Unity and Disunity in the Light of John 6* [Valley Forge, Pa.: Trinity Press International, 1996]) argues that the various elements in John's Christology reflect not various traditions and versions of the gospel (see ch. 8, below) but the author's dialectical thinking.

35. John 4:26; 6:20; 8:24, 28, 58; 13:19; 18:5, 7.

36. John 6:35, 51 (bread of life); 8:12, 9:5 (light); 10:7, 9 (gate); 10:11, 14 (good shepherd); 11:25–26 (resurrection and the life); 14:6 (way, truth, life); 15:1, 5 (true vine).

37. Garnsey, *Food and Society.*

38. On the temple economy, see Hanson and Oakman, *Palestine*, 99–159; for the temple in John, see M. Coloe, *God Dwells with Us: Temple Symbolism in the Fourth Gospel* (Collegeville, Minn.: Liturgical, 2001).

CHAPTER 4

Other Characters

We move from discussing the presentation of God and Jesus to look at four sets of characters with whom Jesus interacts and among whom God's purposes accomplish different things: the Jews, disciples, women, and various others who make brief but important appearances. These interactions advance the plot, highlight aspects of Jesus' significance, and disclose God's life-giving purposes.

The Ioudaioi

The first group is often referred to as "the Jews." But this translation of the term *hoi Ioudaioi* (οἱ Ἰουδαῖοι) is problematic for various reasons, not the least of which is that almost all characters in the gospel, except those designated Samaritans and Gentiles/Greeks or those who are obviously Roman, such as Pilate, are Jews. Jesus is explicitly identified as a Jew in 4:9; salvation comes from the Jews (4:22). Yet in about seventy instances the gospel designates a group of characters with the plural term "the Jews." The translation and interpretation of this term have been much debated.[1] Compounding the issue is the fact that although these complex characters are often presented negatively, there are also positive references to *Ioudaioi* (e.g., 11:19, 31, 33, 36, 45). Moreover, in our post-Holocaust world, interpreters of John are rightly very alert to the ways in which references to the *Ioudaioi* in John can feed a long and regrettable tradition of hateful anti-Judaism.

The *Ioudaioi* first appear in 1:19: "The Jews [*Ioudaioi*] sent priests and Levites from Jerusalem to ask him [John the Baptist], 'Who are you?'" The scene (which extends to v. 28) offers at least seven pieces of information about the *Ioudaioi* and raises important questions that require us to read on to find answers:

1. Since John the Baptist is a Jew, the *Ioudaioi* must be a distinctive group among Jewish people and the term does not designate all Jewish people.

2. They are people with power, for they send others to carry out their investigation.

3. Twice the verb "send" underlines their power (1:19, 22; two different verbs in Greek). Sending is a defining characteristic for God as we saw in chapter 3 above. Do the *Ioudaioi* act as agents of God, participating in God's work of sending, or are they rivals or opponents of God?

4. They are based in Jerusalem (1:19), the city of the temple and the ruling elite—the chief priests, allies of Rome.

5. They send "priests and Levites," who are temple personnel. This suggests that the group's power is based in the temple and that the Jerusalem priesthood is a likely part of it.

6. Their investigation of John the Baptist is not friendly or open to his ministry. Their aggressive, intimidating interrogation centers on John's identity ("Who are you?" 1:19, 22) and his baptizing activity (1:25). Why do they want to know? They seem so busy spying on him, assessing his credentials, exerting their power over him, controlling what happens in their society, that they do not engage John as "a man sent from God" (1:6) who bears witness to Jesus (1:7–8). The scene suggests an oppositional rather than an accepting posture, and a great concern with acceptable teaching. Will they remain this way? How will they treat the one to whom John bears witness, Jesus?

7. In 1:24 these Jerusalem- and temple-based *Ioudaioi* are identified as "the Pharisees" (also in 9:13–18; 11:47–54). The Jewish historian Josephus allies leading Pharisees with Jerusalem's ruling elite, the chief priests.[2] Together they were allies of Rome, serving as dependent retainers as part of the power elite.[3] John's gospel reflects these realities in associating Pharisees with the rulers (3:1), the chief priests (7:32, 45), and the temple (8:13–20).

The next few references to the *Ioudaioi* both confirm this initial picture of a group of powerful leaders based in Jerusalem and extend the term's referents. In 2:6, 13 the term seems to take on a much more general meaning in referring to Jewish cultural and religious practices (purity observance; Passover a feast "of the Jews [*Ioudaioi*]"). This use recurs throughout the gospel (4:9, 22; 5:1; 6:4; 7:2; 11:55; 19:42) in association with practices that express a "national but not geographically limited religious, political and cultural identity."[4] It may also be that even in these references something of the sense of "the ruling authorities" is present, since often these leaders promoted and oversaw these temple-based celebrations.

In 2:13–22 some of the clues about the identity of a distinctive group emerging in 1:19–28 are confirmed. Jesus attacks the Jerusalem temple, calling it "my Father's house," accusing the authorities of making it "marketplace," and ordering them to "destroy" it. The temple authorities or leaders are identified as the *Ioudaioi* (2:18, 20) who preside over a religio-politico-economic institution of great power that Jesus condemns.[5] They immediately (and reasonably) question Jesus' right to attack the temple, thereby defending their heritage, power, wealth, and status. And when he orders them to "destroy this temple" and says that he will raise it in three days, they do not understand that he is referring to his own body (nor do the disciples; 2:19). This first encounter with Jesus occurs in the context of their great societal power, based in the Jerusalem temple; it includes conflict, is marked by their questioning of Jesus' legitimacy, and evidences their nonunderstanding.

The interactions of the *Ioudaioi* with Jesus quickly deteriorate as conflict with Jesus increases. In chapter 3 Jesus ridicules the powerful, high-status Nicodemus, "a Pharisee . . . a leader of the Jews [*Ioudaioi*]" (3:1). This "teacher of Israel" is unable to understand Jesus' teaching about being born from above (3:3–15). In chapter 5, after Jesus has healed a paralyzed man on the Sabbath (5:10) and made claims about his relationship with God, the "Jews" want to kill him (5:16–18). Chapters 6–12, often in the context of festivals (6:4; 7:2; 11:55), emphasize their resistance to his teaching (6:41, 52; 8:57), their nonunderstanding (7:11, 15, 35; 8:22, 48, 52; 10:24), their intimidation of the people and Jesus' followers (7:13; 9:22; 12:42), their alienation from Jesus (11:54), and their desire to arrest (7:30, 32, 44; 10:39; 11:57) and kill Jesus (5:18; 7:1, 19–20, 25; 8:37, 40; 10:31–33; 11:53).

Not all the references, however, are negative. A division occurs among the *Ioudaioi* over Jesus (10:19). Some believe in Jesus (8:31; 11:45; 12:9–11). Others show great support and sympathy for Mary and Martha at Lazarus's death (11:19, 31, 33, 36). Some of the authorities believe in Jesus but fear the social consequences of public confession (12:42).

Apart from one reference, the *Ioudaioi* are absent from chapters 13–17 (13:33). But these societal leaders figure prominently in chapters 18–19 as they exert their power over Jesus in his arrest (18:12–14), appearance before the high priest (18:19–20), appearance before and condemnation by Pilate (18:31, 36, 38; 19:7, 12), crucifixion (19:20, 31), and burial (19:38). Seven of the fifteen references to the *Ioudaioi* in 18:31–19:21 identify Jesus as "King of the Jews," a title that both asserts his power over them and signifies their rejection of him. They appear just once in the resurrection account, where their intimidating presence cannot contain God's activity (20:19).

The term *Ioudaioi*, then, predominantly refers to a group of ruling authorities or leaders based in the Jerusalem temple who oppose Jesus and execute him. What drives this deadly conflict? What aggravates them to the point that they, in association with the Roman governor, crucify Jesus? Most often the narrative presents these leaders from Jesus' perspective. Jesus initiates the attack on their temple and societal leadership in 2:13–22. In chapters 5–12 he accuses them of not having heard the Father's voice (5:37); not having the Father's word abide in them (5:38a); not believing Jesus (5:38b, 40, 43); not knowing how to interpret the Scriptures (5:39); not having love for God (5:42); not being able to discern who comes from God (5:43); not seeking God's glory (approval, honor) but seeking it from others (5:44; 12:43); being accused (condemned?) by Moses (5:45); not keeping the law (7:19); not knowing God (7:28; 8:19); having the devil as their father (8:44); remaining in sin (9:41); hating the Father and Jesus (15:24).

Many of the accusations concern (from Jesus' perspective) the leaders' lack of experience of God, their unfaithfulness to their heritage, and their inability to discern God's presence and enact God's purposes for human society. Since the gospel presents Jesus as the revealer of God's presence and purposes, it is not surprising that the leaders are presented as misunderstanding or rejecting all the central claims about Jesus. They do not know his origin from God (6:41–42; 9:29); his destiny in returning to God (7:33–35; 8:22, they wonder about suicide); his authority as sent by God (7:29–30); his identity as God's agent (8:25); his identity as the Christ/Messiah (10:24), Son of God (19:7), king of Israel (19:21) (they think he is a Samaritan [8:48], possessed by demons [8:48, 52], mad [10:20], a sinner [9:24]); his unity with God (5:17; 10:31–33); his mission to save from sins (8:24–25) and reveal God (8:26–27) and God's purposes (7:16–24); the meaning of his words (2:20; 6:52; 8:27; 18:20–23); the significance of his works (6:26, 30; 10:31–33; 11:47).

Jesus accounts for their negative interaction with him in several ways. He declares that they have false commitments. They love darkness and so do evil deeds (3:19–21). They love human glory or honor befitting their elevated societal status and power, instead of seeking God's honor (5:42–44). He declares them to be spiritually blind, unable to see God's purposes manifested in himself (9:39–41). They cannot embrace Jesus because they are not "of" God. They do not belong to God; they are not committed to God's purposes. Rather they are "of" or from the devil and serve sin in lives of falsehood and murder that embody the devil's ways (8:39–47). In his most sustained attack, Jesus denies the identity and heritage of being God's people that they assert for themselves as children of Abraham and children of God (8:39–47).

Scholars have established that much of this harsh, condemnatory talk is standard polemic in the ancient world.[6] It is not objective, researched, reasoned discourse but reflects struggles over how competing and conflicting groups with vastly different perspectives establish their own legitimacy and assert their Jewish identity while disqualifying others. Though the gospel's perspective is always pro-Jesus and the Jewish leaders are depicted negatively as his opponents, we do get some sense of why these powerful leaders resist Jesus and put him to death.[7]

Based in the temple, these leaders represent and uphold fundamental cultural values, define societal boundaries concerned with Jewishness, and defend societal structures and order that benefit the elite. They experience Jesus as one who threatens central and longstanding Jewish affirmations and challenges their societal power and order. Five issues at least seem to be to the fore:

1. Monotheism: The affirmation that there was one God (Exod 20:1–6; Deut 6:4–6) defined Israel's distinctive identity and provided a boundary over against "pagan" nations, who worshiped other gods, often engaging in idolatry (e.g., 1 Kgs 16:31–18:46; Isa 41). The leaders charge Jesus with violating this understanding in John 5:16–18 when he claims to be sharing in God's workings, "thereby making himself equal to God."[8] Similarly, in 8:56–59, after he uses the divine name "I am" to claim existence before Abraham, they mock him and try to stone him—the penalty for blasphemy. In 10:30–33, after Jesus claims, "The Father and I are one," they again want to stone him for blasphemy "because you . . . are making yourself God."

2. Revelation: The leaders oppose Jesus' claim to be the revealer of God's will and purposes. They identify themselves as "disciples of Moses" to whom "God has spoken" on Mount Sinai. But they do not think God has spoken to Jesus, no matter what origin he claims (9:28–29). They have plenty of evidence that God has not

spoken to Jesus: Jesus has accused them, the nation's leaders and teachers (3:10), of not knowing how to interpret Moses and has claimed, strangely, that Moses speaks about him (5:45–47; cf. 1:45). Jesus has shown little regard for Moses' teaching about the Sabbath (5:1–18; 9:1–12, 16). He has claimed to exceed Moses' revelation (6:32–35). He has accused the leaders of not obeying Moses' teaching (7:19) and misinterpreting it because they opposed his healing "a man's whole body on the sabbath" (7:23).

3. Covenant community boundaries: The leaders reject Jesus' attempts to redefine God's covenant people, the children of Abraham, as comprising only those who believe in Jesus. They uphold descent from Abraham as determining Abraham's children. They are deeply offended when Jesus declares that they are children neither of Abraham nor of God because they do not believe in Jesus (8:39–47). Only a Samaritan outcast or a demon-possessed man would ignore ethnic and cultural factors and seek to circumscribe God's people in such a limited way (8:48–52).

4. Jesus' identity: The leaders do not think that Jesus is sent from God or is the Messiah or God's Son or agent (9:16). And they find his public claims about himself and his demands for a believing response unacceptable. In their view, he is leading the people astray (7:12, 32–47), turning them "from the way in which the LORD your God commanded you to walk" (Deut 13:1–11, quoting v. 5). This makes Jesus a false prophet for whom the penalty is death by stoning (Deut 13:10). Several times they try to carry out this penalty (8:59; 10:31–33; 11:8).

5. Societal power, status, and Roman alliances: The leaders exercise their economic, political, religious, and cultural power, based in the Jerusalem temple, by Rome's favor,[9] reaping rewards of privilege, wealth, and status but inheriting the task of maintaining the status quo for the elite's benefit. Jesus challenges this order in attacking the temple (2:13–22). Using the common image of a shepherd for political leaders and evoking the blistering condemnation of Israel's exploitative leaders in Ezek 34, Jesus attacks the legitimacy of their rule, calling them thieves and bandits who abandon or threaten and do not care for the people/sheep (John 10:1, 8, 12). By contrast, Jesus cares for and transforms people's existence (the crippled man, ch. 5; the blind beggar, ch. 9). The leaders fear that Jesus' popularity as a miracle worker (11:47), popular attempts to declare him king (6:15), and

his vision of societal existence that includes abundant life (10:10), health (4:46–54; chs. 9, 11), and fertility (ch. 6) for all will upset their power alliances with Rome and their societal authority, privileged status, and self-beneficial order. "If we let him go on like this, everyone will believe in him, and the Romans will come and destroy our holy place and our nation" (11:48). Their loyalty is to Caesar (19:12–15). Only one response is possible for the power elite. "It is better . . . to have one man die . . . than to have the whole nation destroyed" (11:50). They plan to kill him (11:53) so as to stop his erosion of their control (12:9–11, 12–19). They oppose this figure, who shows by his actions of healing, feedings, and inclusion of women, Samaritans, the physically damaged, the poor, and those ignorant of the law that God's just and life-giving purposes extend to all people and envision vastly different societal structures.[10]

These leaders, claiming God's blessing, seem passionately and legitimately committed to maintaining their traditions, Jewish identity, and the current societal order against the threat that Jesus poses. Central to their opposition appears to be the securing of boundaries that define Jewish identity. Monotheism, following Moses, descent from Abraham, and the societal inclusion of those excluded by the elite's system are nonnegotiable items that Jesus seems to contest. To challenge these affirmations is to be a false prophet, one who misleads the people. He challenges the leaders' power and societal order secured in alliance with Rome.

The Disciples

In contrast to the Jewish leaders, the disciples are presented as those who receive Jesus' ministry (1:12–13), but they are by no means perfect or ideal characters. Like the opponents, disciples frequently misunderstand Jesus, though in contexts of commitment to him rather than rejection. And like the leaders, their interactions with Jesus advance the plot, highlight aspects of Jesus' significance, and disclose God's life-giving purposes.

John's gospel refers to this group character about seventy-eight times and names those who commit to Jesus. It does not highlight a group of twelve male disciples as do the Synoptics. Of the only four instances in which it refers to twelve disciples, three come in 6:67–71, in a context that indicates there are many other disciples.[11] Nor does the gospel list the names of twelve disciples as the Synoptics do. We cannot assume, then, that when the gospel refers to "disciples," it has twelve male disciples in view. The term denotes believers in Jesus, both male and female. At various points, the gospel singles out particular disciples for attention. It explicitly identifies seven male disciples (Andrew, Philip, Peter, the beloved disciple, Nathanael, Thomas, and Judas) and a number of female believers (such as the unnamed Samaritan woman, Mary and Martha, and Mary Magdalene).

"Disciples" make their first appearance in 1:35–51 as John bears witness and two of his disciples follow Jesus. Unlike the Synoptics, where people become disciples as a result of Jesus' call (Mark 1:16–20 par.), these characters become disciples because others bear witness about Jesus. Three times a character bears witness to another, who follows Jesus and confesses Jesus' identity. The three opening scenes in the chart establish important characteristics of disciples. Their commitment to, relationship with, and understanding of Jesus are signified in "following," "abiding/remaining," and "seeing" Jesus, three verbs that have double meanings and signify discipleship.[12] Disciples bear witness to and confess Jesus' identity as God's agent.

Verses	Who bears witness?	Witness about Jesus	To whom?	Immediate consequence
1:35–39	John the Baptist	Lamb of God (1:36)	two disciples (1:37), including Andrew (1:40)	They follow Jesus (1:38); see and abide (1:39)
1:40–42	Andrew (1:40)	The Messiah (1:41)	Simon his brother (1:41)	Jesus renames Simon Peter/Cephas (1:42)
1:43–51	Philip, called to follow by Jesus (1:43)	"him about whom Moses . . . and also the prophets wrote" (1:45)	Nathanael (1:45)	He comes and sees (1:46); Jesus exhibits special knowledge (1:47); Nathanael confesses "Son of God" and "King of Israel" (1:49).

In this context, disciples witness Jesus turning water into abundant wine at Cana (2:1–11). They are able to discern not just a miracle or display of power but a sign, a work of "glory," the powerful presence and life-giving purposes of God manifested in Jesus. They entrust themselves to Jesus (2:11) whereas, in contrast, Jesus does not entrust himself to those who cannot see past the work of power to his identity and the revelation of God's purposes in him (2:23–25).

In chapters 3–6 they accompany Jesus and witness his ministry (3:22). Their numbers grow and they baptize (4:1–2). They procure food (4:8, 31, 33). They are surprised that Jesus talks to a Samaritan woman, but they say nothing (4:27). He teaches them directly about his task to do God's will (4:31–38), and they (over)hear his teaching and dispute with the *Ioudaioi* in chapters 5 and 6. Their characterization does not take place in direct conflicts with the *Ioudaioi* but by implicit contrasts.

Two further characteristics emerge. First, despite their impressive start in chapters 1–2, they often lack understanding. They do not understand that when Jesus refers to the temple, he means himself (2:20–22); that when Jesus refers to food, he means God's commission (4:31–34); that Jesus can feed the hungry crowd (Philip has no idea [6:5–7]; Andrew has a boy's small lunch but sees no possibilities [6:8–10]); that Jesus can walk on the stormy sea (and so they are frightened) (6:16–21). Second, disciples take offense at Jesus' teaching and abandon him (6:60–71). They have heard him declare his identity as the bread that God has sent from heaven, and that eating this bread means life forever (6:25–59). But some do not believe this hard word and abandon Jesus (6:60–66).

At least twelve disciples emerge in this context as a remnant of followers (6:66–71). Peter is the group's spokesperson in declaring, "You have the words of eternal life. We have come to believe and know that you are the Holy One of God" (6:68–69). The confession sounds wonderful. Peter seems to have understood the significance of Jesus' words, his central revelation of eternal life, the necessity of believing, Jesus' identity as God's agent. But there are three problems. Why does Peter use language of "the Holy One" when much of the gospel has focused on Jesus as Christ and Son? Second, Jesus goes on immediately to talk of being betrayed by a disciple, Judas, and labels him a devil (6:64, 70–71). And third, Peter is unable subsequently to understand that this divine agent must die. He does not seem to know the implications of his confession.

Apart from being exhorted to abide or remain in Jesus' word (8:31), the disciples accompany Jesus (7:3; 11:7) but receive little press until chapter 11, when their lack of understanding comes to the fore. They take literally Jesus' metaphorical reference to Lazarus's sleep and so fail to understand that he has died (11:11–13). Jesus is still trying to elicit faith from them (11:15). Thomas, making his first appearance, declares that their journey to Judea means death for all of them (11:16). Judas Iscariot, again described as the one who will betray Jesus (12:4; cf. 6:64),[13] complains that Mary should not have wasted money on expensive ointment with which to anoint Jesus but instead should have used the money on the poor. The narrator undercuts this comment, however, by observing that Judas stole money from the group's common funds, and

by having Jesus side with Mary, not Judas (12:4–7). They do not understand Jesus' entry to Jerusalem (12:16). Philip does not know what to do
when some Greeks want to see Jesus (though Andrew does, 12:20–22).

An important contrast shapes the interaction between Jesus and the
disciples in John 13–17. In these chapters Jesus is alone with the disciples. His teaching is framed by his imminent crucifixion and their future lives in his absence. Jesus' actions and teachings, together with the
actions of the beloved disciple, present dimensions of ideal discipleship
whereas, in contrast, the disciples continually indicate how little they
understand about Jesus. Assuming the slave's role, Jesus washes their
feet to exemplify his service of giving his life and the love that they
should have for one another (13:4–20, 34–35; 15:12–17). He identifies
Judas as the one who will betray him, knowledge that he imparts to the
beloved disciple but denies to Peter (13:21–30). Jesus assures them that
he goes to prepare a place for them and will return to take them to be
with the Father. In the meantime the Paraclete, John's term for the Holy
Spirit, will be with and in them (14:16–17) to teach them (14:26;
16:12–13). He exhorts them to abide or remain in him (15:1–11), even
in difficult circumstances marked by opposition (15:18–16:4).

The beloved disciple, who appears for the first time in 13:23, exhibits key characteristics of disciples.[14] He enjoys close relationship with
Jesus (ἀνακείμενος . . . ἐν τῷ κόλπῳ τοῦ Ἰησοῦ; *anakeimenos . . . en tō
kolpō tou Iēsou;* lit., "lying close to the breast of Jesus"). The phrase εἰς
τὸ κόλπον was used in 1:18 to describe the intimate relationship between God and Jesus that provides the basis for Jesus' revelation of
God's purposes. The beloved disciple continues this task and evidences
the truth of Jesus' teaching that disciples share intimate relationship
with God and Jesus (17:21). Moreover, by being presented as the "the
disciple whom Jesus loved," this disciple is defined by the love that both
God and Jesus show for the world and disciples (3:16; 13:1). He participates in the loving relationship between Father and Son (3:35; 5:20) by
loving the Son (14:23; 16:27) and lives in loving relationship with
disciples (13:34–35).

By contrast, the other disciples named in this section do not do well:

- Satan enters and controls Judas to betray Jesus (13:2, 27). Jesus
  knows what Judas will do (13:21–30).

- Peter, despite his confession at 6:68–69, refuses to have his feet
  washed by Jesus; he is unable to understand Jesus' self-giving action (13:6–8). Then Peter overcompensates, demanding that
  Jesus wash his hands and head; he fails to understand that he is
  already clean (13:9–11).

- Peter does not know where Jesus is going, rejects Jesus' teaching that Peter will follow there later, demands to go there now, and declares that he will die for Jesus (13:36–37). Jesus does not believe him and predicts that Peter will betray him (13:38).

- Thomas does not know where Jesus is going or that Jesus reveals the way to encounter God (14:5).

- Philip does not know that Jesus has already revealed God to him (14:8–13).

- Some of the disciples do not understand Jesus' teaching about his destiny and his return (16:17–18).

- Jesus does not seem convinced that they believe (16:31).

Nevertheless Jesus prays in chapter 17 that God's purposes will be accomplished through his followers.

The passion narrative continues some of these elements. Judas betrays Jesus (18:1–5). Jesus serves the disciples by insisting that they not be arrested (18:8). Peter continues to resist Jesus' death, drawing his sword to attack those who arrest Jesus (18:10–11). Peter denies he is Jesus' disciple three times (18:17, 25, 27). Alone of the disciples, the beloved disciple is present at the cross (19:25–27); the rest seem to be in hiding (cf. 16:32; 20:19). A secret disciple, Joseph of Arimathea, overcomes his "fear of the Jews" to provide burial for Jesus (19:38–42).

The resurrection narrative looks to the future roles of disciples (chs. 20–21):

1. The beloved disciple will bear witness. He discerns the significance of the empty tomb, something not said of Peter (20:8). Again the beloved disciple overshadows Peter (cf. 13:21–30). Jesus rebukes Peter's question about the beloved disciple but indicates that the beloved disciple will remain until Jesus returns. This disciple continues to bear witness, enabling the writing of the gospel (21:20–25).

2. Peter's future is as leader and martyr. Jesus questions Peter's love for him, commissions him to the role of leading the disciples, and predicts his martyrdom (21:15–19). Peter becomes the good shepherd in Jesus' absence (cf. John 10).

3. At the tomb neither the beloved disciple nor Peter knows the Scriptures (20:9), and neither stays to encounter the risen Jesus as Mary does (20:11–17).

4. Thomas, who was absent from the risen Jesus' appearance to disciples, refuses to believe unless he touches the nail marks on Jesus. Eight days later he sees the risen Jesus, who blesses him for seeing and believing and blesses others (the gospel's readers) for believing the account without literally seeing the risen Jesus (20:24–29).

5. Jesus appears to the disciples, commissioning them to continue his mission, doing greater works (14:12), and bearing fruit (15:8). Jesus empowers them with the Spirit (20:19–23).

These male disciples, though committed to following Jesus in contrast with the leaders, generally do not exhibit constant, discerning, and faithful discipleship (the beloved disciple is an exception, as is the man born blind in John 9; see below).

Women Characters

Consistently the male disciples are outperformed by a small number of women who often present examples of positive responses—believing in or entrusting themselves to Jesus. Some of these women live outside the conventional power structures of their male-dominated society. They witness and discern Jesus' revelation of God's purposes and play key roles in accomplishing them.[15] In so doing, they also contribute significantly to the characterization of Jesus.[16]

Jesus' mother

Though unnamed, Jesus' mother appears in two crucial scenes. In 2:1–12, at the wedding at Cana, she is the one who informs Jesus that the wine has run out (2:3). His enigmatic response declares that it is not his "hour" and strongly asserts his independence. Yet she confidently expects him to act and tells the servants to obey his command. In so doing, she seems to exhibit some theological insight, setting up the sign whereby Jesus turns water into wine and reveals the will and life-giving, abundance-bringing purposes of God to the disciples ("his glory," 2:11).

She reappears in 19:25–27 at the cross with the beloved disciple. Jesus' hour has come. He addresses both of them, and uses family terms ("your son"; "your mother") to link them in a new household. As witnesses of his ministry, they are bound to each other as the nucleus of a new, distinctive community, the "children of God" (1:12), that continues Jesus' ministry with greater works (14:12), much fruit (15:8), and mission (20:21). In both scenes she participates in and furthers God's purposes.

The Samaritan woman (John 4)

The Samaritan woman's long conversation with Jesus contrasts with Nicodemus's in John 3. Nicodemus is named; she is not. He is a privileged male; she, an inferior female. He is a Jew; she, a member of the enemy people, a despised and hated Samaritan (4:9).[17] He is a powerful, high-status member of the ruling elite (3:1); she, a non-elite villager, one of the poor who make up 97 percent of the population.[18] He brings previous experience and understanding of Jesus and his signs (3:1–2); she encounters a stranger. He is unable to understand Jesus' theological teaching; she is theologically perceptive, understanding and receiving Jesus' revelation.

The woman's discernment of Jesus' identity and role grows through the chapter:

- 4:9: She encounters Jesus as a stranger and identifies him as a Jewish man wanting a drink.

- 4:12: She asks if Jesus is greater than her ancestor Jacob in supplying water that offers eternal life.

- 4:15: She asks for the water of eternal life, although she seems to understand it literally.

- 4:19: She asks if Jesus is a prophet, since he has revealed that she has had five husbands (4:16–18).[19] His revelation about her husbands does not condemn her but enables her insight about him. She pursues the relationship further by asking about the divisive issue of the place of worship (not the God worshipped). As in 2:4, Jesus again mentions the "hour."

- 4:29: After Jesus' revelation about worshipping in spirit and truth, the woman indicates her expectation for a messiah. Her naming this category sets Jesus up to reveal his identity (4:26). She includes his identity as prophet (his knowledge of her) and wonders about his identity as the Messiah in her report of the conversation (4:29, 39).

The scene ends with her missionary activity in her village. She participates in Jesus' mission by inviting the villagers to encounter Jesus, with the same language, "Come and see" (4:29), that he used to invite the first disciples (1:39; also 1:46). They come because she bears witness (cf. 1:35–51; 4:39). Jesus "stayed" with them (4:40; cf. 1:38–39). They encounter Jesus for themselves, believe *his* word, and name him as

"Savior of the world" (4:41–42). The title, a polemic against a common designation for the Roman emperor, attests the universal extent of God's life-giving purposes and sovereignty, Jesus' identity as the king who represents these purposes, and the inclusion of these Samaritans, widely regarded as outcasts (4:9), in God's purposes.[20] Her mission activity thus participates in God's purposes and furthers Jesus' work (4:34) even while the male disciples struggle to understand Jesus' cross-cultural mission (4:27) and their own mission (4:31–38).

Mary and Martha

In addition to the display of God's life-giving power in Jesus' raising Lazarus from the dead, two features mark this scene in John 11. First, there are numerous indications of the intimate friendship and hospitality that Mary and Martha (supported by caring, neighborly Jews, 11:19, 31, 33–36) and their brother Lazarus share with Jesus (11:2–3, 5, 11, 34–36). And second, the words and actions of both women set the context for the revelation of God's purposes through Jesus. They initiate Lazarus's raising by informing Jesus of Lazarus's illness (11:3).

Martha's conversation with Jesus exhibits her bold confidence that, as a miracle worker, Jesus can do something (11:21–22). By thinking in terms of future eschatology, when the dead will be raised at the end of the age (Dan 12:1–3; 2 Macc 7), she misinterprets his claim that Lazarus will rise (11:23). Jesus corrects her by revealing his own identity and mission, in 11:25–26, as the one who manifests God's resurrecting, life-giving power in the present. She responds with an accurate confession of Jesus' identity as "the Messiah, the Son of God" (11:27). But her subsequent protest in 11:39 against Jesus' command to remove the stone from Lazarus's tomb because there will be an odor suggests that, like Peter in 6:69, she does not understand the implications of her confession.

Mary's interaction is more by action than words. She also boldly expects Jesus to be able to do something about Lazarus (11:32). Mary leads both Jesus and the Jews to the tomb. For Jesus, it is a place to manifest God's life-giving purposes (11:41–44). For these Jews, it is a place of belief (11:45). By contrast, for the Jerusalem authorities, this life-giving action is the final catalyst for his death (11:46–57; 12:9–11). The first scene of chapter 12 elaborates a strange and brief reference in 11:2 to Mary anointing Jesus' feet. The scene (12:1–8) emphasizes four aspects of her action: (1) It is costly. She uses expensive perfume consisting of nard, which was used for cosmetics, medicines, and burial treatments (12:3). Judas protests its expense (12:5–6), but the rebukes from the narrator and Jesus indicate that Judas has missed the point (12:6–8). (2) The perfume pervades the house (12:3b). The scene recalls and contrasts the odor of death mentioned by Martha in 11:39, replacing it with an aroma of devotion and insight. (3) She "wiped" Jesus' feet (12:3, also 11:2), a verb that will be used in 13:5 when Jesus wipes the disciples' feet. Her act of service and devotion anticipates his. (4) Her action anticipates and prepares for his death. The narrative does not attribute any motive to her and does not explicitly indicate her discernment that he must die. But Jesus interprets her action in precisely those terms by linking it to "the day of my burial" (12:7). In contrast to Peter, she seems to know the inevitable fate of one who challenges Rome's allies.

Mary Magdalene

In the resurrection narrative of John 20, Mary Magdalene plays a prominent role.[21] She is the first to find Jesus' tomb, which she proclaims to Peter and the beloved disciple (20:1–2); stay at the tomb weeping (20:11–13) while the others return to their homes (20:10); see Jesus after he has been raised by God's life-giving power (20:14–16) (recognition comes as he pronounces her name [20:16]; Jesus' disciples recognize his voice and he knows their names [20:3–4; cf. 10:3–4]); be commissioned by the risen Jesus to announce the good news (20:17); proclaim the gospel of the risen and ascended Jesus (20:18).

Although these women characters are not perfect, they consistently outperform the male disciples in manifesting positive responses to Jesus. Often outside the power structures of their male-dominated society, they discern God's life-giving purposes revealed in Jesus.

Minor Characters

Numerous other characters appear in the gospel, often for limited but important interactions with Jesus, moving the action forward and highlighting aspects of his significance. These characters include the crowds, John the Baptist, Nicodemus, a leader of the Jerusalem elite (ch. 3),[22] the royal official (4:46–53), the lame man (5:2–16), Jesus' brother (7:2–10), the blind man (ch. 9), Lazarus (chs. 11–12), and Pilate (chs. 18–19). Two of these characters are discussed here.

The man born blind

The one appearance of the man born blind in John 9 is memorable for its depiction of his developing understanding of Jesus' identity.[23] The first seven verses depict the miracle as Jesus uses saliva, mud, washing in the pool of Siloam, and the man's obedience to turn the man's blindness into sight. The rest of the chapter concerns the reactions of his neighbors (9:8–12), the authorities (Pharisees/Jews, 9:13–41), his parents (9:18–23), and the man himself as they try to make sense of what has happened. The healed man interacts with the authorities and gains insight as well as sight in the context of, and frequently in contrast to, the resistance of the Jews/ Pharisees. He sees Jesus as "the man" (9:11), then the "prophet" (9:17), then "from God" (9:33), and finally as the "Lord" and "Son of Man" (9:35–38). His initial reports of what happened (9:11) become direct confession (9:38). The more pressure the authorities place on him, the more confrontational (9:27), insightful, and confessional he becomes (9:13–17, 24–34). Meantime the leaders become more "blind" (9:39–10:21), identifying Jesus as "not from God" (9:16), a "sinner" (9:24), and confessing that they do not know his origin (9:29). They put the man out of the synagogue community (9:22, 34).[24]

Pontius Pilate

The Roman governor appears in a long judgment scene in 18:28– 19:16a.[25] In seven alternating subsections, Pilate shuffles between his allies—the *Ioudaioi*, or Jerusalem authorities/leaders—outside his praetorium, or headquarters, and the arrested Jesus inside. Pilate has sent troops to arrest Jesus and so knows he must remove this threat (18:3–11). His interactions with the Jerusalem leaders exhibit an efficient and at times astute working relationship marked by impatience, tension, and taunts (e.g., 18:31, 38; 19:6, 12) as they negotiate each other's power in taking care of this threat from a provincial kingly pretender (18:33). Although Pilate has greater power, he needs their support as his allies, yet he continually reminds them of their dependence on him in making them beg for his action (19:4–7, 12). Although they need his patronage, they also remind this representative of Rome that his task is to protect the emperor's interests (19:12–16). Yet he secures from them an amazing statement of loyalty to Rome (19:12). His interactions with Jesus are marked by his nonunderstanding of Jesus' words and his inability to discern anything of God's purposes expressed in Jesus (18:33–38a; 19:9–11). The resurrection of Jesus displays God's life-giving power, reveals the limits of the power of Pilate and the Roman Empire, which he represents, in that they cannot keep Jesus dead, and judges Pilate as one who, in judging Jesus, judges himself as an opponent of God's just purposes.

Conclusion

The interactions of these characters with Jesus contribute at least three things. They move the plot forward, highlight the significance of Jesus, and manifest aspects of God's life-giving and just purposes.

1. The plot: Jesus' conflict with the Jerusalem authorities is central to the plot. This conflict develops through scenes of direct attack (the temple, 2:13–22; chs. 8, 10), but more often the authorities respond to Jesus' actions with the "minor characters" or the accompanying spoken claims that he makes (5:1–18; ch. 9, healing on a Sabbath; claims about relationship with God, chs. 5, 8, 10). The Lazarus scene functions as the final catalyst for Jesus' death, accomplished by the alliance of Rome (Pilate) and Jerusalem (11:46–57; chs. 18–19). The disciples and characters such as the man born blind generally provide contrasting, positive interactions to this conflict and hostility. But even here there are further nuances. Whereas the women characters seem to elicit and receive Jesus' revelations, the male disciples often do not understand, although they remain loyal (Thomas, Philip). Some trust Jesus' word (4:1–42; 4:46–54); some are attracted to Jesus' miracles (2:23–25); some seem interested in his teaching but get no further (Nicodemus); and others abandon him (6:66; Judas, Peter).

2. Jesus' significance: These interactions constantly engage the issue of Jesus' identity, mission, and significance. The Jerusalem authorities decide that God does not speak through one of unknown origin; he is a sinner and blasphemer (unlike Moses, 9:28–29). By contrast, the Samaritans, Peter, the man with (in)sight, and Martha confess him as the Savior of the world, Holy One, Son of Man, Messiah, and Son (4:42; 6:69; 9:35; 11:27). Others decide that he is a king (6:14) and debate his identity (chs. 6–7).

3. God's purposes: Throughout the gospel Jesus reveals God's life-giving purposes. These are not to be spiritualized. Encounter with God (eternal life in 17:3) means a new way of life including abundant fertility in wine and food (2:1–11; 6:1–14); physical wholeness (4:46–54; 5:1–18; 9:1–8; ch. 11), which Jesus interprets as utterly expressive of God's will (7:23); the end of hierarchical and exploitative socioeconomic structures, replaced by communities of new power relations expressed in service and love (2:13–22; 13:12–20, 34–35; ch. 10); and the end of social structures secured by gender, ethnicity, cultural traditions, and social status (ch. 4).

Notes

1. Among numerous summaries and contributions, see U. C. Von Wahlde, "The Johannine 'Jews': A Critical Survey," *NTS* 28 (1982): 33–60; "'The Jews' in the Gospel of John: Fifteen Years of Research," *Ephemerides theologicae lovanienses* 76 (2000): 30–55; Culpepper, *Anatomy,* 125–32; R. Kysar, "Anti-Semitism and the Gospel of John," in *Anti-Semitism and Early Christianity: Issues of Polemic and Faith* (ed. C. Evans and D. Hagner; Minneapolis: Fortress, 1993), 113–27; S. Motyer, *Your Father the Devil? A New Approach to John and "the Jews"* (Carlisle, Eng.: Paternoster, 1997), 46–57; D. Rensberger, "Anti-Judaism and the Gospel of John," in *Anti-Judaism and the Gospels* (ed. W. R. Farmer; Harrisburg, Pa.: Trinity Press International, 1999), 120–57; the essays by H. de Jonge, M. de Boer, R. Collins, P. Tomson, and A. Reinhartz, in R. Bieringer, D. Pollefeyt, and F. Vandecasteele-Vanneuville, eds., *Anti-Judaism and the Fourth Gospel* (Louisville: Westminster John Knox, 2001); A. Reinhartz, *Befriending the Beloved Disciple: A Jewish Reading of the Gospel of John* (New York: Continuum, 2001), 46–48, 70–75, 84–95.

2. See Josephus, *J.W.* 2.411; *Life* 189–198; for the chief priests as the rulers of Judea, Josephus, *Ant.* 20.251.

3. Saldarini, *Pharisees.*

4. Reinhartz, *Befriending,* 72–75, esp. 74. Reinhartz convincingly rejects the argument of M. Lowe ("Who Were the *Ioudaioi?*" *NovT* 18 [1976]: 102–7) that the term should be translated "Judeans." See also S. J. D. Cohen, *The Beginning of Jewishness: Boundaries, Varieties, Uncertainties* (Berkeley: University of California Press, 1999), 69–106.

5. On the power of the Jerusalem temple, see Hanson and Oakman, *Palestine,* 63–159.

6. L. T. Johnson, "The New Testament's Anti-Jewish Slander and the Conventions of Ancient Polemic," *JBL* 108 (1989): 419–41.

7. See Reinhartz; *Befriending,* 84–95; M. de Boer, "The Depiction of 'The Jews' in John's Gospel: Matters of Behavior and Identity," in *Anti-Judaism and the Fourth Gospel* (ed. R. Bieringer, D. Pollefeyt, and F. Vandecasteele-Vanneuville; Louisville: Westminster John Knox, 2001), 141–57, esp. 149–57.

8. W. Meeks, "Equal to God," in *The Conversation Continues: Studies in Paul and John in Honor of J. Louis Martyn* (ed. R. Fortna and B. Gaventa; Nashville: Abingdon, 1990), 309–21; J. A. Ashton, "Bridging Ambiguities," in *Studying John: Approaches to the Fourth Gospel* (Oxford: Clarendon, 1994), 71–89.

9. E.g., the Roman governor appointed the chief priest (Josephus, *Ant.* 18.33–35; 20.197) and, until the late 30s, kept the high-priestly garments under Roman supervision in the Antonia fortress (Josephus, *Ant.* 18.90–95; 20.6–14).

10. Karris (*Jesus,* 102–7) argues that conflict develops because Jesus "waters down the 'election' of Israel by bringing into God's people the marginalized" (p. 104). My reading suggests that matters of a just and life-giving societal vision and structures based on understanding of the divine purposes are to the fore.

11. Also John 20:24.

12. For these verbs of discipleship, see 8:12; 10:4–5; 21:19 ("follow"); 15:1–12 ("abide"); 3:3, 36 ("see"). Brown, *Gospel according to John,* 1:501–3, 510–12.

13. Judas is also identified as "son of Simon Iscariot" (6:71; 13:26). "Iscariot" has been interpreted to mean membership in a rebel group, the Sicarii; Judas's falseness, evoking a Hebrew word; his act of handing Jesus over, likewise evoking a Hebrew word; his occupation (a red dyer or fruit grower); or his place of origin, either the village Kerioth in southern Judea or "from the city," referring to Jerusalem. W. Klassen, "Judas Iscariot," *ABD* 3:1091–92.

14. For further discussion, see ch. 9, below.

15. See, e.g., S. Schneiders, "Women in the Fourth Gospel and the Role of Women in the Contemporary Church," *Biblical Theology Bulletin* 12 (1982): 35–45; Culpepper, *Anatomy*, 132–44; M. Scott, *Sophia and the Johannine Jesus* (JSNTSup 71; Sheffield, Eng.: Sheffield Academic Press, 1992), 174–240; R. Maccini, *Her Testimony Is True: Women as Witnesses according to John* (JSNTSup 125; Sheffield, Eng.: Sheffield Academic Press, 1995); O'Day, "John," in *Women's Bible Commentary* (ed. Newsom and Ringe); Conway, *Men and Women;* M. M. Beirne, *Women and Men in the Fourth Gospel: A Genuine Discipleship of Equals* (JSNTSup 242; Sheffield, Eng.: Sheffield Academic Press, 2003).

16. A. Fehribach (*The Women in the Life of the Bridegroom: A Feminist Historical-Literary Analysis of the Female Characters in the Fourth Gospel* [Collegeville, Minn.: Liturgical, 1998]) recognizes their ambivalent roles: they are positive paradigms of faith responses yet they are marginalized because they maintain androcentric and patriarchal structures in contributing to the gospel's presentation of the male hero, Jesus.

17. Samaritans originated in the interaction between Assyrian imperialists and inhabitants of the northern kingdom (2 Kgs 17). Around 300 B.C.E., the Samaritans built a temple on Mount Gerizim to rival the Jerusalem temple (John 4:20; Josephus, *Ant.* 11.306–328). Jewish troops destroyed it in 128 B.C.E. (Josephus, *Ant.* 13.254–258). The dispute was bitter and ongoing.

18. Whittaker, "The Poor."

19. Commentators have made much of her supposedly poor record with men and her supposed immorality. Two observations are important: First, five previous husbands and a man who is not her husband do not necessarily mean she was immoral. She could be involved in levirate marriage, with the sixth man refusing the role (Gen 38, Tamar; Deut 25:5–10; Ruth). So O'Day, "John," in *Women's Bible Commentary* (ed. Newsom and Ringe), 384. Second, whatever the reason and circumstances, Jesus does not dwell on her moral condition or condemn her.

20. Koester, "'Savior.'"

21. S. Schneiders, "John 20:11–18: The Encounter of the Easter Jesus with Mary Magdalene—A Transformative Feminist Reading," in *Readers and Readings of the Fourth Gospel* (vol. 1 of *What Is John?* ed. F. F. Segovia; SBLSymS 3; Atlanta: Scholars Press, 1996), 155–68.

22. Rensberger, *Johannine Faith,* 37–63.

23. Culpepper (*Anatomy,* 139–40) notes eleven similarities with the healing of the lame man in 5:1–17.

24. For John 9 as a possible window into the experience of John's community, see ch. 8, below.

25. Rensberger, *Johannine Faith,* 87–106; Carter, *Pontius Pilate,* 127–52.

CHAPTER 5

Johnspeak: The Gospel's Distinctive, Dualistic Language

As we have examined John's plot and characters, it is clear that John uses very distinctive and at times strange language. For instance, the scene of Jesus turning water into wine at the Cana wedding ends with the observation that Jesus performed "the first of his signs . . . and revealed his glory, and his disciples believed in him" (2:11). What are his signs? Why not call them miracles or works of power, like the Synoptic Gospels? What is "his glory"? What does it mean to "believe in him," and how is this related to his signs?

Subsequent scenes raise further questions. During the vicious dispute between Jesus and the Jerusalem leaders in chapter 8, Jesus declares, "you will know the truth, and the truth will make you free" (8:32). To what sort of "knowing" does Jesus refer? And Pilate is not the only person in human history to wonder, "What is truth?" (18:38). And free from what and for what?

Subsequently, in chapter 10, Jesus contrasts his own societal vision and mission with that of the destructive leadership of the temple-based leaders in Jerusalem. He describes them as bad shepherds who are thieves and bandits/rebels. The language of shepherds, thieves, and bandits/rebels is associated with political leaders. Jesus, identified, by contrast, as the good shepherd, declares, "I came that they may have life, and have it abundantly" (10:10). What is life, and what is the eternal life about which Jesus constantly talks (3:16–18) and to which the gospel bears witness (20:30–31)? How does it contrast with the life offered by the bad shepherds?

A crucial aspect of understanding John's distinct and strange language is to recognize that it is often bipolar, dualistic. Our discussion of John's plot and characters highlighted the conflict that Jesus' ministry provokes and the division it creates. Jesus' ministry causes a crisis of decision for the characters (and for the gospel's readers).[1] They must decide whether to believe Jesus' claims and revelation. In this context, the gospel frequently employs pairs of opposite terms (life-death; light-dark; truth-falsehood; above-below) to depict two very distinct and contrasting realities and identities. What realities does this language describe? How does the starkly dualistic language relate to the numerous characters who, as we observed in the chapter 4, above, often evidence mixed characteristics? Disciples follow Jesus and believe, but they often understand little and Judas and Peter betray him. The Jerusalem leaders seek to put Jesus to death, but "many of the Jews" (11:45), "many of the authorities," believe in him (12:42). Why use such clear-cut language, which establishes two separate realities, when many of the characters in the story are by no means so cut-and-dried?

The gospel's dualistic language performs two social functions. One is to depict in the clearest terms possible the distinctive and alternative identity of those in the community who have committed themselves to follow Jesus. This dualistic language constructs a view of the world that centers on God's cosmic purposes. It divides those who encounter God's saving purposes from those who do not and locates both in relation to God's saving purposes. But it would be a serious misunderstanding to think of this salvation only in individual and "spiritual" terms. For John, this new life lived in relation to God, manifested in Jesus and yet to be completed, is ecclesial, ethical, societal, and cosmic. The gospel's dualistic language elaborates these dimensions. The negative depiction of those who do not believe Jesus is the unfortunate corollary of presenting salvation and new life in terms of the new life of believers. This negative depiction of "the other" in this dualistic language functions to secure the privileged and distinct identity of believers as part of a counter-community or antisociety alienated from, and alternative to, the rest of society.[2]

M. A. K. Halliday describes an antisociety as "a society set up within another society as a conscious alternative to it. It is a mode of resistance."[3] It has its own system of values, behaviors, sanctions, rewards, and punishments that differ significantly from the dominant society. An antisociety generates its own way of talking that Halliday calls an antilanguage. This antilanguage reflects a "form of closed community." It functions to secure "inner solidarity under pressure" and is both a reflection and a source of an "alternative identity." The distinctive antilanguage is a "reality-generating system" that socializes community members into a different way of experiencing and understanding the world as members of a community in opposition to, and in tension with, the rest of society.[4] The antisociety's antilanguage functions to "express, symbolize, and maintain [its] social order."[5] It is helpful to think of John's gospel as an example of this sort of antilanguage. The distinctive dualistic language reflects, creates, and maintains an alternative identity and understanding of the world for its readers. The language constitutes an antisociety in tension with, and counter to, dominant values. (Chapters 8–9, below, will return to the likely experiences of those for whom the gospel was written.)

But although John's distinctive dualistic language constitutes an antisociety, the force and starkness of John's "either this or that" language point to a second social function. The stark dualism suggests that the gospel is addressing readers who are not especially clear on their identity and who live in ethical and social circumstances that are confusing and somewhat ambiguous. The gospel's language attempts to clarify their identity and circumstances for them by sharply differentiating them from those who do not think and experience the world as they do. (See chapter 8, below, for further discussion of this second function.)

John's polarizing language can be seen in the examples in the table.[6] The gospel gives the first column positive weighting and the second, negative.

Belonging to God	Belonging to the devil
From above	From below
Not from this world	The world
Believe	Not believe
Save	Condemn/judge
Life	Death
Light	Darkness
Love	Hate
Truth	Falsehood

Belonging to God or the Devil

Jesus' condemnation of the Jerusalem authorities in 8:42–47 provides the heading for the two columns in the table.[7] In verses 42–43, by pointing to their negative response to him, Jesus counters the leaders' claim in verse 41 to have God as their father. He declares, "If God were your Father, you would love me, for I came from God." While asserting his own origin from God, Jesus interprets their not accepting his word as evidence of their origin: "You are from your father the devil" (v. 44) and "are not from God" (v. 47). Their actions reflect their father in that they seek to kill Jesus and prefer lies or falsehood (vv. 44–46). By contrast, "whoever is from God hears the words of God" (v. 47).

John's dualistic language refers to the whole cosmos. It is not just about "good" and "bad," believing or nonbelieving people. It is about their origin and commitments in relation to two superhuman powers, God and the devil. These powers are very involved in human affairs, they struggle against each other to elicit human loyalty, and they seek to establish their contrasting purposes through their human offspring or agents. For John, they are not equal powers, and God's victory is certain.

Depicting the devil, John employs a long Jewish tradition that sees the devil (known by names such as Satan, Azazel, and Beelzebul) as the opponent of God's purposes and as malevolent toward humans:

1. As a father, the devil has human offspring who carry out his wishes (8:44). Here these offspring include the Jerusalem leaders ("you are from your father"). This link suggests a comprehensive condemnation of the world over which they and their Roman allies rule. It suggests that their hierarchical world, which benefits the elite at the expense of the rest, is contrary to God's purposes. The devil's human agents also include Judas, who carries out Satan's agenda of resisting God's purposes, manifested in Jesus, by betraying Jesus to death (6:70; 13:2, 27). Origin from the devil means commitments that are contrary to God's purposes.

2. The devil is associated with sin, especially lies and murder (8:44). Several Jewish traditions attribute sin's origin to the devil's lies (Wis 2:24) and interpret the serpent of Gen 3 as the devil.[8] This sin is also seen in Cain's murder of Abel (Gen 4). The devil's agents, the Jerusalem authorities, manifest the devil's characteristics in their actions of rejecting Jesus' teaching and putting him to death. The offspring imitate and replicate their father.

3. This link between the devil and his human agents suggests further meanings for the gospel's phrase "ruler of this world." Commonly this phrase is understood to be the devil. Jesus says that this ruler will be driven out (12:31), warns that the ruler is coming (14:30), and declares that the ruler has no power over him (16:11). John uses the language of ruler also for the Jerusalem authorities, who, as Rome's allies, exercise power over their world, including synagogues (3:1, Nicodemus; 7:26, 48; 12:42).

The common terminology suggests that the gospel depicts the Jerusalem leaders as allies of the devil. Also allied with the devil is Rome's representative, the governor Pilate. The framing of references to the "ruler of this world" in future terms (12:31; 14:30) anticipates Pilate's entry into the narrative in chapters 18–19. He is a ruler or authority (though the term "ruler" is not used for Pilate). He is a murderer in putting Jesus to death. He is "false" in opposing Jesus and certainly not interested enough in truth to wait for Jesus' answer (18:38). And as Jesus declares in language resembling 14:30, Pilate has no power over Jesus (19:11). Jesus, who is "from God," announces certain victory over the devil and his agents, the Jerusalem leaders and their Roman allies. He announces judgment on the world that rejects God's good and just purposes for all people (12:31).

To be "from your father the devil," then, locates someone in John's great divide between these two cosmic superpowers, God and the devil. The phrase denotes people's identity in terms of their cosmic allegiance ("from/of" the devil) and their lived commitments because the lives of humans replicate their father's nature, commitments, and actions. This origin *shapes* how humans live. In turn, human living reveals people's origin and their commitments to replicate their father's commitment. More important, origin *explains* why one lives in a particular way. Those who live consistently with God's purposes manifested by Jesus demonstrate that they originate from God. Jesus is from God, since he does God's will. Jesus' opponents seek to kill Jesus. They are not from God but replicate their father the devil. Cosmic origin, human community, and ways of living are interconnected.

From Above, From Below (8:23a)

Earlier in chapter 8, Jesus uses the dualistic language of "from above" and "from below" to make the same point. He declares to the audience in the temple that they cannot go to God the Father and that they will die in their sins (8:20–22). They do not understand, prompting him to employ a spatial metaphor in declaring, "You are from below, I am from above" (8:23).

Jesus has previously employed spatial language to assert his own origin and identity of being sent from God. As the Son of Man (a heavenly figure in Dan 7:13), he "descends" or "comes down from heaven" (John 3:13). He is "the bread that came down from heaven" (6:41–42, 50–51).

Heaven is "above," the traditional abode of God (12:28), who sent him (6:38). He "came from God" (8:42; 13:3; 16:27–30). Through the Spirit's action, also sent by God to accomplish God's purposes (14:26), humans can also be born from above, that is, by God's action (3:3–8). Since "above" is the sphere of God's activity, "below" is that of the devil.

Not of This World, Of This World (8:23b)

Jesus further elaborates "from/of" "God/the devil" and "from above/below" in 8:23b with another pairing: "you are of this world, I am not of this world." "World," which John employs about seventy-eight times, is a complex but important term for the gospel, embracing positive and negative connotations and embracing both the created and the human realms.[9] It can be used positively to denote the universe (17:5, 24), God's physical creation (1:10b cf. 1:3), and the realm of human interaction (1:9–10; 16:21). It is also used positively in terms of God's loving purposes for human beings (3:16).

But the term also has a negative meaning that dominates the gospel and is especially evident in chapters 14–18. This negative usage refers not to physical creation (which is good in both Gen 1 and John 1:1–3) but to human lives and society that resist God's life-giving purposes. In this negative sense, "the world" denotes life not as God intends it, life in opposition to God's purposes. "The world" fails to know or believe Jesus (1:10). It has refused to acknowledge its Creator and has accepted another, Satan with his human agents, as its ruler (12:31). It is unable to understand itself as created by, dependent on, and accountable to God with a mandate to structure its life according to God's life-giving purposes (1:10b). Its deeds are evil (3:19; 7:7). Its "peace," evoking the *pax romana* (Roman peace), the unjust imperial order imposed by Rome, is contrary to God's peace or wholeness, in which all people and resources are justly related (14:27). It does not know God (17:25). It hates Jesus (7:7) and disciples (15:18–19; 17:14) but loves its own, those "of the world" (15:19), who, in contrast to disciples and Jesus (17:14), reject God's purposes (15:19). "The world," then, comprises the hierarchical, unjust society that the ruling authorities have established for their own benefit and defend with violence (18:36). It is contrary to and opposed to God's purposes. So the world sins in refusing to acknowledge Jesus' identity as revealer of God's just and life-giving purposes and in thereby spurning those purposes (7:7; 16:10).

Yet God loves the world (3:16) and actively seeks to "save the world" and transform its destructive existence (1:9; 3:17; 12:47). Jesus, who is not of the world (17:14; 18:36), is the agent of this salvation (4:42; 6:14) in the world (1:10; 9:5; 13:1). Jesus is sent by God into the world (3:17), commissioned to reveal God's purposes (8:26). Jesus comes into the world (3:19; 11:27), giving life to the world (6:33, 51; 8:12) and not judging it (12:47). He is its Savior (4:42), its light or salvation (8:12; 9:5), its bread (6:33, 51), the one who takes away its sin (1:29).

But the world, true to itself, hates Jesus (15:18–19) and his followers who continue his mission (17:14) in the world (17:11). The world rejects Jesus because he exposes its deeds as evil (3:19–20; 7:7), contrary to its Creator's purposes. Its rejection of Jesus confirms the world's identity and way of life as antithetical to God's purposes. Judgment results (9:39; 12:46–47; 16:11); its ruler is condemned (12:31). Yet God continues the saving mission through disciples (17:18, 23) who are also sent into the world (20:21) and who also experience rejection (15:18–19) and danger from Satan and his agents (17:15).

Hence, although Jesus can be "in the world" (as the domain of humans and marked by rejection of God's purposes) and he can leave this domain to return to God at the end of his mission (13:1; 16:28), he does not originate from or belong to "the world" (8:23b; 17:14). His "kingdom," the revelation of God's order and rule for human interaction and society, is "not of this world." It is vastly different, not sharing, for example, the world's commitment to violence (18:36). Jesus does not belong to the world, this order that rejects and opposes God's good and just purposes (17:16). He does not originate in it or share its commitment because, contrary to the world, his commitment is to God's purposes. In sharing this commitment to God's purposes, his disciples, too, "do not belong to the world" (17:14, 16).

But the Jerusalem leaders and their allies, committed to maintaining a social structure contrary to God's purposes, are "of this world" (8:23). Hence they do not understand his words (8:22, 27); they do not know that he is the revealer of God's purposes (8:25). They reject God's life-giving purposes for human society. Their incomprehension and rejection reveal their identity as well as their origin from, and allegiance to, the devil. Being "from below," being "of the world" means they reject God's purposes. They will die in their sins unless they change their stance toward Jesus and believe in him (8:24).

Determinism and Decision

Our focus on origin and the commitments expressed in a person's way of life raises the question of the power of this origin. Is it so determinative of identity and lifestyle that it can never be changed? Does John suggest that humans are fated or destined to play a fixed and inevitable role? Are humans programmed robots? Does free will play any part? What is the relationship between determinism and human responsibility? Can humans do anything to become children of God?[10]

The gospel seems to offer a no/yes answer. The "no" stems from its emphasis on divine action and human impossibility. God gives power to become God's children; it cannot happen any other way (1:12–13). God "gives" believers to Jesus as though God arbitrarily chooses some and not others (6:39, 65; 17:2, 6, 9). God draws people to Jesus (6:44).

The "yes" reflects the gospel's emphasis on believing as a human responsibility or choice and as a process in which people journey through hardship and challenge to insight and commitment (the Samaritan woman in John 4; the man born blind in John 9). Although God loves the world (3:16) and draws *all* people (12:32), only some believe. The language of "everyone who believes/whoever believes" (3:16, 36) suggests the opportunity for any and all to choose to believe. If choosing to believe as an act of human will did not exist, there would be little point in the disciples' ongoing mission (17:21), in the commands to believe (8:24; 12:36; 14:1), or even in the act of writing the gospel (20:30–31). In 1:12–13, although divine power is needed to create children of God, this power takes effect when people have received Jesus and are believing: "to all . . . who believed in his name, he gave power to become children of God." Perhaps some believing is required first; begetting seems to happen while one is believing.

It seems, then, that the gospel recognizes both God's activity and human decision in this crucial act of believing. God continues to work for the world's salvation, but the responsibility remains with humans to accept this work and decide to participate in God's purposes. This paradox respects the mystery of faith, claiming neither too much (totally God's work) or too little (a totally human decision).

Believing, Not Believing

But what does John mean by "believing"?[11] Is this English word the most adequate translation for this rich concept? Five factors provide some insight into the experience of believing:

1. "Believe" is a verb: Nearly one hundred times John uses the verb "believe." The gospel never uses the noun "faith" or "the faith" or "belief." A particular form of the verb appears frequently,

namely, the adjectival or substantive participle that denotes a person's identity as "one who believes" or "a believing one." Whatever else the word means, the use of the verb rather than the noun suggests "believing" is not static, not an inner possession, not a private disposition. It is an action or activity that constitutes and expresses an identity in an ongoing way of life, an active and continuing commitment. It has the sense of living faithfully and loyally, of acting with fidelity.

2. Context: Further insight comes from the contexts in which "believe" is used. For example, in 2:11 the disciples "believed in him." In 2:23–24 the same verb appears twice but is translated in two quite distinct ways with two different subjects (in italics): "many *believed* in his name because they saw the signs that he was doing. But Jesus on his part would not *entrust* himself to them." We will return shortly to the relationship between signs and believing. Notice here, however, the difference a translation makes. In the second instance, it makes little sense to say "Jesus did not believe himself to them." Hence the need for another English word; "entrust" is a good choice. But what difference would it make if we used this same English word, "entrust," to translate the previous use of the same Greek verb? A translation such as "many entrusted (themselves) to his name" conveys a dynamic sense of attachment and commitment and foregrounds the element of active trust. These dimensions are often missing from our English word "believe."

Another dimension emerges from some other contexts. In 4:39 "many Samaritans . . . believed in [entrusted themselves to] him" because of the testimony of the woman at the well. Yet in 4:42, after Jesus has visited with them, some say that they do not believe/entrust any more because of her word but because of being with Jesus. Believing is not a single act but often a process, as is evident in John 9. The man born blind confesses in 9:38, "I believe [entrust myself]," but only after he has regained his sight, experienced the interrogation of the Jerusalem authorities, suffered abandonment (again) from his parents, been expelled from a synagogue (9:34), and met with Jesus. Believing/entrusting is a process that includes insight, adversity, and social interaction.

3. Believing what/who? "Believe" does not always have an object and can be used on its own (3:18). But attending to its object offers further insight.

a. As we would expect, believing or entrusting is explicitly directed to Jesus or to God. In more than one-third of its uses, the verb "believe/entrust" is followed by prepositions (either εἰς, *eis*, or ἐν, *en*), so that it literally means "believe/entrust into or on." A few times God is the object (14:1), but over thirty times Jesus (or his name) is the object (3:16–18). This use suggests a sense of personal commitment to Jesus—a relationship with him marked by ongoing fidelity and loyalty—of actively entrusting oneself to him.

b. A second use is related to this sense of commitment and loyalty. The verb can also indicate believing (or not believing) in Moses (5:46), the Scriptures (2:22), or Jesus' word (4:50; 5:47).

c. The verb also introduces "that" (ὅτι, *hoti*) clauses containing affirmations about Jesus. Believe "that I am he" (8:24), "that you are the Messiah, the Son of God" (11:27), "that I am in the Father and the Father is in me" (14:10–11), "that I came from God" (16:27), "that you have sent me" (17:21), "that Jesus is the Messiah, the Son of God" (20:31). These are central Johannine understandings about Jesus (see ch. 3, above). They could easily be combined into the form of a creed. "Believing/entrusting" here includes not only commitment to, and relationship with, Jesus but also understanding of, and consent to, statements that accurately assert Jesus' origin, identity, authority, mission, and relationship with God. These statements express God's perspective on Jesus, and so believing/entrusting oneself to them means allying oneself with God's verdict. Clearly, these are affirmations with which nondisciples do not agree. What one believes functions, then, not only in establishing and maintaining relationship with God but also socially, in identifying those who belong to John's distinctive community and marking a division with outsiders.

4. Synonyms: These dimensions—commitment to, entrusting of oneself to, relationship with, fidelity to, understanding, and allying with God—are also expressed in verbs that are synonyms for "believe." "Believe"/"entrust" is used with "see" (1:50; 4:48; 6:30, 40; 11:40, 45; 12:44–45; 20:8, 25, 29), "know" (4:42; 6:69), "hears my word" (5:24; 12:45–46), "comes to me" (6:35), "comes and eats/drinks" (6:47–57; 7:37–38), "continue in my word" (8:31),

"worship" and "see" (9:38–39), "know and understand" (10:38), "loved me" (16:27), "received and know" (17:8). These synonyms emphasize various dimensions of believing/entrusting.[12] "Seeing" denotes not just physical sight but insight into, perception of, and commitment to Jesus' identity, mission, and God's purposes (14:9). "Hearing" likewise indicates not just physical hearing but hearing that discerns the significance of Jesus. "Knowing" signifies both intellectual knowing and, in the Hebrew Bible tradition, the experiential, relational encounter with God. "Coming to" expresses not physical movement but a dynamic seeking after, and commitment to, Jesus. In 14:12 to believe is to do the life-giving works that Jesus does (and even greater): believing/entrusting means a way of life in God's service.

5. Antonyms: The verb "believe"/"entrust" is commonly negated (3:12, 18; 6:36; 10:38). Not surprisingly, to not believe/entrust oneself to Jesus/God is to have other commitments (5:44), to value social status and honor more than God's purposes (12:41–42), to love evil deeds (3:18–19), to disobey the Son and his revelation (3:36), to reject his claims (6:36; 8:45), to not belong to his people (10:26).

A further issue needs consideration. What role do Jesus' miracles or "signs" have in the act and life of believing/entrusting? The gospel offers several scenarios that present signs as ambiguous and difficult to interpret. Four scenarios identify four interactions between signs and faith:

1. Signs conceal Jesus' identity. Some witness Jesus' signs or miracles but see no evidence of God's presence or purposes (12:37). The authorities, for example, respond with suspicion and hostility in 5:16–18 to Jesus' healings, throughout chapter 6 in discourse with Jesus, and in chapter 9 with aggressive questioning of the man born blind and with his expulsion from the synagogue community (9:34). Hostility is also evident in chapter 8 as they conclude that Jesus, far from being an agent of God's purposes, is a despised Samaritan and demon-possessed (8:48). The leaders find in Jesus' signs a reason to put him to death (11:47–48). They can discern no sign of God's presence or purposes.

2. Signs conceal and reveal a little of Jesus' identity, thereby misleading some. Some characters witness Jesus' miracles and see something of God's purposes and presence. They do not exhibit

hostility or great insight, but they follow him as a miracle worker, a prophet, or a popular king (6:14; 11:47–48). Jesus is suspicious of this response (2:23–25) and exhorts such people to discern the revelation of God's purposes in the sign (6:25–40; note 6:26).

3. Signs reveal Jesus' identity and lead to confession. Some who witness the signs discern God's purposes at work in Jesus and understand his role as agent of God's life-giving purposes. The sign contributes to a process of believing/entrusting themselves to Jesus. Thus, when Jesus turns water into wine at Cana, he "revealed his glory" (2:11). In the Hebrew Scriptures, the term "glory" can mean praise or honor (so 12:43), but it frequently refers to the power and presence of God manifested among the people in a special way (Exod 16:10; 24:16). Jesus' miracle at Cana, for those with eyes to see, manifests God's power and presence. The disciples discerned this revelation (how?) and "believed in him" (2:11). They then spend the rest of the gospel trying to put together the various pieces of the Jesus puzzle, frequently misunderstanding, at times betraying, but persevering (see ch. 4, above).

In other signs, Jesus' words also play a prominent role in fostering believing/ entrusting. In the second sign, when the royal official asks Jesus to heal his son, Jesus declares, "Unless you see signs and wonders you will not believe" (4:48). The statement has been understood variously as a rejection of signs, or a tolerant rebuke for demanding them, or a test for the official, or a disparagement of signs-based believing. But it seems rather to be a statement from Jesus recognizing that signs can have a helpful role in fostering a life of believing/entrusting. Subsequently, the man believes/entrusts himself to Jesus' word of healing, journeying home to find his son alive (4:50). He then "believed"/ "entrusted," together with his whole household (4:53–54). Sign and word interact in his journey to faith. Similar developments or growth (or "faith journeys") take place in chapter 9 when the blind man is healed and progressively comes to believe. In chapter 11 Martha knows that Jesus the miracle worker could have prevented Lazarus's dying, but in conversation with Jesus she comes to confess Jesus as "the Messiah, the Son of God," before the miracle of Lazarus's raising (11:20–27). And the whole gospel narrative combines Jesus' signs and words to form "these [things that] are written" to arouse and confirm believing/ entrusting (20:30–31).

4. Signs are unnecessary for some; faith results from testimony about Jesus. The third position anticipates this fourth response with its reliance on Jesus' words rather than on miracles. Jesus' conversation with Thomas evidences both an affirmation for the role of signs and a preference for Jesus' words. Thomas refuses to believe, entrust himself to, the accounts that Jesus is alive. He demands to see and touch Jesus' wounds in order to believe (20:24–25). A week later Jesus appears to Thomas and Thomas believes/entrusts. Jesus asks, "Have you believed because you have seen me?" Thomas's reputation for doubting or demanding proof is unjustified because his experience of believing/entrusting after seeing the risen Jesus is no different than that of Mary Magdalene or the other disciples. But then Jesus goes on to announce a blessing: "Blessed are those who have not seen and yet have come to believe" (20:29). This blessing refers to the gospel's readers who have no opportunity to see Jesus' signs (although John expects disciples to do works similar to and greater than Jesus', 14:12) but must believe the accounts. Finally Jesus' words seem to matter more. Several times the gospel presents characters who believe/entrust "because of" words, either the verbal testimony of others or Jesus' words (4:39, 41, 50, 53; 17:20).

These last three ways of understanding the interaction between signs and believing/entrusting may help explain the lack of insight and receptivity evident in the first position and the fact that it is the dominant response of the Jerusalem leaders or authorities. The last three positions assume some openness to the possibility that God intervenes and works to transform the current social structure and difficult experience. The authorities, despite their power base in the Jerusalem temple, are not presented as people concerned about being accountable to God for how they structure and rule society. Having structured it for their own benefit, they are not very interested in the harmful and sickening effects. And they are certainly not interested in God's life-giving and transforming intervention, which would displace their power and status. That is, some openness to God's intervention seems to be a precondition for discerning the power and purposes of God in Jesus' signs. It is the first step in a journey to discerning Jesus' identity and God's purposes.

Believing/entrusting is, then, the means whereby humans encounter God's salvation (3:16). It is the means of participating in God's work of rescuing the world from its present way of life and transforming it to enact God's life-giving purposes. God has been enacting such work for a long time in creation (1:5, 10; 4:22; 12:20–26). Believing/entrusting is a process, and the gospel uses several pairings to denote the transfer that takes place, describing what resists God's saving work and what participates in it. Believing means salvation, not condemnation; life, not death; light, not darkness; truth, not falsehood.

From Death to Life

Whereas the Synoptic Gospels present "the kingdom/reign/empire of God/of the heavens" as central to Jesus' ministry,[13] John uses such a phrase only a few times (3:3, 5; 18:36). Instead he makes "life" central to his story of Jesus.[14] Giving life constitutes Jesus' mission (10:10). It is Jesus' identity (11:25–26; 14:6). It is the purpose of the gospel that "through believing you may have life in his name" (20:31). To believe is to pass from death to eternal life and to be not under judgment (5:24). As we know from our daily lives, the term "life" can have all sorts of meanings, depending on who is using it and in what context. And since all the characters in the gospel are "alive" in some sense, what does John mean by using this particular term?

One way of beginning to understand what the gospel means by life is to notice what it is opposed to in the gospel's dualistic language. In 5:24 life follows death. What does the gospel mean by death?[15] Since Jesus dies (19:30), more than physical death seems to be in view.

Before Jesus' statement in 5:24 about passing from death to life, he has been talking about the two main tasks that the Father has given to him: giving life (5:21) and judging (5:22–23). "Judgment," as 5:23 makes clear, is for an existence that does not "honor" God or Jesus. Since "honoring" God is what Jesus does (8:49), an existence that honors God consists of what Jesus does. It is a life that participates in God's life-giving purposes (5:21). Jesus reveals these purposes in his actions and words (5:24); those who serve and follow him live a death-free life (8:51–52) and are in turn honored by God (12:26). Not to honor God, then, is to live an existence that does not participate in God's life-giving purposes, that is not honored by God, and that is already under God's judgment (3:18). The gospel describes as death this existence of not participating in God's life-giving purposes. That is, death is not just a matter of ceasing to have physical life. It denotes a type of existence that ignores or resists God's purposes. Humans, however, can pass from this existence, known as death and under judgment, to an existence called life by hearing Jesus' revelation, by recognizing him as the definitive revealer sent from God, and by believing/entrusting themselves to his revelation (5:24).

But to what do humans pass? What is life? The adjective "eternal," which accompanies the noun "life" seventeen times in the gospel, provides another important clue. For us, "eternal" often has the primary meaning of unending time. But for John, "eternal life" includes much more than that. The Greek adjective translated "eternal" literally means "agely," denoting "agely life" or "life of the age." The word "age" refers to a way of understanding history that developed in some Jewish eschatological texts just before and around the time of Jesus. Although there are variations, essentially this way of thinking divided history into two ages. Suffering and oppression mark the present age. The "age to come" is the final age, or eschaton, in which, after God's intervention and judgment, God's life-giving and just purposes are established in a new world in which there is no rejection of God's purposes. The phrase "eternal/agely life" in Dan 12:2 refers to this future new age, free of the oppression of the tyrant Antiochus Epiphanes, in which those martyred in faithful resistance are raised to new life. "Life of the age," or "agely life" (eternal life), is, then, not just about quantity (never-ending time); it also concerns a particular quality of life. It is life that participates in this final age, in which God's just purposes for all creation are established. It is *eschatological* life, life of the age, life of the eschaton.

This claim to manifest God's good purposes for never-ending life marked by justice has a polemical edge to it. Rome claims to be the eternal city (*Roma aeterna*) with a never-ending empire (*imperium sine fine*).[16] Such language claims that Rome's hierarchical way of life, which secures the power, status, and wealth of the small elite at the expense of the rest, lasts forever. John's notion of eternal life, which upholds the establishment of God's just and life-giving order, challenges Rome's claims, promises its downfall, and points to God's alternative way of life.

John employs this tradition of "life of the age" with at least two modifications: here "life of the age" includes *realized eschatology* and is *christological.* For John, eternal/"agely" life is experienced *now* and by believing/entrusting in *Jesus.* This life, which constitutes the very purposes and existence of God (5:26), is mediated now by Jesus' words (5:24; 6:63b, 69) and actions (4:53–54; 11:25–44). The life of the future age, eschatological life, is available now. Those who believe in/entrust themselves to Jesus already have eternal life (3:16, 36). Already now they participate in a life free from what is contrary to and opposes God's purposes. John identifies the existence that is contrary to God's purposes not only as the world but also as death. To believe/entrust is to have already passed from death to life, from condemnation to salvation (5:24).

At its heart, life of the age is to know God (17:3). To know is to participate in or to experience God. John does not mean that before Jesus no one encountered God. The Hebrew Scriptures, full of marvelous encounters with God, invalidate this claim. Rather, to have life of the age now is to encounter God, who is undertaking the final and definitive act of establishing God's purposes once and for all. These purposes include ordering all of human life according to God's good purposes, defeating the devil (12:31), ending death, and condemning for sin (5:24).

These statements are not to be understood only in terms of individual and private spiritual experience. God's life-giving purposes embrace all of creation; they are physical and material. The end of the "ruler of the world" involves, as argued above, the end of exploitative rulers who do not enact God's just ways and cause much human misery through misrule. It means a new form of *societal* life marked not by domination and self-interest but by seeking the good of the other in humility, love, and service (13:12–17, 34–35). This "agely" life is also *somatic*. God's purposes include the resurrection of bodies from death to life (5:24–29; 11:38–44), the supplying of abundant wine and food (2:1–11; 6:1–14), and the restoration of wholeness and health to a sick world damaged by imperial power (4:46–54; 5:1–16; ch. 9). The prophet Isaiah (and other writings contemporary with John, such as *2 Baruch* and *4 Ezra*) envisaged that the establishment of God's reign over all opponents included great fertility, abundant food, and physical wholeness (Isa 25; 35:1–10).

But although the gospel emphasizes the huge scope and "now-ness" of God's life-giving work and the importance of believing as the means of participating in it, it also recognizes that God has not yet completed this work. The resurrection of the body (6:39–40, 54), the full establishment of life of the age (12:25), judgment (12:48), and the return of Jesus (14:3, 18, 28) are yet to take place. Then God's life-giving and just purposes will be completed.

Light and Darkness

This transfer from death to life is also described with another dualistic pairing, the metaphor of darkness and light (12:35–36). Light is a common metaphor in the Hebrew Bible for God's life-giving creative power (Gen 1:1–5, 14–19), salvation (Ps 27:1), and deliverance from oppressive imperial powers (Isa 9:1–2). John describes life contrary to God's purposes (death; world; from below; of the devil) as darkness. This life is marked by evil deeds and hatred of the light, God's saving purposes (3:19–20).

God is at work overcoming resistance in various ways (1:4) but especially in Jesus, the light of the world (1:8–9; 8:12; 9:5). He has "come as light into the world, so that everyone who believes in me should not remain in the darkness" (12:46). "Darkness" and "the world" are synonyms for opposition to God's purposes. It is precisely among such opposition that God's saving purposes are manifested by Jesus as he exposes the evil of this way of life (3:20). Those who choose to entrust themselves to Jesus encounter the light, God's salvation, that creates a different way of life (eternal life). This life is marked by "deeds [that] have been done in God" (3:21), by works that imitate and continue Jesus' life-giving mission (13:12–17, 34–35; 14:12). Salvation and ethical existence are intricately connected.

Love and Hate

In referring to love for the darkness and hate for the light (3:19–20), the gospel employs another dualism.[17] Hate is a hallmark of the world, denoting its commitments and priorities, which are displayed in its false way of life, opposed to God's purposes. It hates the light (3:20), Jesus (7:7), the Father (15:23–25), Jesus' followers (15:18–19; 17:14). It loves human status and applause (12:43).

Jesus seeks to reverse this hate or opposition to God's purposes. He wants people to "hate their life in this world" in order to experience eternal life (12:25). Believing/entrusting means receiving God's love or transforming, powerful favor, which is manifested in Jesus and concerned to save or rescue the world from its false commitments and structures (3:16; 15:9). Love is God's life-giving power at work, transforming the world that is not structured according to God's purposes. This love or profound commitment to establish God's purposes is shared by Father and Son (3:35; 14:31; 17:23), so much so that the Son gives his life to further it (10:17). Believing/entrusting means participating in these purposes, reciprocating this love for both the Son and the Father (8:42; 14:21, 23). It means living in a new community marked by reciprocal love and service (13:34–35; 15:9–17) and by living Jesus' teaching (14:15, 21, 23).

Truth and Falsehood

Commitment to "truth" and not to "falsehood" is another metaphor for encountering God's salvation ("agely" life; light; from above; not of the world; of God). What does John mean by truth (18:38)?[18]

In English, "truth" or what is "true" can mean several things. One cluster of meanings concerns what is accurate, correct, genuine, authentic, real. The "truth" about a matter claims to be an accurate or correct or real (with nothing hidden) account. A second cluster of meanings concerns faithfulness or reliability. Someone's word is true, meaning that it can be relied on. Or if we say that he is true to her, we mean he is faithful to her and trustworthy. Although it has been much debated, John's use of "truth" seems closer to the second, but the first is not entirely absent.[19]

In the Hebrew Bible, the term "truth" primarily, though not exclusively, refers to God acting in faithfulness or loyalty to the covenant promises to be Israel's God. Frequently the term is translated "faithfulness," as in Exod 34:6 to describe the God who gives the covenant at Sinai. God is celebrated as one who loves steadfastly and acts faithfully, who can be relied on to keep the covenant, to instruct and forgive the people, to redeem Israel (Ps 25:10). Psalm 40:10–11 pairs God's faithfulness with God's steadfast love and salvation. Psalm 108 celebrates God's saving of Israel because of God's steadfast love and faithfulness (108:4; also 89:14), and Ps 146 celebrates God's faithful intervention with justice and transformation (salvation) for the oppressed and broken (146:7). God seeks a comparable faithfulness or truthfulness among humans in living faithful or truthful to God's will as manifested, for example, in the covenant requirements.

John describes God as the "true God" (17:3), thereby depicting God as acting in faithfulness to God's commitments to save the world. Jesus is introduced in 1:14, 18 as a manifestation of God's "grace and truth," a revelation of God acting in faithfulness to God's life-giving purposes to transform human existence. Jesus identifies himself as "the truth" in 14:6, with the same meaning; likewise he is the "true bread" (6:32), the "true" judgment (8:16), the "true vine" (15:1). Accordingly, for people to "know the truth" (8:32) is to encounter or participate in God's faithful activity of saving people from what is contrary to God's purposes as they are manifested by Jesus. Such an encounter means that "the truth will make you free" from all that is contrary to God's purposes (sin, 8:34). Jesus' mission is to bear witness to God's faithful saving activity ("the truth"); those who are open to God's work "hear" or understand or embrace or "believe, entrust themselves to," his message, being set free from what opposes God's faithful purposes. These believers are "of the truth," committed to, and participating in, God's faithful work (18:37). Conversely, Pilate, who oversees an order opposed to God's purposes, has no idea about "the truth" (18:38). Likewise, the devil does not participate in God's faithful saving work but is committed to oppose it (lies or falsehood, 8:44).

God's faithfulness does not end with Jesus' return to the Father. Rather, God sends the Spirit of truth (14:17; 16:13), the Paraclete, to continue God's faithful saving work among believers (14:16–17). The spirit teaches them (15:26). They worship "in spirit and truth" as participants in God's faithful saving work. This focus is much more important than a particular place (4:24). The Spirit, or Paraclete, guides them into "all the truth," the "things that are to come" (16:13), namely, eternal life or the full, final, and faithful establishment of God's salvation (15:26). Just as the world by definition rejected Jesus, so it rejects the Spirit ("neither sees him nor knows him," 14:17).

Conclusion

This chapter has looked at some of John's distinctive language, especially his common dualistic language, and has tried to decode a number of these pairings to understand how John uses them. Many of the terms are somewhat synonymous, with overlapping meanings denoting the experience and process of salvation (or its opposite).

John uses this dualistic language to depict the distinctive and alternative identity of those who have entrusted themselves to follow Jesus. It does so in part by contrast, denoting in negative terms human existence that does not participate in God's life-giving purposes. Positively, John's dualistic language also describes God's salvation and the distinctive life it creates, lived in relation to God, manifested in Jesus, and yet to be completed. This life is individual, ecclesial, ethical, societal, and cosmic, an alternative to that of life in Rome's world.

This dualistic language, however, is not just a matter of perspective. It has important social functions. It identifies consenting readers of the gospel as believers in Jesus and sharply distinguishes them from nonbelievers by depicting the latter in negative terms. The negative depiction of "the other" in dualistic language functions to secure the privileged and distinct identity of believers as part of a countercommunity or "antisociety" alienated from, and alternative to, the rest of society.

Notes

1. R. Bultmann, *Theology of the New Testament* (2 vols.; London: SCM, 1961–1955), 2:63.

2. For "antilanguage" and "antisociety," see M. A. K. Halliday, "Antilanguages," *American Anthropologist* 78 (1976): 570–84. The concept was applied to John by B. J. Malina, *The Gospel of John in Sociolinguistic Perspective* (Protocol of the Colloquy of the Center for Hermeneutical Studies in Hellenistic and Modern Culture 48; Berkeley, Calif.: Center for Hermeneutical Studies, 1985); and N. R. Petersen, *The Gospel of John and the Sociology of Light: Language and Characterization in the Fourth Gospel* (Valley Forge, Pa.: Trinity Press International, 1993), 87–89; for a similar understanding, see Rensberger, *Johannine Faith*, passim; and J. Neyrey, *An Ideology of Revolt: John's Christology in Social-Science Perspective* (Philadelphia: Fortress, 1988), 106; R. Rohrbaugh, "The Gospel of John in the Twenty-First Century," in *Literary and Social Readings of the Fourth Gospel* (vol. 2 of *What Is John?* ed. F. F. Segovia; SBLSymS 7; Atlanta: Scholars Press, 1998), 257–63.

3. Halliday, "Antilanguages," 570.

4. Ibid., 572–76.

5. Ibid., 580.

6. There has been much discussion about the origin of, the parallels to, and the significance of John's dualism: e.g., Bultmann, *Theology*, 2:15–32; Dodd, *Interpretation;* G. Ladd, *A Theology of the New Testament* (Grand Rapids: Eerdmans, 1974), 223–36; Ashton, *Understanding*, 205–37 (an Essene, 205); R. Kysar, *John: The Maverick Gospel* (rev. ed.; Louisville: Westminster John Knox, 1993), 58–77, 78–127.

7. L. Keck, "Derivation as Destiny: 'Of-ness' in Johannine Christology, Anthropology, and Soteriology," in *Exploring the Gospel of John: In Honor of D. Moody Smith* (ed. A. Culpepper and C. C. Black; Louisville: Westminster John Knox, 1996), 274–88.

8. *Life of Adam and Eve* 33:3; Rev 12:9.

9. Brown, *Gospel according to John*, 1:508–10; N. H. Cassem, "A Grammatical and Contextual Inventory of the Use of κόσμος in the Johannine Corpus with Some Implications for a Johannine Cosmic Theology," *NTS* 19 (1972–1973): 81–91; S. Morrow, "Κόσμος in John," *CBQ* 64 (2002): 90–102; also Painter, "Earth Made Whole."

10. Schnackenberg, *John*, 2:259–74; Kysar, *John: The Maverick Gospel*, 70–74.

11. Bultmann, *Theology*, 2:70–92; Brown, *Gospel according to John*, 1:512–15; Ladd, *Theology*, 270–75; Schnackenburg, *John*, 1:558–75.

12. For discussion, see Ladd, *Theology*, 259–63; Brown, *Gospel according to John*, 1:501–3, 512–15.

13. The Greek word βασιλεία, *basileia*, usually translated "kingdom" or "reign" in the gospels, also means "empire" and commonly refers to the Roman Empire.

14. Brown, *Gospel according to John*, 1:505–8; Ladd, *Theology*, 254–69; Schnackenburg, *John*, 2:352–61.

15. John 5:24; 8:51–52; 11:4, 13; 12:24; 18:32.

16. *Roma aeterna* or *urbs aeterna*, Livy (4.4.4; 28.28.11), Tibullus (2.5.23), Ovid (*Fasti* 3.72); *imperium sine fine* ("empire without end"), Virgil, *Aen.* 1.278–79.

17. S. van Tilborg, *Imaginative Love in John* (Leiden: Brill, 1993).

18. Ladd, *Theology*, 263–69; Schnackenburg, *John*, 2:225–37; I. de la Potterie, *La vérité dans saint Jean* (2 vols.; Analecta biblica 73–74; Rome: Biblical

Institute Press, 1977); also A. Lincoln, *Truth on Trial: The Lawsuit Motif in the Fourth Gospel* (Peabody, Mass.: Hendrickson, 2000).

19. Some scholars have argued that the first option represents a Greek meaning and is John's use (so R. Bultmann, "ἀλήθεια," *TDNT* 1:232–51; Dodd, *Interpretation*, 170–79, "the ultimately real"); others have argued that the latter represents a Hebrew meaning and is John's use (so Ladd, *Theology*, 263–69).

CHAPTER 6

Telling the Story: John's Style

Just as John's language is significantly different from that used in the Synoptic Gospels, so too is the style that John employs to tell his story of Jesus, the revealer of God's life-giving purposes.[1] Gone are the Synoptics' familiar parables and almost all talk of the reign or empire of God.[2] John's Jesus speaks much more about himself, describing himself with metaphors such as "the good shepherd," "the true vine," "the way, the truth, and the life." At the same time, he declares that if he bears witness to himself, his testimony is not true (5:31). Jesus' pithy one-liners, which triumphantly clinch victory over opponents in brief conflict scenes in the Synoptics, yield in John to much more extended narratives (e.g., John 4; 9; 11–12; 21).[3] Miracle stories become signs stories with much larger discourses and disputes (e.g., John 5 and 6). The episodic style of the Synoptics, which piles up short scenes (much like television soap operas), does not completely disappear (1:19–2:25). It is, however, overshadowed by longer narratives.

John's style, or way of telling his story, like so much in the gospel, can best be described with a paradox. On the one hand, John's style reveals God's mysterious, life-giving purposes; on the other, it hides God's purposes and creates confusion. We will examine some of the stylistic features or techniques that the gospel's author employs to create both confusion and revelation. These features reinforce the gospel audience's understanding about Jesus and secure the identity of "those in the know" as a countercommunity or antisociety distinct from those who do not understand.

How Skillful Is the Gospel's Author?

How good a writer is the author of John's gospel? The question is worth asking, especially when we notice contradictions and enigmatic sequencings in the gospel. Often referred to as aporias, they will feature prominently in our next two chapters. Here are a few examples:

1. Problems of sequencing: In John 5 Jesus is in Jerusalem, but 6:1 locates him on "the other side of the Sea of Galilee." The word "other" suggests that Jesus has just been on one side of the sea— which cannot be so, given the location of Jerusalem. In 14:31 Jesus seems to end the chapter-long sermon he has spoken to the disciples, but then he talks for two more chapters (chs. 15–16) and prays in yet another (ch. 17). In 20:30–31 the gospel seems to end, but then a whole chapter follows.[4]

2. Problems of inconsistent content: In 3:22 Jesus is said to be baptizing, but just fifteen verses later, 4:2 says Jesus does not baptize. In 7:8 Jesus says he is not going to Jerusalem, but in 7:10 he goes.

3. Problems of inconsistent theology: Do signs lead to faith (2:11), or is faith without signs preferable (20:29)? Does the gospel emphasize sacraments (6:51–58), or does it indicate that they are not important by leaving out the institution of the Lord's Supper? Are God's eschatological or end-time purposes known in the present (5:24) or in the future (5:28–29)?

How to make sense of such enigma? We could conclude that these ambiguities and puzzles (along with other puzzling details of grammar)[5] indicate that the author is not very skillful in handling sources (see ch. 7, below); and/or had only simple knowledge of Greek in translating an Aramaic original;[6] and/or was, as a person in cultural transition, working with "immigrant" Greek;[7] and/or was not very competent in shaping a coherent narrative and characters. If we were reading a publication from our own time, we might conclude that the author was not very good at telling a story.

But some scholars have pointed out that features such as contradictions and awkward sequences may suggest the opposite conclusion. In the world from which John's gospel originates, such mysteries can be signs of great skill employed to give appropriate presentation to the gospel's profound content.[8]

Treatises from around the time of the gospel that advise how to write about religious themes emphasize three qualities: *sublimity,* or eloquent speech to express lofty thoughts; *obscurity* to provide emphasis and maintain the mystery of the material and ensure that only insiders understand it; and *solemnity* to articulate matters relating to God or the gods. John's frequent use of ambiguity (discussed below), even contradiction, and his double meanings, varied terms, symbolic language, and abrupt narrative transitions are examples of the lofty and evocative literary style that embody these values. These techniques seem appropriate for expressing his profound and paradoxical understandings of God's purposes manifested in Jesus. Such "grandeur of rhetoric" produces in its audience not only emotional, intellectual, and spiritual stimulation and wonder in experiencing divine mysteries but also an identity of belonging to a privileged group that is distinct from outsiders because it has encountered special revelation of God's purposes.

Clear Explanations

Although such sublimity and grandeur evoke mystery, writing clearly so that one's audience understands also matters. More than fifty times, John's author offers explanations that provide helpful information or perspective. These explanations include:[9]

- translations of Hebrew or Aramaic words into Greek, notably the titles or names of persons (1:38, 41, 42; 4:25; 20:16, 24) or places (9:7; 19:13, 17);

- clarifications of time (7:2; 9:14; 19:31) and/or place (6:23; 8:20; 10:22, 23; 11:18, 30; 19:42; 21:8), which facilitate links in the narrative (6:23) or supply contextual information necessary to understand the action, such as those referring to Sabbath days or festivals (7:2);

- explanations of customs, as in 4:9, which supplies information crucial for the exchange between Jesus and the Samaritan woman ("Jews do not share things in common with Samaritans");

- reliable narration, in which the author presents himself as one who reliably perceives (1:14, 16) and guarantees truth about Jesus (19:35; 21:24) and who has the "inside scoop" on Jesus' relationships (13:23);

- references to disciples when they fail to understand Jesus' teaching (8:27; 10:6; 13:28; 20:9) or later gain further insights (2:22; 12:16);

- narrative color (4:2; 6:23) and information about a character's internal thoughts or motives (2:9, 24–25; 7:5; 11:51; 12:6), the referents of Jesus' speech (6:71; 7:39), or the significance of an action (19:36; 20:30–31; 21:19);

- enumerations that connect actions (2:11; 4:54; 21:14);

- identifications of persons either to link them with other scenes (7:50; 11:2; 18:14) or to supply further information about them (18:10, 40);

- emphasis on Jesus' special knowledge of situations or people (2:23–25; 6:6, 64; 13:11);

- theological explanations that elaborate Jesus' mission (3:16–21, 31–36; 12:37–43).

Some of this information helps the audience make narrative connections, and other information facilitates understanding of the gospel's theological claims.

Repetition

Another technique that facilitates effective communication is repetition. Many public speakers and teachers have heard the old adage "Tell them what you're going to tell them, tell them, then tell them what you have told them." As noted in chapter 3, above, John's prologue (1:1–18), in one sense, declares what the gospel will narrate, the gospel then narrates it (1:19–20:29/ch. 21), and the conclusion of 20:30–31 tells the audience what the gospel has narrated.

In addition, repetition of vocabulary and themes ensures that the gospel's audience is aware of and can understand important emphases. For instance, about twenty-five times, the gospel introduces sayings of Jesus with a repeated word, "amen, amen" (ἀμήν ἀμήν), often translated in the old King James Version as "verily, verily" and in more recent translations as "truly, truly" (RSV) or "very truly" (NRSV). The repeated word functions to underline the importance of the saying as setting forth a fundamental truth.

> Truly, truly, no one can see the kingdom of God without being born from above. (3:3)

> Truly, truly, whoever believes has eternal life. (6:47)

Truly, truly, whoever receives one whom I send receives me; and whoever receives me receives him who sent me. (13:20)[10]

We have also noted John's frequent use of verbs for "sending" to emphasize God's authorization of Jesus' revelation, origin, and identity as God's agent as well as Jesus' commissioning of disciples to continue his mission of revealing God's life-giving purposes (20:21). The frequently used preposition "from" also highlights Jesus' origin and reliable revelation. The verb "believe/entrust," used almost a hundred times, continually underlines the desired response to Jesus' ministry. The presence or absence of this verb, along with its positive and negative use ("do not believe/entrust"), establishes the line between insiders and outsiders.

Jesus' farewell discourse to the disciples (chs. 13–16) repeats important themes:[11] Jesus departing to God (13:1–3, 33, 36; 14:1–7, 28–29; 16:5–7, 16–22, 28); a new commandment, to love one another (13:34–35; 15:12–13, 17); to love Jesus and keep the commandments (14:15, 21–24; 15:10, 14); the Paraclete, or Spirit (14:16–17, 26; 15:26); Jesus' presence with disciples (14:18–20; 15:4–9); Jesus choosing disciples (15:15–16, 19; 16:7–11, 13–15); prayer in Jesus' name (15:16; 16:23–24, 26). In the context of Jesus' imminent departure and long-term absence from the disciples, the repetition of these themes underlines his absence, identifies means of continuing presence, and provides assurance for disciples.

Repeated accounts of Jesus' works enable the audience to understand their significance. The repeated healings (4:46–54; 5:1–18; ch. 9; ch. 11; with 2:23 and 21:25 suggesting many others) and the provision of abundant resources of drink and food (2:1–11; 6:1–14) function as signs of Jesus' identity. He is the one in whom God's powerful presence and purposes are revealed. But they are also signs of God's just purposes to give life to all. The wholeness and abundance enacted by Jesus' works anticipate the fertility and plenty that various prophetic and apocalyptic traditions indicate will mark the full and final establishment of God's purposes (Isa 25:6–10; 35:5–6; *2 Bar.* 29:4–8; 73–74).

Repetition thus facilitates the process of revelation. Over and over again the gospel emphasizes Jesus' origin, identity, mission, rejection, death, resurrection, destiny, and revelation. Such repetition employs various narrative techniques to keep key emphases before the audience, ensuring that they do not miss something important, securing their understanding, assisting the formation of a coherent and unified reading, and establishing their identity as believers who, in contrast to outsiders, receive John's proclamation.

At the same time, repetition functions to cast a negative verdict on those who do not believe. We all know the experience of making repeated efforts to explain something to someone who, despite our best efforts, still does not "get it." Our frustration often leads to negative thoughts and words about this person. Is the person that stupid, or is the person deliberately being difficult? The gospel's repetition casts a similar negative verdict on Jesus' opponents.

But not all of the gospel's rhetoric is readily understood, and for good reason. In order to highlight some of the complexity of the gospel's language, we will look at five often overlapping and interrelated techniques that scholars have identified in its rhetoric. The gospel frequently employs ambiguous language, riddles, misunderstandings, irony, and images. I do not want to suggest that these techniques operate in isolation from each other. They cannot be readily distinguished from each other, as is evident when scholars often discuss the same examples under different categories. The purpose here is to highlight aspects of John's complex language that often operate simultaneously in the gospel's rhetoric. Ambiguity recognizes that words with multiple levels of meaning are in play. Riddles pose dilemmas that need solving and introduce the risk of getting it wrong. Misunderstandings occur when wrong choices concerning meanings and type of language (literal or metaphorical) are made. Irony employs not only double levels of meaning but also degrees of unawareness. Symbols are often multivalent and not fixed in meaning. Taken together, such language games readily create confusion even as they effect revelation of God's mysterious purposes in Jesus.

Ambiguous Words

The gospel employs ambiguous words. Sometimes it is a matter of whether a word means one thing or another. But often it also entails discerning whether the language is to be taken literally or metaphorically and whether the word can appropriately have several meanings. Characters who do not receive Jesus' revelation misunderstand whereas followers of Jesus choose the right meaning:

1. In 3:3–5 Jesus tells Nicodemus, "no one can see the kingdom of God without being born from above [ἄνωθεν, *anōthen*]." The word *anōthen* is ambiguous. It can have a temporal meaning ("again"), or it can mean origin ("from above"). The latter is metaphorical, the former is literal. Nicodemus chooses the former meaning and in bewilderment asks, "How can anyone be

born after growing old? Can one enter a second time into the mother's womb and be born?" The answers betray his misunderstanding, making him look ridiculous. But although Jesus' choice of word confuses Nicodemus, it also reveals. Readers of the gospel already have clues that Jesus employs the latter meaning, "from above," to refer to origin in God's action. John has said as much in the opening prologue: "But to all who received him, who believed in his name, he gave power to become children of God" (1:12).

2. In 3:14 and again in 8:28 and 12:32, Jesus indicates that he must be "lifted up" (*hypsoō*, ὑψόω). At one level, the verb refers to Jesus' inevitable crucifixion, literally, his "lifting up" on the cross to die. In one sense, his crucifixion is the victory of his opponents. Yet readers know that his crucifixion is part of a much more significant lifting up, namely, his exaltation through resurrection and ascension to God at the completion of his life-giving mission (cf. 13:1–3). The verb has several meanings.

3. In 11:50 Caiaphas, the chief priest appointed by Rome and Rome's ally, declares that "it is better for you to have one man *die for* the people." Caiaphas means that Jesus' death will remove the risk that Jesus' ministry poses to the exploitative Roman order. Jesus dies "instead of" the people suffering Rome's punitive action, vicious retaliation, and forceful reinforcement of its order (11:48; cf. 18:14). But readers of the gospel know that Jesus, the good shepherd, *dies for* the benefit of the people in accord with God's purposes (cf. 10:15). He dies "for the sake of" the people so that they might encounter a new way of life shaped by God's purposes.

4. In 19:30, when Jesus dies, he says, "It is finished" (τετέλεσται, *tetelestai*). For the Roman and Jerusalem authorities, and for those gathered at the cross (19:25–27), this seems to refer to Jesus' death. They are not wrong but their understanding is very incomplete. Readers of the gospel have read 19:28, which uses the same verb to present Jesus' inner knowledge ("Jesus knew that all was now finished"). Previous statements of Jesus' special knowledge have concerned his God-given mission (1:47–48; 2:25; 6:61, 64; 13:1–3; 18:4), especially his mission to reveal God's purposes (4:34; 5:36; 17:4). Jesus' ambiguous words from the cross reveal the triumph of God's love and life-giving purposes (3:16) and the lengths to which the defenders of Rome's death-bringing order will go in their opposition.

In each instance, at one level the ambiguous words express a very inadequate understanding of what Jesus is about. At another level, the words express central understandings about Jesus and his mission. These understandings are revealed to insiders but remain elusive to outsiders. The ambiguous words reinforce the identity of the understanding insiders as a distinctive and countercultural group or antisociety.[12]

Misunderstandings

Evident in these examples of words with multiple levels of meaning, what we call polyvalent language, are numerous instances of misunderstanding. Alan Culpepper notes a threefold pattern that occurs at least eighteen times in the gospel:

- Jesus makes an ambiguous statement.

- His conversation partner misunderstands it, either by interpreting it literally (Nicodemus) or by asking an inappropriate question.

- Jesus or the gospel narrator explains his statement (though at times this explanation is missing).[13]

Eight times, for example, Jesus' opponents, the Jerusalem leaders, misunderstand Jesus, especially when he speaks about his death/resurrection/ascension and the freedom and new life ("agely" [see ch. 5, above] or "eternal" life) that he offers to the children of God (2:19–21; 3:3–5; 6:51–53; 7:33–36; 8:21–22, 31–35, 51–53, 56–58). Their misunderstanding demonstrates their rejection of his claims and mission.

The threefold pattern can be seen in 2:19–21:

- Jesus declares, "Destroy this temple, and in three days I will raise it up."

- The confused Jerusalem leaders respond literally, referring to the Jerusalem temple: "This temple has been under construction for forty-six years, and will you raise it up in three days?"

- Readers familiar with the whole story know from the references to "three days" and the verb "raise" that the temple about which Jesus speaks is not the Jerusalem temple, where the scene is set, but a reference to himself, crucified and raised. But just in case some of the gospel's audience are confused, the author clarifies the mystery: "But he was speaking of the temple of his body.

After he was raised from the dead, his disciples remembered that he had said this; and they believed the scripture and the word that Jesus had spoken" (2:21–22).

Jesus' disciples, confused at the time, come to understand the reference later in the light of Jesus' resurrection. But there is no mention of the leaders' subsequent understanding, indicating that they remain opposed to Jesus' revelation. The misunderstanding emphasizes the significance of Jesus' death and destiny, a crucial understanding if the gospel's purposes of securing belief and eternal life are to be accomplished (20:30–31).

The gospel's audience also learns from the disciples' misunderstanding. Eight times, the disciples (and others who exhibit belief) misunderstand Jesus. In 4:31–34, for instance, the same threefold pattern is evident. The disciples urge Jesus to eat.

- Jesus responds to their literal statement with a metaphorical one: "I have food to eat that you do not know about."

- The confused disciples answer with a question that maintains their concern with literal food: "Surely no one has brought him something to eat?"

- Jesus then explains: "My food is to do the will of him who sent me and to complete his work."

They have missed the metaphorical dimension of Jesus' statement about his identity as the agent of God's purposes. Subsequently they will misunderstand his revelation of life that overcomes death (11:11–15), of resurrection (11:23–25), the necessity of Jesus' death (13:36–38), Jesus' return to the Father (14:4–6), Jesus' revelation of God (14:7–9), Jesus' promise to return to take disciples to be with himself (16:16–19), and the gift of the Spirit (14:17).

On two occasions the crowds misunderstand Jesus. In 6:32–41 they misunderstand Jesus' statement about being "the bread from heaven," a statement about Jesus' origin, identity, and mission, which derive from God. They claim to know his parents! In 12:32–34 they misunderstand Jesus' statement about his death, destiny, and return to God through crucifixion, resurrection, and ascension (his glorification) by claiming that "the Messiah remains forever."

These misunderstandings accomplish at least four things in the narrative: (1) They create mystery and revelation, befitting for narratives that deal with matters of divine purpose and presence. (2) They confuse and reveal, dividing people between those who understand and those who misunderstand. They present a view of human society centered on, and divided by, allegiance to Jesus as the revealer of God's just purposes for human life. (3) They focus attention on central aspects of John's presentation of Jesus: his origin from God, mission, death, resurrection, ascension or return to God and his revelation of God's purposes, his gift of life according to God's purposes (eternal life), his ongoing presence with disciples, and the presence of the Spirit. The misunderstanding scenes provide opportunity for readers to gain understanding of these central matters. (4) In such scenes the gospel's readers are drawn into the circle of those "in the know." The purpose is to secure the reader's identity as one of Jesus' comprehending followers, distinct from his misunderstanding opponents (20:30–31).

Riddles

By noticing another feature, we can press the question of how these ambiguities and misunderstandings function for the gospel's readers. The notion of a riddle helps to clarify how John's language can simultaneously create confusion and offer revelation. Riddles employ ambiguities in posing a dilemma that needs to be solved.[14] They draw us readers in, catching our attention, challenging us to solve the mystery correctly. Their effect is to divide those who "get it" from those who do not. They divide insiders and outsiders. They define the antisociety. Those who truly understand John's good news, those who are really in the know, can, or should be able to, solve the riddles about Jesus. But for outsiders and opponents, such riddling language remains confusing and elusive.

Sometimes the narrative signals these riddles explicitly. In 10:1–5, for example, Jesus speaks to the Jerusalem leaders, the Pharisees (9:40), about himself as the good shepherd whose voice the sheep hear and follow. "Shepherd" is a common metaphor for leaders, rulers, and kings (so Ezek 34), and Jesus uses it to contrast himself with false leaders or "strangers" such as the Jerusalem leaders. The narrator says, "Jesus used this figure of speech [riddle] with them but they did not understand what he was saying to them" (10:6). They fail to understand themselves as false leaders, or Jesus as the true representative and revealer of God's just purposes.

But often the narrative signals riddles not by naming them but by showing the confused and often ridiculous responses they elicit. For instance, Jesus announces, "Whoever eats of this bread will live forever; and the bread that I will give for the life of the world is my flesh" (6:51). His opponents' cannibalistic interpretation highlights the riddle and makes them look ridiculous: "How can this man give us his flesh to eat?" They try to understand his saying literally instead of understanding it as a metaphor for believing or entrusting oneself to Jesus and living in his presence (6:47, 56). Jesus attempts to dispel their confusion in the next five verses but seems only to intensify the mystery. Jesus' disciples also struggle to understand, although they do not appear as silly as the opponents. They say, "This teaching is difficult; who can accept it?" (6:60).

The riddle in 8:21–22 again exposes the confusion and misunderstanding of Jesus' opponents. Jesus says, "I am going away, and you will search for me, but you will die in your sin. Where I am going, you cannot come." The leaders interpret his comment as referring to suicide. Their response reveals both the riddle and their failure to comprehend it: "Is he going to kill himself? Is that what he means . . . ?" Jesus' statement fails to reveal to them his return to God. Significantly, his words are strikingly similar to his statement in 7:33, which made the same point and which they also did not understand. In both instances their misunderstanding underlines the ambiguity of Jesus' mysterious way of talking and reveals them to be on the wrong side of the divide. By 10:24 the leaders have had enough of Jesus' riddles and appeal to him for plain speaking.

Not only do Jesus' opponents not understand him. Language that is meant to reveal confuses his disciples, who also misunderstand him (see 11:11–16). In 16:16–24 they misunderstand a statement similar to those in 7:33 and 8:21–22 about Jesus' destiny. Readers who identify themselves as disciples are warned to examine their own (mis)understandings about Jesus and God's purposes.

A riddle appears in 11:23–27 that seems to be solved successfully. After Lazarus's death, Jesus assures Lazarus's sister Martha that her brother "will rise again" (11:23). Martha responds in terms reminiscent of the expectation of some first-century Jews: "I know that he will rise again in the resurrection on the last day" (11:24). Her expectation of the future resurrection, however, is contrary to Jesus' intention to raise Lazarus to life now. So Jesus counters her future tense by using the present tense and identifying himself: "I am the resurrection and the life. Those who believe in me, even though they die, will live. . . . Do you believe this?" (11:25). Martha confesses her belief and accurately identifies Jesus as "the Messiah, the Son of God" (11:27). It seems that Martha has understood the mysteries of God's power that are at work in the present world and that Jesus reveals. She seems to have solved the riddle. But twelve verses later, when Jesus orders the stone removed from Lazarus's tomb, it is death, not resurrection and new life, that Martha expects: "Lord, already there is a stench because he has been dead four days." Her protest brings a sharp retort from Jesus reminding her of the imminent demonstration of God's powerful presence (11:39–40).

Jesus seems to signal a change of approach in 16:26–30. After sixteen chapters and about thirty-six riddles, he announces the imminent end of riddling. After explaining again to the disciples his imminent departure to the Father, he declares, "I have said these things to you in figures [the same word as in 10:6; riddles]; the hour is coming when I will no longer speak to you in figures [riddles], but will tell you plainly of the Father" (16:25). But this statement about the end of riddles is a riddle! What "hour" does Jesus speak about when he can speak to them plainly? Does he refer to the ongoing work of the Spirit with disciples after his return to God,[15] or does he speak of the imminent revelation on the cross?[16] The disciples confidently declare in 16:29 that they can tell that Jesus is now "speaking plainly, not in any figure of speech [riddle]!" But Jesus is not convinced and replies by warning them in 16:32 that they will soon abandon him (cf. 18:27; 20:19).

Throughout, the riddles in Jesus' speech have enacted both confusion and revelation. In them he has referenced the significance of his origin (8:38), life (10:1–6), mission (4:32; 9:39), actions (2:16; 11:11–15), words (8:26), death and resurrection (2:16–18), and return to God (7:34; 8:21). He has spoken of discipleship: its origin (3:3–5), abiding in his words (8:31–32, 51), the ongoing relationship (14:19), the future destiny (16:16). For such elevated matters, mystery is appropriate. Revelation occurs in solving his riddles correctly, thereby joining the antisociety of those who believe Jesus to be the agent of God's life-giving purposes for the world.

Irony

Irony pervades the gospel, involving its big theological themes, its plot, its presentation of characters, and shaping individual scenes and exchanges.[17] For example, the Word becomes flesh, comes to his own people, is not recognized by many of them, but is welcomed by others who form a distinctive community, a countercommunity or antisociety. The revealer of God's loving and just purposes for the world often encounters resistance and noncomprehension. Irony is present in many of the instances discussed above.

Paul Duke defines irony thus: "Irony as a literary device is a double-leveled literary phenomenon in which two tiers of meaning stand in some opposition to each other and in which some degree of unawareness is expressed or implied."[18] This definition picks up on elements of ambiguity, misunderstanding, and riddles that we have already noted. Duke emphasizes that irony is double-layered and presents opposing perspectives. But it also draws attention to a further aspect, the element of unawareness. Like riddles, irony engages the gospel's readers. It functions positively to delight and secure the audience's insight, emphasizing central aspects of the gospel's worldview and inviting the audience to share this perspective, which is contrary to false understandings of Jesus. Negatively, it functions to attack and expose confused ways of (mis)perceiving Jesus and God's purposes. It often ridicules those, especially the powerful and of high status, who either make false declarations about God's purposes or Jesus' identity or speak without full awareness of what they are saying. They ought to know better, but they do not.[19] Irony thus plays an integral role in the interplay of confusion and revelation.

Many of these features of irony are evident, for instance, in 6:42 and 7:27–28.[20] In the latter passage, the Jerusalem crowds ponder Jesus' identity: " 'Yet we know where this man is from; but when the Messiah comes, no one will know where he is from.' Then Jesus cried out as he was teaching in the temple, 'You know me, and you know where I am from.'" The crowd claims to know Jesus' origin. In 6:42 they declare that Jesus is the son of Joseph and that they know his mother and father. But such knowledge, though partially correct, displays their ignorance. His origin is double-layered. Jesus comes from God. They offer a partial perspective, mistakenly thinking it to be the whole story. Their claims to know his parental origin mean that they cannot see his true origin and identity as the Messiah, the one anointed, or commissioned, by God. They have had the opportunity to know otherwise. Eleven verses earlier, Jesus declared his teaching to come from God (7:17) and himself to be "sent" from God (7:18). He repeats the latter claim in 7:29, only to be met by efforts to arrest him. Jesus' comment in 7:28 thus ridicules them for claiming to know something that they do not and defines them as opponents.

Further instances of irony attack the opponents' false claims to knowledge. Jesus exposes the ignorance of Nicodemus, a teacher of Israel who does not know how God works among humans (3:10). Jesus mocks their opposition by asking which of his works of mercy merit his death (7:23; 10:32). His origin is an issue in 7:41b–42 and 7:52b (the Messiah is not to come from Galilee). They accuse Jesus of being possessed by demons (7:19; 8:48) and of being a sinner and evildoer (9:24; 18:30), when he has declared that he is the agent of God sent to manifest God's purposes (4:34). In 9:29 they claim (rightly) not to know Jesus' origin, after declaring to know that God has spoken to Moses. But their claimed knowledge does not extend to knowing that Moses has spoken of Jesus (5:45–47) and that God has sent Jesus.

Irony is also present in the opponents' incredulous questions expressing false assumptions about Jesus while simultaneously and without awareness expressing some truth about Jesus' origin and identity. They posit but reject the notion, for example, that Jesus (who the audience knows was in the beginning with God, 1:1) could be greater than Jacob (4:12), or Abraham (8:53, 57). They wonder how Jesus could have education when he has never studied (7:15), thus alluding to but ignoring Jesus' claims that he reveals what he has seen and heard directly from God (5:19–20; 8:26, 38). They accuse the one who comes from God of making himself God and not being from God (10:33; 9:16). The irony exposes their opposition, ridicules them, and invites the audience to enjoy the correct knowledge of these central Johannine affirmations about Jesus' authority, identity, origins, and relationship to Israel's traditions.

The opponents also unwittingly announce aspects of Jesus' mission, death, and return to God. In 7:35–36, in response to Jesus' statement about going away where they will not be able to find him, they wonder, "Where does this man intend to go that we will not find him? Does he intend to go to the Dispersion among the Greeks and teach the Greeks?" Their guess is completely wrong. Jesus speaks about returning to God. But at another level they unwittingly speak truth. Jesus' mission concerns the whole world, Jew and Gentile (3:16). In 12:20–24 some Greeks "wish to see Jesus," an event that signals the time for Jesus' death. And their guess about teaching Gentiles anticipates the mission activity of John's church, activity that embraces Jew and Gentile.

In 8:22 the opponents make another guess about Jesus' reference to going away. This time they guess that Jesus intends to kill himself. Again they are wrong in that they, in alliance with Pilate, will put Jesus to death. Yet at another level they again unwittingly speak correctly. Jesus gives himself to die (10:17–18).

The chief priest, Caiaphas, in 11:48–50 unknowingly predicts several future events. His rationale for putting Jesus to death is that "if we let him go on like this," three things will happen: everyone will believe in him, the Romans will destroy the temple, and the Romans will destroy the nation. Caiaphas is wrong, since none of these things happens while Jesus lives. He and his Roman allies put Jesus to death. Yet in the resurrection Jesus does live on, something Caiaphas facilitates, not prevents. And reading the gospel after 70 C.E., the audience knows that the latter two events happened in Rome's destruction of the temple in 70, and a number have believed.

Another person of power, Caiaphas's ally, the Roman governor Pontius Pilate, also unwittingly reveals Jesus' mission and identity.[21] Mockingly he presents the whipped, condemned, and crowned Jesus to the chief priests and their agents with the scornful words "Here is the man!" (19:5). Yet thirteen times the gospel has presented Jesus as the man from heaven, sent from God, the Son of Man. As Son of Man, Jesus descends from and ascends to God, dies, is exalted and glorified, gives life, and exercises judgment.[22]

Pilate makes a similar unwitting declaration of Jesus' identity with his repeated focus on Jesus as "King of the Jews" (18:33, 39; 19:3, 14–15).[23] He places a notice on Jesus' cross that so identifies Jesus in three languages (19:19–22). Pilate intends the notice as an insult to Jews and a warning, to all, of what Rome does to those who rebel against Rome's rule and claim power without Rome's authorization (cf. 19:12, 15). But without Pilate knowing it, the notice proclaims in three common languages for those in the know that Jesus is a kingly figure who manifests God's sovereign and just purposes among people (cf. Ps 72). Jesus' kingship is not comparable to the emperor's because it is given by God, not derived from or marked by the "world's" way of doing kingship (oppressive and beneficial only to the elite), and not marked by violence (18:36). Pilate intends to signal defeat. In reality, his notice proclaims that God's life-giving purposes are manifested precisely in the midst of oppression, suffering, and death. Pilate intends to emphasize the power of crucifixion. In reality, he ensures a coronation, as God's power will trump death and Jesus will be glorified in being raised and returning to God. Pilate intends to signal Jesus' condemnation but shows himself to be judged and condemned by Jesus. Without knowing it, Pilate, along with Jesus' other opponents, testifies to central aspects of Jesus' origin and destiny, his mission and identity.

Although irony is a central element in the presentations of Jesus' opponents, it is also employed, somewhat sparingly and less viciously, for Jesus' disciples. Nathanael disparages the notion that "anything good [could] come out of Nazareth," the town of Jesus' origin (1:45–46). In 11:16 and 13:37, Thomas and Peter declare that they will die with Jesus. They are correct that Jesus will die, but they do not realize that his purpose is to lay down his life for them (10:17–18). And their bravado is exposed when he dies alone (16:32). They abandon him (18:15–18, 25–27) and hide in fear and disbelief (20:19, 24–29). In 16:16–18 they, like the opponents, fail to understand Jesus' declarations about going away. Instead of guessing at its meaning like the opponents (7:35–36; 8:22), they repeat aspects of his declaration three times before admitting that they do not know. The repetition emphasizes to us, the gospel's readers, the importance of the issue and invites us to supply the correct understanding. Later, in 16:29–30, they declare that they understand and believe, entrust themselves to, Jesus, declaring that he comes from God. This is a crucial and correct insight, but it is only part of the story. Their statement responds to only half of Jesus' statement in 16:27–28, which is about both his origin and his destiny. Despite claiming understanding, they still do not know where Jesus is going. Jesus notes how inadequate their claimed understanding is (16:31–32).

Throughout, irony exposes opposition to, and incorrect understandings of, Jesus. It ridicules Jesus' opponents. It reveals confused thinking as characters speak with double meanings and, unintentionally, more truly than they are aware. It constantly challenges the audience to affirm and enjoy their correct knowledge of central Johannine affirmations about Jesus' authority, identity, relationship to Israel's traditions, revelation, death, resurrection, origin, and destiny. Irony plays an integral part in John's mysterious presentation of Jesus, the revealer of God's life-giving purposes.

Images

John uses images from everyday earthly existence to represent divine purposes. For example, Jesus makes numerous statements that begin with "I am" and in which the predicates employ images from everyday life:[24]

I am the bread of life. (6:35)

I am the bread that came down from heaven. . . . I am the living bread that came down from heaven. (6:41, 51)

I am the light of the world. (8:12; 9:5)

I am the gate [door] for the sheep. (10:7, 9)

I am the good shepherd. (10:11, 14)

I am the resurrection and the life. (11:25)

I am the way, and the truth, and the life. (14:6)

I am the true vine. (15:1, 5)[25]

Such images—and this list identifies only one type of the numerous images the gospel uses—can be called symbols, pointing beyond themselves to something or someone else and placing two things in some sort of relation to each other. Or they can be described as metaphors, speaking of one thing ("I") in terms of another ("bread of life") and requiring the audience to find connections or transfer between the two.[26] With either term, the links between the two entities are not clear. Images are complex, creating a puzzle that requires imagination and insight to solve and also poses the risk of getting it wrong. They challenge or invite the audience to make connections, to discover meaning, to experience revelation. If the audience cannot do so, the misunderstanding is exposed.

The "I am" way of talking is not unique to John.[27] Various Hellenistic religious groups depict revealer figures presenting and identifying themselves with the language of "I am" and a predicate, a phrase that describes their identity or activity. The goddess Isis declares, "I am Isis, the queen of every land. . . . I am the first that devised fruit for people. I am mother of King Horus."[28] Poimandres, the revealer god of the Hermetic literature (literature associated with the Egyptian god Thoth, known in Greek as Hermes Trismegistus, originating probably in the second century C.E.), declares, "I am Poimandres, the Mind of the Sovereignty. I know what you wish and I am with you everywhere."[29]

In the Hebrew Bible, this "I am" language is used for God in several ways. First, the language of "I am" is used without a predicate. God reveals himself to Moses in the burning bush: "I am who I am" (Exod 3:14). In John's gospel, Jesus uses the same construction, "I am" without a predicate, in 6:20; 8:18, 23, 24, 28, 58; 13:19; 18:5. English translations sometimes obscure this Greek construction.

Several chapters later in Exodus, the second use of "I am" language, with a predicate, appears. God reveals himself in terms of what God will do to save the people: "I am the LORD your God, who has freed you from the burdens of the Egyptians" (Exod 6:7). In Isa 40–55 the "I am" language with a predicate reveals God's saving actions in setting the exiles free from Babylonian captivity:

> Who has roused a victor from the east [the deliverer Cyrus;
>   see Isa 44:28–45:1],
>   summoned him to his service?
> He delivers up nations to him. . . .
> Who has performed and done this,
>   calling the generations from the beginning?
> I, the LORD, am first,
>   and will be with the last. (Isa 41:2–4)

It also emphasizes that there is no other God: "I am the LORD, and there is no other" (Isa 45:18).

In the context of these examples in the Hebrew Bible, John's use of "I am" presents Jesus as the authoritative revealer of God. He is the only one to see God (1:18), to witness God at work (3:11–13; 5:19–20), to hear God's words (3:32–34; 8:26). He reveals God's saving work in overcoming the injustice and death that the current sociopolitical order under Rome's control imposes (chs. 18–21). His actions reveal the life of wholeness and abundance that God will establish (e.g., 5:1–18; 6:1–14).

The predicates that complete the "I am" sayings ("bread," "light," etc.) appear in numerous religious traditions.[30] In the Hebrew Bible, they are frequently associated with God and God's saving work:

1. Bread: John 6 echoes the exodus story of God saving the people from Egyptian oppression and sustaining them with bread or manna in the wilderness (Exod 16). In wisdom literature, bread is a common metaphor for encountering God's presence and living a just life based on God's teaching (e.g., Prov 9:5; Sir 15:3). The final establishment of God's purposes over all that resists God's life-giving purposes is imaged as a banquet in which all enjoy abundant food (Isa 25:6–10; Isa 55). The image denotes God's redemption of all life, including the material, physical, and sociopolitical.

2. Light: The image evokes God's provision of light in ordering the created world according to God's purposes (Gen 1:3–5, 14–19). It evokes God's deliverance of the people from Egyptian tyranny. God provided light to guide the people by night (Exod 13:21–22). The psalmist sums up God's saving, powerful actions, declaring, "The LORD is my light and my salvation; whom shall I fear?" (Ps 27:1). Perpetual light is a feature of the final accomplishment of God's purposes and establishment of God's just reign in Zech 14:7 (14:8 refers to "living waters" that flow from Jerusalem to the nations).

For audiences who know such contexts, the images provide revelation of God's mysterious purposes. For other audiences who do not make appropriate associations, such as in John 6, the images confuse more than they reveal.

In a helpful discussion of the images of Jesus as the gate or door for the sheep and as the good shepherd in John 10, Robert Kysar identifies some of the ways in which the audience experiences these images as revelation.[31] Kysar outlines John 10 thus:

10:1–3a: the image of entering the sheepfold

10:3b–5: the image of what the shepherd does and what the sheep do

10:6–7a: the narrator's comment and transition

10:7b–10: the image of the door and the sheep

10:11–15: the image of the good shepherd

10:16: an expansion of the image of the good shepherd

10:17–18: a theological image

The passage contains four "I am" statements, in verses 7 and 9 (door) and 11 and 14 (good shepherd). How do these images function?

1. The placement of these statements in a larger scene that involves different places (sheepfold, pasture), characters (thieves, robbers, strangers, hirelings, shepherd), activity (calling, hearing, leading, etc.), contrasts (hearing and not heeding, killing and saving, laying down one's life and fleeing, sheep and wolves), and rapidly shifting images (door, good shepherd) engages the audience's imagination and secures *participation*.

2. The audience is asked to inhabit this picture world and to make *comparisons* between the changing images, life as they know it, and life in relation to Jesus.

3. Some of the images are *shocking* or disturbing in that they emphasize the danger that exists for the sheep from thieves, robbers, and wolves that steal and kill (10:5, 8, 10, 12). In keeping with the common use of shepherds as an image for political leadership (Ezek 34; Suetonius, *Tiberius* 32), the "false shepherds" depict the Roman and Jerusalem leaders who preside over a world that endangers well-being.

4. Yet *paradoxically* Jesus is imaged as the door and good shepherd who protects and provides intimate relationship and eternal life free of destructive forces and marked by abundance and wholeness.

5. Like much of the gospel's language, the two worlds depicting everyday life and life with Jesus are starkly *contrastive and oppositional*, highlighting different ways of living and different consequences.

6. They require the audience to *decide* which world to inhabit, to cast their lot with the status quo or with the new life that Jesus reveals, namely, the "life of the age" (see ch. 5, above), or eternal life, in which God's just and life-giving purposes are accomplished.

Kysar thus highlights the participatory character of the images, their shocking effect, their use of paradox, their contrastive and oppositional features, and their decisional quality. By these means the images can be revelational. Audiences who are unwilling to engage the images in this way find them confusing.

Conclusion

The gospel's style functions to reveal and to confuse. The gospel works hard to convey its central claims about God manifested in Jesus by explaining data and repeating information. But it also employs a series of interrelated and overlapping techniques—ambiguous language, misunderstandings, riddles, irony, and images—that have a divisive effect. Some people find revelation, others know only confusion. The division reinforces the identity and way of life of followers of Jesus as a special group that understands the mysterious and life-giving purposes of God. John's antilanguage functions to constitute a distinctive or countercultural community or antisociety committed to Jesus' revelation of God's life-giving purposes in a world that more often than not finds the revelation to be confusing and elusive.[32]

Notes

1. For some aspects, see Barrett, *John*, 5–10; J. P. Louw, "On Johannine Style," *Neot* 20 (1986): 5–12; Brown, *Introduction to the Gospel*, 278–97; also E. Schweizer, *Ego eimi: Die religionsgeschichtliche Herkunft und theologische Bedeutung der johanneischen Bildreden, zugleich ein Beitrag zur Quellenfrage des vierten Evangeliums* (Forschungen zur Religion und Literatur des Alten und Neuen Testaments 38; Göttingen: Vandenhoeck & Ruprecht, 1939), 82–112.

2. The obvious exceptions appear in John 3:3, 5; note also 18:36.

3. H. Windisch, "John's Narrative Style," in *The Gospel of John as Literature: An Anthology of Twentieth-Century Perspectives* (ed. M. Stibbe; Leiden: Brill, 1993), 25–64.

4. B. Gaventa, "The Archive of Excess: John 21 and the Problem of Narrative Closure," in *Exploring the Gospel of John: In Honor of D. Moody Smith* (ed. R. A. Culpepper and C. C. Black; Louisville: Westminster John Knox, 1996), 240–52.

5. Examples in F. Thielman, "The Style of the Fourth Gospel and Ancient Literary Critical Concepts of Religious Discourse," in *Persuasive Artistry: Studies in New Testament Rhetoric in Honor of George A. Kennedy* (ed. D. F. Watson; JSNTSup 50; Sheffield, Eng.: JSOT Press, 1991), 169–83, esp. 169–72; E. D. Freed, "Variations in the Language and Thought of John," *Zeitschrift für die neutestamentliche Wissenschaft* 55 (1964): 167–97, esp. 170–71.

6. Grammatical limitations result from the influence of a possible Aramaic original; so, e.g., C. F. Burney, *The Aramaic Origin of the Fourth Gospel* (Oxford: Clarendon, 1922).

7. S. Ringe, *Wisdom's Friends: Community and Christology in the Fourth Gospel* (Louisville: Westminster John Knox, 1999), 12–13.

8. Following Thielman, "Style"; see also C. C. Black, "'The Words That You Gave to Me I Have Given to Them': The Grandeur of Johannine Rhetoric," in *Exploring the Gospel of John: In Honor of D. Moody Smith* (ed. R. A. Culpepper and C. C. Black; Louisville: Westminster John Knox, 1996), 220–39.

9. Following, with modifications, M. C. Tenney, "The Footnotes of John's Gospel," *BSac* 117 (1960): 350–63. Subsequent scholarship has expanded the number of "footnotes" or asides; J. O'Rourke ("Asides in the Gospel of John," *NovT* 21 [1979]: 210–19) identifies 109; T. Thatcher ("A New Look at Asides in the Fourth Gospel," *BSac* 151 [1994]: 428–39) identifies 191 in four categories: staging asides (44), defining asides (46), and asides that explain discourse (48) and actions (53).

10. These three quotations from the NRSV have been modified by using "Truly, truly." For other examples, see 3:5; 6:53; 8:51; 13:16; for origin, see R. A. Culpepper, "The Origin of the 'Amen, Amen' Sayings in the Gospel of John," in *Jesus in Johannine Tradition* (ed. R. T. Fortna and T. Thatcher; Louisville: Westminster John Knox, 2001), 253–62.

11. From the extensive literature, see D. F. Tolmie, *Jesus' Farewell to the Disciples: John 13:1–17:26 in Narratological Perspective* (Biblical Interpretation Series 12; Leiden: Brill, 1995); F. Moloney, "The Function of John 13–17 within the Johannine Narrative," in *Literary and Social Readings of the Fourth Gospel* (vol. 2 of *What Is John?* ed. F. F. Segovia; SBLSymS 7; Atlanta: Scholars Press, 1998), 43–65.

12. On the meaning of the term antisociety, see ch. 5 n. 2, above.

13. Culpepper, *Anatomy*, 152–65.

14. Following T. Thatcher, "The Riddles of Jesus in the Johannine Dialogues," in *Jesus in Johannine Tradition* (ed. R. Fortna and T. Thatcher; Louisville: Westminster John Knox, 2001), 263–77. Thatcher identifies thirty-eight riddles (including most of Culpepper's "misunderstandings"): 1:15; 2:4b,16, 19; 3:3, 5; 4:7, 10, 20, 32; 6:5, 32, 51; 7:23, 34, 37–38; 8:4–5, 18, 21, 24, 26, 31–32, 38, 51, 56; 9:2, 39; 10:1–5, 34–36; 11:11, 23, 25–26; 12:32; 13:10, 21, 33; 14:4, 7, 19; 16:16; 21:18, 22.

15. Schnackenburg, *John*, 3:161–62; Brown, *Gospel according to John*, 2:733–35.

16. Moloney, *John*, 453.

17. P. Duke, *Irony in the Fourth Gospel* (Atlanta: John Knox, 1985); O'Day, *Revelation*; Culpepper, *Anatomy*, 165–80; R. A. Culpepper, "Reading Johannine Irony," in *Exploring the Gospel of John: In Honor of D. Moody Smith* (ed. R. A. Culpepper and C. C. Black; Louisville: Westminster John Knox, 1996), 193–207.

18. Duke, *Irony*, 17.

19. Ibid., 36–42.

20. Drawing throughout on Duke, ibid., 43–115.

21. For discussion, see Rensberger, *Johannine Faith*, 87–106; Carter, *Pontius Pilate*, 127–52.

22. John 1:51; 3:13–14; 5:27; 6:27, 53, 62; 8:28; 9:35; 12:23, 34c-d; 13:31.

23. Duke, *Irony*, 126–37.

24. For some discussion, see Schweizer, *Ego eimi*; P. B. Harner, *The "I am" of the Fourth Gospel* (Philadelphia: Fortress, 1970); Schnackenburg, *John*, 2:79–89; D. Ball, *"I Am" in John's Gospel: Literary Function, Background, and Theological Implications* (JSNTSup 124; Sheffield, Eng.: Sheffield Academic Press, 1996).

25. For "I am" without a predicate (6:20; 8:18, 23, 24, 28, 58; 13:19; 18:5), see below.

26. The discussion is extensive. See, e.g., Culpepper, *Anatomy*, 180–98; D. Lee, *The Symbolic Narratives of the Fourth Gospel: The Interplay of Form and Meaning* (JSNTSup 95; Sheffield, Eng.: Sheffield Academic Press, 1994); C. Koester, *Symbolism in the Fourth Gospel: Meaning, Mystery, Community* (Minneapolis: Fortress, 1995); D. Lee, *Flesh and Glory: Symbolism, Gender, and Theology in the Gospel of John* (New York: Crossroad, 2002).

27. Ball, *"I Am,"* 24–45.

28. A. Deissmann, *Light from the Ancient East* (New York: Hodder & Stoughton, 1911), 135–36.

29. *Corpus hermetica* 1.8–9, cited in C. K. Barrett, *The New Testament Background: Selected Documents* (London: SPCK, 1980), 82; for other examples, see R. Bultmann, *The Gospel of John* (Philadelphia: Westminster, 1971), 225–26 n. 3.

30. See, e.g., Dodd, *Interpretation*.

31. R. Kysar, "Johannine Metaphor—Meaning and Function: A Literary Case Study of John 10:1–8 [i.e., 10:1–18]," *Semeia* 53 (1991): 81–105; also "The Making of Metaphor: Another Reading of John 3:1–15," in *Readers and Readings of the Fourth Gospel* (vol. 1 of *What Is John?* ed. F. F. Segovia; SBLSymS 3; Atlanta: Scholars Press, 1996), 21–41.

32. See ch. 5 n. 2, above.

PART TWO

JOHN: INTERPRETER

Chapter 7

John: Interpreter of Scriptures and Sources about Jesus

We now turn to John the interpreter. Where did the material that makes up John's gospel come from? Given the material discussed in chapter 1, above, about the gospel's genre, it is not likely that the author made it up. Was the author an eyewitness who wrote down his own memories? As we also saw in chapter 1, this probably did not happen. More likely, the author (or authors; see ch. 8, below) worked with existing traditions about Jesus, interpreting them to tell the story of Jesus in a way appropriate to the changing circumstances of their community.

That is, the Gospel of John did not come into being in a cultural or historical vacuum. It did not just drop out of the sky or show up mysteriously on someone's e-mail one day. Rather, in telling this story of Jesus, this author (or authors) interpreted various traditions about Jesus and about God, interacting with changing human experiences and societal circumstances. John's interpretive interaction is identified with three factors: the Hebrew Bible, traditions about Jesus, and the changing circumstances of the community for whom the gospel was written.

Interpreting the Hebrew Scriptures

The New Testament had not been formed when John was written. Accordingly the Scriptures for John's audience were the Jewish writings known to us in the Old Testament, or Hebrew Bible. Twenty-two times,

John's gospel refers to these Scriptures as "writing(s)" and identifies them as God's word for the people (10:34–35).[1]

But these Scriptures have to be interpreted in the right way. For John's gospel, the correct and distinctive way of interpreting them is to read them in reference to Jesus. The Scriptures testify to Jesus (5:39); Moses wrote about Jesus (5:46–47). The gospel's author reads them, as it were, wearing his Jesus glasses, finding references to Jesus in numerous passages. This reading strategy was typical of early Christians. Followers of Jesus saw references to Jesus in the Scriptures where no other reader saw them. Members of the community at Qumran had a similar strategy, reading the Scriptures in relation to their community's experiences and history. They found references to themselves that those who were not members of their group could never see.

Several examples of John's Jesus-centered interpretation of the Scriptures follow; they are not, however, comprehensive. The use of these passages of the Scriptures locates Jesus in the larger context of God's previously revealed purposes (John 4:22), shows Jesus to be enacting these purposes, and elucidates his identity and mission as God's agent.[2]

Explicit Citations

The author explicitly quotes Scripture about sixteen times with the prophets dominating, five from Isaiah and two from Zechariah. He interprets them in relation to what takes place in Jesus' ministry, especially Jesus' mission and death.[3] These citations are commonly introduced in one of these ways: "it was/is written" (2:17; 6:31, 45; 12:14); "to fulfill the scriptures" (13:18; 19:24, 28, 36); "in their law" (15:25). On several occasions the introductions specify the prophet Isaiah ("as the prophet Isaiah said," 1:23; 12:38, 39). In 12:13 there is no introduction. In 5:46 the gospel claims that Moses writes about Jesus (also 8:17), a claim with which Jesus' opponents strongly disagree.

In some citations, it is not always clear which text is being quoted. For instance, does 6:45 ("And they shall all be taught by God") cite Isa 54:13 or Jer 31:34? In some instances several passages of Scripture may be combined. John 7:42 seems to combine 2 Sam 7:12, Mic 5:2, and Ps 89:4, 36–37. Nor is it always clear whether John cites the Greek (the Septuagint) or Hebrew form of the verse,[4] though often he seems closer to the Greek form of the Scriptures.[5] Does he copy or paraphrase or quote from memory?[6] In 7:38 Jesus claims to quote "the scripture," but no matching passage of Scripture has been found. Perhaps the author generally evokes Ps 78:15–16, Ezek 47:1–11, and Zech 14:8.[7]

It is important to notice how John interprets the Scriptures in applying them to Jesus. The quoted verses, of course, do not refer explicitly to Jesus in the Hebrew Scriptures. It is the gospel's author who links them to Jesus, understanding them to denote situations that clarify God's purposes manifested in Jesus. Some examples follow:

1. Isaiah 40:3, cited in John 1:23, does not mention John the Baptist. Rather, it refers to Babylon's control of Jerusalem in the sixth century B.C.E. Isaiah 40 announces God's imminent action to set Jerusalem free from Babylonian imperial power. The author of John's gospel rereads Isa 40:3 christologically, interpreting it—by applying it to John the Baptist—as announcing a fresh revelation of God's saving and life-giving power in Jesus' ministry.

2. John 2:17 cites Ps 69:9, a lament psalm in which the psalmist cries out to God for rescue from unnamed enemies. The unknown psalmist claims that one of the reasons for the opposition and his suffering is his "zeal for your house." Whether this house is the temple or the line of Davidic kings (see 2 Sam 7:4–12 for both meanings) is not clear. Perhaps the psalmist has attacked unjust practices and demanded just dealings. The author of John's gospel reads it in relation to Jesus' attack on the temple, the center of the elite's power, status, and wealth in Rome-supervised Jerusalem. Citing the psalm foreshadows the elite's opposition to Jesus (the "enemies" of Ps 69) but also casts Jesus as the righteous sufferer who will be vindicated by God.

3. John 6:31 cites Exod 16:4, 15: "He gave them bread from heaven to eat." In Exod 16 the bread refers to the manna that God supplies to the people in the wilderness after they have left Egypt. John uses the text as the basis for Jesus' discourse in John 6. John 6:32–48 interprets "He gave them bread from heaven" to refer to Jesus as the source of all life (including literal bread in 6:1–14). John 6:49–58 interprets "to eat" by emphasizing entrusting oneself to God's purposes.[8]

4. John 12:13 and 15 cites two passages of Scripture in relation to Jesus' kingship manifested in his entry to Jerusalem. Neither passage explicitly refers to Jesus, but the gospel's writer interprets them to locate Jesus' action in relation to God's purposes. The first comes from Ps 118:25–26, a psalm of thanksgiving that

celebrates God's steadfast love in delivering the people from hostile nations. The second comes from Zech 9:9, part of the vision of the establishment of God's reign on earth, victorious over the nations and all that oppose God's life-giving purposes. The use of both passages underlines Jesus' role as the agent of God's purposes and anticipates the overthrow of Roman power and its Jerusalem allies.

5. Psalm 41:9 is cited in John 13:18, the meal scene in which Jesus predicts that Judas will betray him. Psalm 41 says nothing explicitly about either Judas or Jesus. Rather, it describes a situation, common in the Psalms, in which a faithful person suffers in various ways, including through a friend's faithlessness (one who "ate of my bread"). Despite such human treachery, the psalm proclaims, God remains faithful and vindicates the afflicted person. The author of John cites Ps 41:9, inviting readers to understand Judas's betrayal of Jesus in this larger context. It identifies Jesus as the faithful but betrayed sufferer, to whom God remains faithful and through whom God's life-giving purposes are accomplished. Similar scenes are evoked by citing Isa 53:1 in John 12:38, Pss 35:19, 69:4 in John 15:25, Ps 22:18 in John 19:24, Ps 34:20 in John 19:36–37, Ps 69:9 in John 2:17, and Ps 69:22 in John 19:28. The scenarios of these psalms demonstrate, as does Jesus' experience, that betrayal, hatred, and the active opposition of enemies do not thwart God's purposes. Rather, they provide the context in which God's life-giving power is revealed through Jesus' death and resurrection.

6. Jesus' death is confirmed in John 19:36–37 when a soldier pierces Jesus' side with a spear. This action means that there is no need to break Jesus' legs (19:33), a frequently employed tactic that expedited death. Not breaking Jesus' legs is said to fulfill or enact the Scriptures that "none of his bones shall be broken." This citation from Exod 12:46 refers not to Jesus but to the animal (often a lamb) sacrificed at Passover. Passover celebrated God's deliverance of the people from slavery in Egypt. The sacrifice of the animal supplied blood for the door lintel to protect the people from God's judgment on the Egyptians (Exod 12:21–27). John's citation of this text places Jesus' death in relation to God's salvation from Egyptian tyranny. Clearly John is not saying that Jesus is literally an animal. Rather, he evokes Passover as a way of thinking about the significance of Jesus' death. God is again acting to deliver people from sin (cf. John

1:29, 36). God is again acting to save people from all that is contrary to God's life-giving purposes in the Roman-dominated world. The use of these passages of Scripture locates Jesus in the larger context of God's previously revealed purposes, shows Jesus to be enacting these purposes, and elucidates his identity and mission as God's agent.

Pervasive Echoes

In addition to these explicit citations, John's interpretation of the Hebrew Scriptures is evident in pervasive echoes of them in John's stories about Jesus and throughout Jesus' long discourses. For example, the gospel begins with echoes of the creation story in Gen 1. It refers to heroes of the Hebrew Bible such as Jacob (his ladder, 1:47, 51; cf. Gen 28:10–17; his well, John 4:5–6, 11–12), Abraham (8:31–38), and Moses (the tabernacle, 1:14; the gift of the law, 1:17; the serpent, 3:14; manna, 6:31–58; water from the rock, 7:38).[9] We noted in the last chapter the gospel's use of the formula of divine self-revelation ("I am"). John thereby shows that all of Jesus' ministry enacts the Scriptures, not just in the instances of the explicit citations.[10] The effect is cyclic. John interprets the Scriptures in relation to Jesus, and the Scriptures interpret Jesus. One example will alert us to what happens throughout the gospel.

Jesus turns water into wine at the wedding at Cana (John 2:1–11). The revelation of God's life-giving purposes in this scene is intricately connected with understanding several of the scene's key elements. First is the setting at a wedding (2:2). The Hebrew Scriptures use the image of marriage to depict the relationship between a faithful God and the people whom God loves forever (Isa 54:4–8). Because of this relationship, God returns to the land of Israel the people exiled in Babylon and protects them from foes forever (Isa 62:4–9). John's Cana scene employs the wedding setting to evoke God's love for the people and commitment to save them. Second, Jesus turns water into wine, supplying more than one hundred gallons (2:6–10). Abundant wine was a common feature of scenes that depicted the anticipated time when God would overcome the people's enemies, defeat injustice, suffering, and death, and establish God's purposes in full for all (Amos 9:13–14; Isa 25:6–10; *2 Bar.* 29:5). John's scene points to God's anticipated act by depicting one element of God's yet-to-be-established purposes. It anticipates abundant resources for all people when God's life-giving justice is established. This is a powerful claim for a people living in Rome's world, in which the ruling elite deprived many of adequate resources.

John's narrative evokes these passages of the Hebrew Scriptures to interpret Jesus' actions as a revelation of God's just and life-giving purposes. The scene closes by connecting this revelation with the term "glory" (2:11). Jesus reveals "glory," namely, the presence, power, and purposes of God.

Subsequent scenes interpret the Scriptures to underline further aspects of God's awaited new world. Jesus' healings enact the physical wholeness that will mark this world (Isa 35:5–6; John 4:46–54; etc.). The feeding of the large crowd with abundant bread in John 6:1–14 continues the emphasis on abundant resources and fertility. The raising of Lazarus anticipates the death of death (John 11; Isa 25:6–10). These dimensions are part of "life of the age" (see ch. 5, above) ("eternal life," 3:16; 10:10; 20:30–31) that Jesus reveals.

Scriptural Paradigms

In addition to explicit scriptural citations and pervasive echoes, John employs and interprets some of the important paradigms that the Hebrew Scriptures use to depict God's activity and purposes. We have already noted frequent references to Moses and the exodus. Kingship is important, as is Abraham. Temple references associated with festivals and life, revelation, the completion of God's purposes, and divine presence are pervasive.[11] Another important paradigm that the gospel employs concerns wisdom as a revealer of God's purposes.[12] This paradigm provides a way of thinking about Jesus' origin, his relationship with God, and his function as revealer among human beings.

Wisdom literature describes an order in creation and human society that shapes human lives and is understood to reveal God's ways. This quest for the order of creation and society developed into a realization of God's active presence in creation and social interaction. Writers personified this presence as a woman, Lady Wisdom, who reveals God's purposes and mediates between the divine and the human.[13] She has a counterpart, Lady Folly, who resists God's ways.

In these traditions, Wisdom is an ambiguous figure. She personifies divine power, presence, and purposes yet protects monotheism. She is immanent in creation yet distinct from it. She is a heavenly figure enjoying intimate relationship with God, yet she is active on earth. She is a revealer who seeks out people, yet she goes away and hides. She reveals God yet is elusive. She frequently ignores traditions about the covenant and exodus, yet she is allied with Torah, the teaching given via Moses. At heart, Wisdom mysteriously manifests God.

Characteristics shared by both Wisdom and Jesus	References in Wisdom literature	References in John 1:1–18
Are preexistent	Prov 8:22, 27–30; Sir 1:4; 24:9; Wis 9:9	1:1
Are "with God"	Prov 8:30; Wis 9:4	1:1
Share divine life	Wis 7:25–26	1:1
Are instruments of creation	Prov 3:19; 8:30; Wis 7:22; 9:1–2	1:3
Are source of life and light	Prov 8:35; Bar 4:1b–2; Wis 7:26	1:4
Cannot be overcome by darkness/evil	Wis 7:29–30	1:5
Come into the world to reveal and manifest God's presence; are sent or descend from heaven	Prov 8; Wis 6:13, 16; 7:27; Sir 24:6–7; Bar 3; 1 En. 42	1:9
Are rejected by humans	1 En 42:2; Bar 3:20–21	1:10b, 11b
Enable receptive humans to relate to God	Wis 7:27; 9:18	1:12–13
Lived among humans	Bar 3:37; Sir 24:8, 11–12	1:14a
Possess unique glory	Wis 7:22, 25	1:14, 18
Know God and make God known	Wis 8:4; 9:9–10	1:18

John interprets this paradigm of the revelation of God's presence and purposes in relation to Jesus, identifying Jesus as wisdom. Jesus and wisdom share at least twelve features (see the above chart).[14] The wisdom motifs in the prologue's presentation of Jesus continue through the gospel.[15] John interprets Jesus as wisdom, the manifestation or revelation of God. To see the Son is to see the Father (12:45; 14:9).

1. Jesus/wisdom mediates divine presence and gifts, especially life:

- Jesus' words and deeds convey what he saw/learned with God (3:11–15; 5:19–46; 6:46).

- To see or know Jesus is to see or know God (14:7–14).

- Jesus manifests God's presence or light (8:12–20; 9:5; 11:9–10; 12:35–36, 46).

- Jesus mediates "eternal life"/"life of the age," which transforms physical suffering (4:46–54), overcomes death (Lazarus, ch. 11), and establishes intimate, everlasting friendship with God (6:35–40, 47–51; 8:51; 10:10, 28; 14:1–4).

- To reject Jesus is to reject God (15:18–25).

2. Some accept and some reject Jesus/wisdom:

- Those who accept become children of God (1:12–13), having been born "from above" (3:1–10).

- They "abide"/"remain" with Jesus and form a new community of love for one another (15:1–17).

- Others, frequently identified as "the world" and as "the Jews" (see chs. 4 and 5, above), reject Jesus (1:10–11) and his followers (15:18–24; 16:1–4).

- As wisdom, Jesus causes divisions, dividing believers from nonbelievers cosmically and socially.

3. Jesus/wisdom reveals God's glory: He displays the presence and power of God ("glory") among humans in his life and death (7:18, 39; 8:50, 54; 11:4; 12:23, 27–29; 13:31–32; 14:13).

4. Jesus/wisdom's saving presence is active among people:

a. He is active in public places, as is Wisdom (Prov 1:20–33; 8:1–36). John 1–11 presents a series of public encounters as Jesus reveals God's purposes: the wedding at Cana (2:1–11), the Jerusalem temple (2:13–21), the Samaritan woman at the well (ch. 4), the official at Capernaum (4:46–53), the sick at the pool with five porticoes at the Sheep Gate (ch. 5), a mountain (6:1–14), and by the sea (6:25–71).

b. He reveals God's saving presence: Jesus/wisdom's origin is "from God" or "with God," and his destiny is to return to God (3:11–21; 7:32–36; 8:21–30; 13:1–3; 14:1–17, 28–31; 16:7). He descends from heaven (6:35–50) but must be "lifted up" to return through crucifixion, resurrection, and ascension (3:14–15; 8:28; 12:34). He is sent from God (5:38; 7:18, 28–29; 12:44; 13:20) to "save the world," or mediate God's redemptive presence (3:16–17; 5:34; 10:9; 12:47). Like wisdom, he gives life (3:16–17). His return to heaven means absence from his followers, and so he reassures them (chs. 14–16) of his abiding presence through the Spirit (14:26; 16:13–14) until they join Jesus in the place he has prepared (14:1–7).

c. He teaches God's ways: As a teacher/rabbi (1:38; 3:2; 8:4; 13:12–14; 20:16), Jesus teaches or reveals God's just, loving (13:34; 14:15–17, 21; 15:10, 12–17), and life-giving ways (6:59; 7:14–24; 8:2, 20, 28; 18:20). The Paraclete continues this task in Jesus' absence (14:26; 16:4–15).

d. He provides nourishment/bounty: Wisdom invites people to feasts as expressions of God's good presence, life, and blessing (e.g., Prov 9:5). Likewise Jesus provides wine (2:1–11), gives "water of life" to the Samaritan woman (ch. 4), feeds the multitude (6:1–14), and describes himself as the "bread of life" (6:25–65). He hosts a meal (ch. 13). He describes the Spirit as abundant living water (7:37–39).

e. He reveals God's presence and gifts in the "I am" (ἐγώ εἰμι, *ego eimi*) sayings: All the predicates to "I am" except "the good shepherd" (God, cf. Ps 23:1) are associated with wisdom (and with God, whom wisdom manifests): the bread (Sir 24:21), the vine (Sir 24:17, 19), the way (Prov 3:17; 8:32; Sir 6:26), the light (Wis 7:26; 18:34), the truth (Prov 8:7; Wis 6:22), the life (Prov 3:18; 8:35–36), the gate/door (Prov 8:34–35). Jesus, like wisdom, supplies necessities, mediates life, and protects from danger.

John employs this wisdom paradigm, this way of understanding God's revealing activity, to assert the identity of Jesus as the revealer of God's life-giving purposes and to interpret the significance of human response to his ministry. As wisdom, Jesus originates with God as the self-revelation of God. Coming from God, in intimate relation with God, and committed to God's purposes and will, he is God's agent (Christ, Son) among humans. In him some encounter God's life, ways, presence, and gifts, which challenge the status quo and anticipate its transformation to manifest God's purposes. Others encounter only a threat that must be eliminated. The gospel employs this ready-made way of understanding God's life-giving purposes to interpret the identity and significance of Jesus. Its use of this wisdom paradigm shows the pervasive influence of the Scriptures on John's presentation. Other examples of John's use of scriptural paradigms to interpret the significance of Jesus include the liberation and exodus from Egypt and Isaiah's understanding of how God uses and judges imperial powers.[16]

Interpreting Traditions about Jesus

In addition to interpreting scriptural traditions to present the significance of Jesus, John interprets existing traditions about Jesus. He employs diverse materials to tell the story of Jesus with a particular perspective, namely, that Jesus reveals God's life-giving purpose. What traditions about Jesus does John interpret, and how? Related to the question of how John interprets are further questions: For whom does John interpret? When and where? And which John (or which of several authors, in some scholars' perspectives) are we talking about? (Chapters 8 and 9, below, will take up these questions.)

Interpreting Memories?

A very common view, with some support in early church writings from the second to fourth centuries, understands the gospel to be the memoirs of an elderly John. Late in his life, so this view goes (see further ch. 9, below), John sat down to write out his memories of Jesus, interpreting them about fifty years later for believers who did not know Jesus. Although this view has a simple appeal, it does not adequately account for numerous difficulties in the gospel, including inconsistent content, rough sequences, and uneven style (such as the aporias discussed in ch. 6, above). Other examples of aporia are listed here:

- The poetic style of 1:1–18, along with some important items of vocabulary ("word," "grace"), is not matched in the rest of the gospel.

- The gospel contains quite different types of material with differing presentations of Jesus. In the narratives, Jesus works miracles. In the discourses, Jesus is the one sent from God to reveal God's purposes.

- John includes a number of short scenes in which Jesus journeys somewhere, setting up what might be a significant scene, but nothing (apart from the passing of time) seems to happen.[17]

- In 3:22 Jesus and the disciples are said to go into the land of Judea, but Jesus is already in Jerusalem in Judea (2:23).

- In 4:23 Jesus says that "the hour is coming, and is now here," a very ambiguous statement at best. And it is not a momentary lapse, since he says it again in 5:25.

- In 5:22 Jesus declares that "the Father . . . has given all judgment to the Son," but in 12:47 Jesus says that he does "not judge anyone who hears my words."

- The content of 5:19–25 about Jesus' life-giving role and relationship with the Father seems mostly to be repeated in 5:26–30. But in the latter section, the eschatological point of view changes from the present to the future.

- A similar repetition occurs in 6:35–50 (Jesus as the bread of life) and 6:51–58, although the latter section heightens the notion of eating and drinking Jesus' flesh and blood.

- In 7:3–4 Jesus' brothers suggest he go to Judea and work signs. But 2:23 and 5:1–9 indicate that he has already worked signs in Judea.

- In 11:2 Mary is identified as anointing Jesus, an action not narrated until chapter 12.

- Chapter 21 has some features of style not typical of the rest of the gospel.

It is most unlikely that a single author is responsible for such glaring inconsistencies of style, content, and sequence. How are we to make sense of these data? We will consider two possibilities: that the gospel writer has interpreted and combined different sources (discussed in this chapter) and/or that the gospel has gone through several editions, with several authors and editors interpreting the story of Jesus for changing circumstances (discussed in ch. 8, below).

Interpreter of Sources

Scholars have suggested three possible sources about Jesus that the author interpreted in writing the gospel: the Synoptic Gospels, independent written sources, and oral tradition about Jesus.[18] Each is discussed here.

Creative Interpreter of the Synoptic Gospels?

One possibility is that the author interprets the Synoptic Gospels to tell a more adequate story of Jesus.[19] Some scholars have suggested that

John's gospel reflects an uneasy relationship with other parts of the early Christian movement (10:16, other sheep not of this fold).[20] In places the gospel seems to indicate rivalry; in other places, harsh rebuke and denunciation; and in one instance, a desire for unity (17:21–22).

Rivalry is especially evident in the gospel's presentation of Peter, the most prominent apostle in other parts of the Christian movement (Matt 16:18; Acts 2–15; 1 Pet 5:1–2). John's gospel recognizes Peter as a legitimate follower (1:40–42) who confesses Jesus' identity (6:68–69). But Peter's actions do not always reflect well on him. He resists Jesus washing his feet (13:6–11), boasts he will lay down his life for Jesus (13:36–38), uses his sword trying to prevent Jesus' arrest (18:10–11), and betrays Jesus (18:15–18, 25–27). Often he is paired with "the beloved disciple" (see further in ch. 9, below) in ways that do not reflect well on Peter. The beloved disciple reclines closest to Jesus, and Peter has to ask him to obtain clarification from Jesus about who will betray him (13:21–26). Both the beloved disciple and Peter race to the empty tomb, but only the beloved disciple, who reaches the tomb first, is described as seeing and believing (20:8). It is the beloved disciple, not Peter, who first recognizes the risen Jesus (21:7).

This presentation of Peter has suggested to some a rivalry between John's believing group, based in the testimony of the beloved disciple, and other Christian groups founded by the proclamation of apostles, such as Peter. John's group is shown to be more perceptive, more closely linked to Jesus, in need of no shepherds other than Jesus (10:1–3, 7–8). By contrast, there are disciples who do not continue to follow Jesus after his declaration about giving his flesh and blood for the life of the world (6:60–66). These disciples are identified as not believing (6:64), and in 8:31–59 they resist Jesus' claims about his identity and mission. Some scholars have viewed these scenes as depicting the gospel's verdict on those who do not accept the claims of John's community.

It is always difficult to reconstruct historical events on the basis of a text such as John (see ch. 8, below). But if these characters do point to other Christian groups, they indicate the gospel's ambivalent relationships with these groups. There is rivalry with some, denunciation for others, and hope for reconciliation (17:21–22). Such speculation provides the context for exploring whether and how John's gospel might use the Synoptic Gospels as sources for its own story of Jesus.

B. W. Bacon argued that John essentially ignored Matthew but reinterpreted Mark, often as modified by Luke. John's very different understanding of Jesus, John's "doctrinal values" or "spiritual truths," significantly influenced the reworking.[21] According to Bacon, John often rearranges Mark's order and omits Mark's "appearance of pettiness" by adding lofty passages such as the prologue.[22] Bacon posited that John rarely quotes Mark verbatim but reworks Mark often in relation to Luke.[23]

This reworking is evident in the narratives. The Nicodemus story in John 3, for example, combines Mark 10:13–22, 12:28–34, and 15:42–46 with Luke 18:18 and Acts 5:34–40. The Samaritan woman episode in John 4, Bacon argues, combines material from Mark 7:24–30 with Luke's mission to Samaria (Luke 9:51–56; 10:29–37; 17:11–19; Acts 1:8; 8:5–25) and the woman who encounters Jesus in Luke 7:36–50. The Lazarus story in John 11 combines Mary and Martha in Luke 10:38–42 with Lazarus in Luke 16:19–31.[24] John follows Luke in breaking up and distributing Mark's collected miracle stories in John 5–6.

Bacon also sees the discourses as John's creation. John follows Luke's reworking of Mark in breaking up Mark's collection of parables (Mark 4), scattering them throughout the narrative and in several instances allegorizing them (John 10:1–16, the good shepherd; 15:1–6, the vine). John creates the dispute between Jesus and the Jerusalem leaders in John 5 by reworking Mark 2:1–3:6. The healing of the paralytic (John 5:1–9; cf. Mark 2:1–12) is the point of departure for the discourse's emphases on the true Sabbath as imitating God's work, especially giving life (John 5:10–18; cf. Mark 2:23–28), and on condemning the scribes who reject Jesus the giver of life (John 5:30–47; cf. Mark 2:18–22). The farewell discourse in John 14–16 reworks Mark's mission (Mark 3:7–6:13) and eschatological material (Mark 4; 13) along with Luke's mission instructions.[25]

Others also have seen John as reworking the Synoptics.[26] C. K. Barrett argues that John reads Mark and that Mark's outline and, at times, vocabulary influenced John's interpretation of Jesus.[27] Barrett notes at least eleven similar events, often in the same order and often with some verbal parallels (see the chart).

Event	Mark	John	Verbal parallels
Work and witness of John	1:4–8	1:19–36	Mark 1:7 = John 1:27
To Galilee	1:14–15	4:3	Mark 1:8, 10, 11 = John 1:26, 32, 33, 34
Feeding of the multitude	6:33–44	6:1–13	Mark 6:37, 38, 43, 44 = John 6:7, 9, 10, 13
Walking on the water	6:45–52	6:16–21	Mark 6:50 = John 6:20
Peter's confession	8:29	6:68–69	Mark 8:29 = John 6:69

To Jerusalem	9:30–31; 10:1, 32, 46	7:10–14	
Entry into Jerusalem and the anointing	11:1–10; 14:3–9	12:12–15; 12:1–8	Mark 11:9–10 = John 12:13; Mark 14:3, 5, 7–8 = John 12:3, 5, 7–8.
Last Supper	14:17–26	13:1–17:26	Mark 14:18 = John 13:21
Arrest of Jesus	14:43–52	18:1–11	Mark 14:47 = John 18:10
Passion and resurrection	14:53–16:8	18:12–20:29	Mark 15:26 = John 19:19
Destruction in the temple	11:15–17	2:14–16	

Barrett suggests that Mark has also read Luke, for Barrett notes similarities in persons that appear only in these two gospels: Mary, Martha, and Lazarus; a second disciple named Judas (John 14:22; Luke 6:16); Annas. There are also some similarities in details. In Luke and John, for example, Satan works in Judas to betray Jesus (Luke 22:3; John 13:2, 27); the servant's *right* ear is cut off (Luke 22:50; John 18:10); and two angels appear at the tomb (Luke 24:4–5; John 20:12).[28]

Neirynck also argues for John's interpretation of Luke, but on different grounds.[29] Instead of attending to shared scenes, vocabulary, or details, he looks for common editorial emphases. In a case study of the resurrection narratives, he argues that John's dependence on Luke is demonstrated in the fact that John elaborates Luke's "editorial composition" (Luke 24:12) in John 20:3–10.

The claim that John has interpreted some of the Synoptic Gospels, especially Mark and Luke, helpfully highlights points of contact among these various expressions of the story of Jesus, especially in the passion accounts. But the case for John's use of Mark and Luke is unconvincing in at least three factors:

1. The details: Barrett's emphasis on some common scenes pays little attention to a detailed comparison throughout the gospels. Likewise, Bacon's attempt at a detailed reconstruction of John's writing process fails to show how the process works out in the details of John's accounts. For example, in claiming that John builds the story of the Samaritan woman out of Markan and Lukan scenes including women and a Samaritan mission (see details above), Bacon demonstrates nothing more than that John, Mark, and Luke tell stories including Jesus, women, and Samaritans. He cannot show the influence of Mark and Luke on John 4 in a detailed discussion of the passage. The limited verbal

parallels point to a similar problem. If John were as steeped in Mark and Luke as Bacon claims, we would reasonably expect numerous verbal connections.

2. The differences and Johannine distinctives: We have noted in the previous six chapters that John's telling of the story of Jesus evidences a distinctive plot (ch. 2), distinctive characters (chs. 3–4), a distinctive dualistic worldview and language (ch. 5), and distinctive style (ch. 6). None of these attempts to claim the Synoptics as John's sources has been able to account for the apparent similarities *and* the very significant distinctives in John's gospel.[30]

3. Dating: The claim of John's dependence on the Synoptics assumes a date for the gospel significantly later than the Synoptics. Although Mark was most probably written ten to fifteen years before John, it is likely that John and Luke were written about the same time and independently of each other (see ch. 9, below).

Creative Interpreter of Independent Written Sources?

A second view has claimed that John interpreted several independent written sources about Jesus. None of these sources survives, but scholars attempt to identify and reconstruct them, to some degree, from the gospel. This approach explains the difficulties (or aporias) of sequence and content noted above as evidence for John's interpretive work with such sources.

Rudolf Bultmann in his 1941 commentary on John made the most influential proposal for written sources. Using criteria employing disparities of style and theology as well as incongruities between a passage and its context, Bultmann proposes four sources for the gospel. (He also claims to identify two versions of the gospel, stemming from the evangelist and a later interpreter or redactor [editor]. We will focus here on the possible sources and in the next chapter take up the theory of multiple versions.) Bultmann proposes four sources that John interpreted:

1. A signs source or collection of miracle stories:[31] John's gospel includes seven miracle stories, several of which are not in the Synoptics (water into wine, 2:1–11; healing the official's son, 4:46–54). Moreover, the first two stories are numbered, suggesting a larger collection:

Jesus did this, the first of his signs. (2:11)

Now this was the second sign that Jesus did. (4:54)

Bultmann also finds evidence for the gospel writer's additions to this miracle material (4:48; 6:4, 6, 14–15).

2. A revelatory-discourse source: Bultmann claims that the author created the gospel's lengthy discourses from a separate source of revelatory speeches whose limits cannot be defined with certainty. He notes in the discourses several typical stylistic forms (such as antithetical parallelism) and a concern with three motifs: the significance of the revealer; an invitation to believe in him; and the consequences of accepting or rejecting him.

3. A passion and resurrection stories source: This written source is independent of the Synoptic accounts.

4. Other sundry sources: These are evident, for instance, in some Synoptic-like scenes, such as the temple scene (2:13–22) and the anointing at Bethany (12:1–8), and in unparalleled scenes, such as the foot washing of 13:1–20.

These proposals have received much evaluation.[32] Particularly telling especially in relation to the revelatory discourse were the critiques of several scholars who applied analyses of John's characteristic style and vocabulary to Bultmann's proposed sources.[33] They found that these distinctive stylistic features appeared in all of Bultmann's proposed sources, thereby pointing to the stylistic unity of the gospel and suggesting that the hypothesized sources were unlikely. Others doubted his claims of distinctive content as a means of identifying sources. These criticisms established that stylistic criteria cannot be a primary means of identifying John's sources. Many found these criticisms convincing, and few efforts have since been made to identify or reconstruct sources for the gospel's discourses.[34]

Yet Bultmann's proposal for a narrative signs source has attracted, in many cases, more positive attention.[35] Robert Fortna, among others, develops this suggestion.[36] He seeks to determine the source's content not on the basis of style but by attending especially to the aporias, or difficulties, of sequence and content, relegating matters of stylistic features and theological content to a supporting role. Fortna not only identifies the passages that comprise the source but reconstructs the order and likely wording of the source. Fortna's reconstructed source is more than a collection of miracle stories; it is a narrative of Jesus' ministry. It begins with the testimony of John the Baptist, followed by the conversion of the first disciples. The miracle stories then follow, and the source concludes with the passion and resurrection accounts and the key verses of 20:30–31. It thereby combines two of Bultmann's proposed sources (signs and passion) to constitute what looks to be a short gospel with its own coherent narrative and theological claim. Fortna argues that the source's function was evangelistic, shaped by the mission activity of its believing readers and their efforts to gain Jewish converts. Its main theological claim was christological, centering on Jesus' messiahship, which is attested by his miraculous deeds, passion, and resurrection.

According to Fortna, John interprets the signs gospel by developing a much more complex view of Jesus and by adding the discourses of Jesus' conflicts and revelation concerning salvation.[37] John affirms the presentation of Jesus as a wonderworking Messiah but extends its meaning. The gospel emphasizes Jesus' heavenly origin and function as revealer. At the same time, it emphasizes that belief in Jesus as the Messiah primarily means encountering salvation. Jesus reveals life comprising eternal coexistence with God the Father and a mystical abiding with Jesus just as he and the Father are one.

The following chart outlines Fortna's reconstructed source, although it is important to recognize that Fortna often omits particular words and phrases from verses.[38] Refer to the gospel to follow Fortna's reconstruction.

Section	Events	Reconstructed source from gospel texts
Introduction	Exordium (beginning)	1:6–7
	Baptist's witness	1:19–21, 23, 26–27, 33–34
	First disciples converted	3:23–24; 1:35b–50
Signs of Jesus	Water into wine	2:1–3, 5–11 (parts of 2:4, 6, 9, 11)
	Noble's son healed	2:12a; 4:46b–47, 49–54
	Catch of fish	21:2–8, 10–12, 14
	Feeding of the crowd	6:1–3, 5, 7–14
	Walking on water	6:15b–22, 25, [67–71?]
	Dead man raised; Samaritan woman	11:1–3, 7, 11, 15; 4:4–7, 9, 16–19, 25–26, 28–30, 40, [42?]; 11:17–20, 28, 32–34, 38–39, 41, 43–45
	Man born blind healed	9:1–3a, 6–7, [8?]
	38-year illness healed	5:2–3, 5–9, [14?]
Death and resurrection	Cleansing the temple; the death plot	2:14–16, 18–19, 11:47a, 53
	Anointing at Bethany	12:1–5, 7, [8?]
	Triumphal entry into Jerusalem	12:12–15
	Last Supper	Fragments in 12–14; 16; based in 13:4–5, 12–14, 26–27, 37–38
	The arrest	18:1–5, 10–11

	High priest's house	18:13, 24, 15–16a, [19?], 20, [21?], 22–23, 16b–18, 25b–28a
	Before Pilate	18:28b, 33, 37–38; 19:15; 18:39–40; 19:6 [12?], 13–14a, 1–3, 16a
	Crucifixion and burial	19:16b–19, [20?], 23–24, 28–30, 25, 31–34, 36–38; 3:1?, 19:39–42
	Resurrection	20:1–3, 5, 7, 8–12, 14, 16–20
Conclusion	Peroration (conclusion)	20:30–31

Fortna's efforts to identify and reconstruct this signs source have been received with both appreciation and skepticism.[39] In the final analysis, his argument is one from silence, since no such document has ever been found. The very nature of his reconstructive task requires him to be speculative. And there is no doubt that his is a complicated explanation for the aporias in John's text. Yet it may be that this factor renders Fortna's argument more convincing, in that his reconstruction is able to embrace more adequately the complexities of the transmission of material and the process of the composition of John's gospel. The content of the proposed signs source also raises some questions, notably the absence of any explicit teaching material from Jesus. Although a document that focuses on Jesus' powerful acts (including resurrection) has some coherence, why would a mission document omit his teaching? Yet it seems clear that if the Synoptic Gospels used sources such as "Q" and Mark (used by Matthew and Luke),[40] it is not improbable that John does also. Fortna's reconstruction offers one tantalizing possibility of what such a source might look like.

Interpreter of Oral Traditions about Jesus?

Some scholars have posited that the author of John is an interpreter of oral traditions about Jesus. This option has taken two forms. It was initially proposed to explain the similarities and differences between John and the Synoptics. Gardner-Smith argued that the differences between John and the Synoptics are so great that the author did not reinterpret the written accounts of the Synoptic Gospels (the first proposal, above). He held that, rather, the small similarities point to an oral "common store of Christian tradition" from which all the gospels, including John, drew.[41] In the 1960s, C. H. Dodd identified a number of sayings common to John and the Synoptics and accounted for their similarities and differences by suggesting that the gospel writers independently interpreted early oral tradition in different ways.[42] In this view, the author of John's gospel worked these sayings into longer discourses, "literary creations" long removed from early traditions and created on the basis of "current Hellenistic models of philosophical and religious teaching."[43] Barnabas Lindars demonstrates this approach in identifying a number of sayings from Jesus that the author of John developed into the major longer discourses in chapters 3, 6, and 8.[44]

A second form of this option presses the oral milieu of John's gospel much further. This emerging approach offers an exciting alternative to the text-centered approaches discussed above. It takes seriously the work in recent decades that has studied the oral nature of communication and tradition in the first-century world. Literacy was restricted to the small, educated elite (perhaps 2–4 percent) and to some urban males (perhaps 15 percent).[45] Most communication took an oral form. It is to such an oral milieu, rather than to written sources, that we might look to describe the nature of John's interpretive work.

Joanna Dewey points out that in oral cultures oral materials are constantly changing by expansion and omission as they are adapted to changing audiences and circumstances.[46] Oral narratives concerned with a hero focus on events, are episodic, additive in nature (similar scenes ensure repetition and variation), frequently polemical and argumentative, and participatory in terms of audience identification and involvement. Teaching from the hero is commonly added to the end of narrative scenes (see, e.g., John 5 and 6). Such communal narratives form quickly as traditional units coalesce and solidify into a single larger story capable, nevertheless, of variation in performance.

This oral milieu exercises a significant impact on how we might conceive of John as an interpreter. Dewey argues that John more likely interprets an existing oral story than written texts. The pervasive oral culture makes a written signs gospel or written passion narrative, such as those proposed by Bultmann and Fortna, unlikely. John's interpretation of an oral story may also be affected by hearing a performance of one of the Synoptic Gospels, such as Mark. Moreover, the narrative inconsistencies and theological tensions pose much less of a problem in an oral context than they do for print-oriented audiences.

This last observation about inconsistencies suggests that the approach of using the aporias in the gospel as the basis for viewing John as an interpreter of written sources may be a misguided effort. Rather, the aporias may reflect the oral milieu in which John is written. Tom Thatcher seeks to demonstrate this point in his study of the gospel's use of riddles, which we discussed in the last chapter.[47] Thatcher argues that riddles are a common form in oral or folkloric cultures and that scholars of John have ignored them because of their attention to written, not oral, forms of communication. Thatcher argues that the pervasive use of riddles in the gospel's discourses derives from the gospel's oral milieu. This milieu was one of conflict over Jesus' identity as revealer of God's purposes. The riddles, as we noted, repetitively focus on Jesus' identity and mission, highlighting the nonunderstanding of his opponents in contrast to the correct knowledge of Jesus' followers. In a context of polemic and conflict, riddles reinforce the boundaries between the two groups and identify Jesus' followers as a distinct community.

The extensive presence of thirty-eight riddles in the gospel's discourses suggests that the riddles may have functioned in such conflictual circumstances and as part of coherent discourses *before* John was written. The so-called aporias or inconsistencies in the gospel would, then, reflect this oral riddling form and polemical context, not written sources. John's interpretive work consisted in preserving these discourses and including them in the gospel instead of creatively elaborating short sayings of Jesus as Dodd, for instance, had suggested.

This recent emphasis on the oral context and sources of John's gospel requires much more exploration. But results are somewhat elusive because, as Dewey points out, oral performances are fleeting and do not leave permanent records for later scholars to examine. Instead scholars have to employ studies of both orality in the ancient world and recent models of oral societies and communications to illumine the possible context of John's gospel, the oral forms of traditions about Jesus, and John's interpretive work with those materials. This work may not yield results as precise as Fortna's reconstructed written signs gospel appears to be, but it may offer more authentic understandings.

Other questions remain unresolved. Why, in this oral milieu, did John do his interpretive work in written form? On at least two occasions, the gospel refers to this act of writing (20:30–31; 21:24). In the first instance (20:30–31), it recognizes that the writing is not comprehensive. Jesus did many other signs not recorded "in this book." Does the author omit them because he relies on oral retelling, or because he could not afford any more writing material or time, or because . . . ? Why give prominence to some by writing them down? The purpose for the writing is stated, namely, that "you" (the Greek indicates a plural) may believe. Why is it necessary to declare this? Were people in an oral society skeptical of the power of writing? Or does the writer feel it necessary to declare his intention because a writer, unlike an oral storyteller, does not receive instant feedback on the impact of his communication? The second instance (21:24–25) repeats these concerns. It emphasizes the "testimony," or witness-bearing role, of the writing. It asserts that this witness is true, and again refers to the incompleteness of the account. Attention to the gospel's oral milieu will help to clarify John's written interpretive work.

Conclusion

The author's interpretive work is complex. We have looked at his interpretation of the Scriptures and of three possible sources about Jesus: the Synoptics, independent written sources, and oral traditions. Another equally complex approach conceives of John's interpretive work as entailing several editions of the gospel, several authors, and changing circumstances for which the story of Jesus is freshly interpreted. We will view this interpretive model in the next chapter.

Notes

1. Γραφή ("writing"): 2:22; 5:39; 7:38, 42; 10:35; 13:18; 17:12; 19:24, 28, 36, 37; 20:9; γράφω ("write"): 1:45; 2:17; 5:46; 6:31, 45; 8:17; 10:34; 12:14, 16; 15:25. J. Beutler, "The Use of 'Scripture' in the Gospel of John," in *Exploring the Gospel of John: In Honor of D. Moody Smith* (ed. R. A. Culpepper and C. C. Black; Louisville: Westminster John Knox, 1996), 147–62.

2. E. D. Freed, *Old Testament Quotations in the Gospel of John* (Leiden: Brill, 1965); D. A. Carson, "John and the Johannine Epistles," in *It Is Written: Scripture Citing Scripture* (ed. D. A. Carson and H. G. M. Williamson; Cambridge: Cambridge University Press, 1988), 245–64; A. T. Hanson, *Prophetic Gospel: A Study in John and the Old Testament* (Edinburgh: T&T Clark, 1991); B. Schuchard, *Scripture within Scripture: The Interrelationship of Form and Function in the Explicit Old Testament Citations in the Gospel of John* (SBLDS 133; Atlanta: Scholars Press, 1992); C. Westermann, *The Gospel of John in the Light of the Old Testament* (Peabody, Mass.: Hendrickson, 1998); J. Clark-Soles, *Scripture Cannot Be Broken: The Social Function of the Use of Scripture in the Fourth Gospel* (Leiden: Brill, 2003); Brown, *Introduction to the Gospel,* 132–38; F. Moloney, "The Gospel of John as Scripture," in *The Gospel of John: Text and Context* (Boston: Brill, 2005), 333–47.

3. John 1:23 = Isa 40:3; John 2:17 = Ps 69:9; John 6:31 = Exod 16:4, 15; John 6:45 = Isa 54:13; John 7:42 = 2 Sam 7:12; Mic 5:2; John 10:34 = Ps 82:6; John 12:13 = Ps 118:26; John 12:14–15 = Zech 9:9; Zeph 3:14–16; John 12:38–40 = Isa 53:1; John 12:40 = Isa 6:10; John 13:18 = Ps 41:9; John 15:25 = Ps 35:19; 69:4; John 19:24 = Ps 22:18; John 19:28 = Ps 69:22; John 19:36 = Exod 12:46; Ps 34:20; John 19:37 = Zech 12:10.

4. Freed, *Old Testament Quotations,* 126–30; Barrett, *John,* 22–24.

5. John quotes the Septuagint verbatim in 2:4 (1 Kgs 17:18), 10:34 (Ps 82:6), 12:38 (Isa 53:1), 19:24 (Ps 22:19) and is close to it in 2:5 (Gen 41:55), 2:17 (Ps 69:10), 10:16 (Ezek 34:23; 37:24), 12:27 (Ps 6:4), 15:25 (Ps 69:5 LXX), and 16:22 (Isa 66:14). Schuchard (*Scripture within Scripture,* xvii, 151–54) argues for the author's exclusive use of the Old Greek tradition. See C. Goodwin, "How Did John Treat His Sources?" *JBL* 73 (1954): 61–75, here 61–63; Freed (*Old Testament Quotations,* 126–30) seems sympathetic to memory though finally he prefers the use of unidentified written texts.

6. Goodwin, "How?" 64–75; compare John 3:14–15 with Num 21:5, 8, 9 for selective borrowing and departure from it; John 1:51 with Ezek 1:1 and Gen 28:12 for conflation, thereby changing the Scriptures' meaning.

7. In 17:12 Jesus refers to the Scripture, but none is cited. Perhaps Ps 41:9 is in view because John 13:18 referred to it in reference to Judas, or perhaps (Freed, *Quotations,* 97) the passage refers to a form of Prov 24:22a that uses similar vocabulary. The unspecified reference to "scripture" underlines the divine plan that is being worked out.

8. The classic study is P. Borgen, *Bread from Heaven* (Leiden: Brill, 1965).

9. R. H. Smith, "Exodus Typology in the Fourth Gospel," *JBL* 81 (1962): 329–42; P. Borgen, "On the Midrashic Character" and "Bread from Heaven," in *Philo, John, and Paul: New Perspectives on Judaism and Early Christianity* (Atlanta: Scholars Press, 1987), 121–29; 131–44.

10. Beutler, "The Use," 147–48.

11. Coloe, *God Dwells with Us.*

12. Summarizing Ringe, *Wisdom's Friends.* Also Scott, *Sophia;* B. Witherington, *John's Wisdom: A Commentary on the Fourth Gospel* (Louisville: Westminster John Knox, 1995).

13. Key passages are Ps 104 and Job 28 (principle of creation); other texts (Prov 8–9; Sir 24; Bar 3:9–4:4; Wis 7–10; *1 En.* 41:1–2; Philo) present Lady Wisdom.

14. C. H. Talbert, *Reading John* (New York: Crossroad, 1992), 68–70.

15. Following Ringe, *Wisdom's Friends,* 54–63.

16. L. Franklin, "There's More Than One Text in This Class: John's Evoking of the Intertext of Isaiah in John 1:23's Citation of Isaiah 40:3" (paper presented at the annual meeting of the Central States Region of the Society of Biblical Literature, St. Louis, April 2002).

17. John 2:12; 3:22; 4:45; 6:1–3; 7:53–8:1; 10:40–41; 11:54b. Identified by C. Hedrick, "Vestigial Scenes in John, or Settings without Dramatization—and Why?" (paper presented at the annual meeting of the Central States Region of the Society of Biblical Literature, St. Louis, April 2004).

18. D. M. Smith, *John among the Gospels: The Relationship in Twentieth Century Research* (Minneapolis: Fortress, 1992); Brown, *Introduction to the Gospel,* 90–104.

19. Smith, *John among the Gospels,* 13–19; B. W. Bacon, *The Fourth Gospel in Research and Debate* (New York: Moffat, Yard, 1910), 367–84.

20. See the discussion in Brown, *Introduction to the Gospel,* 177–80.

21. Bacon (*Fourth Gospel,* 364–66) sees John's Christology as very compatible with Paul's and argues that John is correcting the inadequate Synoptics, especially the anti-Paul Mark.

22. Ibid., 365, 373–77: John omits the temptation, reframes the baptism, recasts the Baptist and the call of the disciples, and omits exorcisms.

23. Bacon (ibid., 367 n. 3) offers three examples of verbatim quoting: John 1:26–27 = Mark 1:7–8; John 12:13 = Mark 11:9; John 13:21 = Mark 14:18. Careful analysis, however, of the first and third examples hardly justifies the claim of "verbatim."

24. John 12:1–8 combines Mark 14:3–9 with Luke 7:36–50; John 1:24–28 combines Mark 1:7 with Luke 3:15–16.

25. Bacon, *Fourth Gospel,* 369, 377–80.

26. Most recently, T. Brodie, *The Quest for the Origin of John's Gospel: A Source-Oriented Approach* (New York: Oxford University Press, 1993). According to Brodie (p. 31), Mark supplies the basis of John's narratives, and Matthew supplies the basis for John's discourses.

27. Barrett, *John*, 34–37, 37–45.

28. Barrett, *John*, 36–37; for discussion of the possible relationship between the gospels of Luke and John, see Smith, *John among the Gospels*, 85–110.

29. F. Neirynck, "John and the Synoptics," in *L'Évangile de Jean: Sources, Rédaction, Théologie* (ed. M. de Jonge et al.; BETL 44; Gembloux, Belgium: J. Duculot, 1977), 73–106; "John and the Synoptics: The Empty Tomb Stories," *NTS* 30 (1984): 161–87; Smith, *John among the Gospels*, 147–58.

30. P. Gardner-Smith, *Saint John and the Synoptic Gospel* (Cambridge: Cambridge University Press, 1938), xi–xii, 88, and passim; Smith, *John among the Gospels*, 37–62.

31. Bultmann, *Gospel of John*, 6–7 and passim.

32. E.g., D. M. Smith, *The Composition and Order of the Fourth Gospel: Bultmann's Literary Theory* (New Haven, Conn.: Yale University Press, 1965), 67–115; Sloyan, *What Are They Saying?* 28–49; Brown, *Introduction to the Gospel*, 46–58.

33. Notably Schweizer, *Ego eimi*; E. Ruckstuhl, *Die literarische Einheit des Johannesevangelium: Der gegenwärtige Stand der einschlägigen Erforschung* (Freiburg, Switz.: Paulusverlag, 1951).

34. T. Thatcher, *The Riddles of Jesus in John: A Study in Tradition and Folklore* (SBLMS 53; Atlanta: Society of Biblical Literature, 2000), 1–41.

35. Kysar, *Fourth Evangelist*, 13–37.

36. R. Fortna, *The Gospel of Signs: A Reconstruction of the Narrative Underlying the Fourth Gospel* (Cambridge: Cambridge University Press, 1970); *The Fourth Gospel and Its Predecessor* (Philadelphia: Fortress, 1988). See also W. Nicol, *The sēmeia in the Fourth Gospel* (Leiden: Brill, 1972). U. C. Von Wahlde (*The Earliest Version of John's Gospel: Recovering the Gospel of Signs* [Wilmington, Del.: Michael Glazier, 1989]) suggests a source with discourse material (p. 65), but his source is limited to narratives.

37. Developed in Fortna, *Fourth Gospel*, passim, esp. 223–314.

38. Fortna, *Gospel of Signs*, 235–45.

39. E.g., Kysar, *Fourth Evangelist*, 33–37; E. Ruckstuhl, "Johannine Language and Style," in *L'Évangile de Jean: Sources, Rédaction, Théologie* (ed. M. de Jonge et al.; BETL 44; Gembloux, Belgium: J. Duculot, 1977), 125–47.

40. See Carter, *Matthew: Storyteller*, 35–76.

41. Gardner-Smith, *Saint John*, 91; Smith, *John among the Gospels*, 37–43.

42. Dodd, *Historical Tradition*, 335–65, 423–32. Dodd discusses (pp. 335–65) sayings common to the Synoptics and John (the four strongest are John 13:16 = Matt 10:24–25; John 12:25 = Mark 8:35; Luke 9:24; Matt 10:39; Luke 17:33; John 13:20 = Matt 10:40; Mark 9:37; Luke 9:48; John 20:23 = Matt 18:18; Dodd also discusses another nine texts); (pp. 366–87) seven parabolic similarities (12:24; 16:21; 11:9–10; 8:35; 10:1–5; 3:29; 5:19–20a); (pp. 388–405) three sequences of sayings (4:31–38; 12:20–26; 13:1–20), and (pp. 406–20) predictions of future events concerning disciples and the death of Jesus and its sequel. For discussion, see Smith, *John among the Gospels*, 53–62; Thatcher, *Riddles of Jesus*, 1–18.

43. Dodd, *Historical Tradition*, 321.

44. B. Lindars, "Discourse and Tradition: The Use of the Sayings of Jesus in the Discourses of the Fourth Gospel," *JSNT* 13 (1981): 83–101. Lindars argues John 5:19 and 8:28–29 develop the sayings of Jesus in Matt 5:45; John 3:3, 5 is a variant of Matt 18:3 and Mark 10:15; John 6:34 develops the petition of Matt 6:11; John 6:35 develops Mark 14:24 and 1 Cor 11:24; and John 8:31–58 develops Matt 5:45, Luke 6:32–35, Matt 17:26, and Mark 9:1.

45. J. Dewey, "The Gospel of John in Its Oral-Written Media World," in *Jesus in Johannine Tradition* (ed. R. T. Fortna and T. Thatcher; Louisville: Westminster John Knox, 2001), 240. On the importance of orality, see P. J. Achtemeier, "*Omne verbum sonat:* The New Testament and the Oral Environment of Late Western Antiquity," *JBL* 109 (1990): 3–27.

46. Following Dewey, "The Gospel of John," 239–52.

47. Thatcher, "The Riddles"; *Riddles of Jesus.*

CHAPTER 8

John: Interpreters for Changing Historical Circumstances

In chapter 7 we examined the gospel author's interpretive work with the Hebrew Scriptures and with possible sources about Jesus, namely the Synoptic Gospels, written collections of Jesus material, and oral traditions. The discussion thus far has referred to the gospel's author as John. This reference assumes that we know the identity of the gospel's author, that the gospel has one author, and that the author is male. In this chapter and the next, it will become clear that this first assumption is very questionable. This chapter examines the second assumption, that there is one author, by engaging theories that several successive authors may have been engaged in producing multiple versions of the gospel. Throughout this discussion, it will be obvious that the third assumption, while reasonable, cannot be absolutely established.

Some scholars have argued that the John's gospel developed through several versions involving several authors who reinterpreted earlier versions for the changing circumstances of their community of believers in Jesus. This interpretive process with several authors is reflected, so this view claims, in the aporias, or inconsistencies of sequence and content, noted in chapter 7, above. According to this approach, attention to these aporias offers the key to identifying several literary strata or versions of the gospel. This view of the ongoing interpretive process with several authors and gospel versions raises questions about what it means to identify this writing as the Gospel according to John.

A second issue also emerges. The view that John's gospel developed through multiple versions with multiple authors emphasizes that the interpretive process was influenced not only by the personalities and perspectives of different authors but also by the changing circumstances among those for whom the gospel was written. That is, to think of John as an interpreter or interpreters is to recognize that interpretive work is contextual. The interpretive work is influenced by, addresses, and results from changing circumstances. The multiple versions of the gospel reflect these changing circumstances and represent an effort to tell the story of Jesus afresh for new situations. This chapter attends to the interaction between changing historical contexts and an ongoing interpretive process expressed in multiple versions of the gospel.

Rudolf Bultmann's Ecclesiastical Redactor

In the last chapter we noted Bultmann's theory concerning the gospel's possible sources. Bultmann also argued for several versions of the gospel, created by different authors or redactors addressing changing circumstances. His theory offers a good starting point for considering the notion of multiple versions.[1]

Bultmann sees the final form of the gospel, with various apparent contradictions, as resulting from the work of an ecclesiastical redactor. This editor, a rather conventional thinker, made several significant contributions to the gospel. First, the redactor added chapter 21 to the gospel's original ending at 20:30–31. Second, it is likely that this redactor reorganized sections of the gospel, thereby creating problems of sequence.[2] On the basis of this theory of "displacement," Bultmann tries to untangle the sequence, reorganizing the gospel by placing chapter 6 before chapter 5 (to make sense of 6:1), inserting 7:15–24 after 5:47 (since it refers to the Sabbath healing), following it with 8:13–20. Further reorganization follows in chapters 7–12 and 13–16; this includes relocating chapter 14 to lead directly into chapter 18 (on the basis of 14:31).

Third, the redactor sought to make this somewhat unusual gospel, produced by the earlier evangelist, more acceptable to the emerging orthodoxy of the second-century church. The redactor worked on two areas of the gospel's content in particular. The first concerned sacraments. The earlier version of the gospel, according to Bultmann, emphasized faith and obedience and had misgivings about baptism and the Eucharist. It recognized that Jesus was baptized (3:22) but omitted the institution of the Last Supper. According to Bultmann, the ecclesiastical redactor sought to overcome this reluctance by giving greater prominence to these sacraments and integrating them into the gospel. Bultmann finds these additions:

- In 3:5 the addition of "of water" links rebirth by the Spirit to baptism.

- John 6:51c–58 is an added passage referencing the Eucharist as a means of encountering the life that Jesus reveals.

- In 19:34b–35 the addition of water and blood identifies Jesus' death as the origin of baptism and the Eucharist.

- The prayer in chapter 17 expresses the eucharistic ideas that the church is grounded in Jesus' death and lives in mystical communion with him.

The second area of content that Bultmann identifies as the redactor's work concerns eschatology. The earlier version of the gospel, according to Bultmann, emphasized the present experience of realities more commonly associated with the still future completion of God's purposes, such as vindication, not condemnation and judgment, and life, not death. But with the larger church's continuing affirmation of these future expectations, the ecclesiastical redactor edited the gospel to make it more conventional by adding passages such as 6:51c–58, a sacramental passage, including a reference to the still future resurrection ("raised at the last day," 6:54); 5:28–29, referring to the still future general resurrection to life and to judgment (in contradiction with 5:21, 24–25, where only those who hear the Son are raised); 12:48, which speaks of judgment "in the last day." Bultmann also sees this ecclesiastical redactor making other changes, attempting to harmonize aspects of the gospel to the Synoptics and heightening the role of the beloved disciple (e.g., ch. 21).

Bultmann's proposal seeks to explain difficulties of sequence and contradictions of content in the finished form of the gospel by assigning them to different authors who interpret the material for different circumstances. Scholars have disputed his reconstruction in various ways. Did a later author highlight and make explicit what was already present in, or assumed by, the gospel instead of significantly recasting it? Did the earlier traditions hold competing emphases that the gospel's author chose to include rather than omit and thereby disenfranchise some perspectives and members of his community? Is it necessary to posit the existence of a later redactor? Perhaps one person's troublesome contradictions are another person's delightful paradoxes. Perhaps the author's own thinking was typically paradoxical.[3] Or perhaps the author edited his own gospel for changing circumstances? Do we know enough to be able to formulate such a reconstruction?

Two Theories

Two of the most influential recent proposals concerning ongoing interpretive work that included changing circumstances, multiple authors, and several versions of the gospel come from J. L. Martyn and R. Brown.[4]

J. Louis Martyn

Martyn proposes a three-stage development including two versions of John's gospel:[5]

Phase 1 and version 1: Martyn sees the first version of John's gospel mainly in terms of Fortna's reconstructed signs gospel (discussed in the last chapter). It consisted mostly of Jesus' miracles or signs. Its purpose was evangelistic, testifying to Jesus' identity as the Messiah. This gospel originated from a small messianic group in a synagogue in an urban context. Some preachers had visited this synagogue to proclaim that Jesus was the Messiah and some had believed their message (1:35–51). These believers remained in the synagogue and continued to announce that Jesus was the Messiah. This phase lasted until the early 80s.

Phase 2: Martyn argues that the synagogue authorities became increasingly concerned about the Jesus, or messianic, group. They demanded exegetical or midrashic support for the claims about Jesus. Their commitment was to Moses (9:28), one who had ascended into the heavens and received heavenly secrets. They understood Jesus to have been a false prophet who led people astray (7:12, 47–48), and they accused his followers of being ditheists, of violating monotheism by worshipping two gods (5:18; 19:7). The synagogue authorities concluded that the affirmation of Jesus as the Messiah was apostasy and that the group should be expelled from the synagogue. To detect and expel members of the messianic group, they employed the Benediction against Heretics (the Birkat ha-Minim; 9:22; 12:42; 16:2). This benediction, recited in worship, was devised, so Martyn argues, by a group of rabbis meeting at the small town of Yavneh after Rome's destruction of Jerusalem and the temple in 70 C.E. It read:

> For the apostates let there be no hope
> And let the arrogant government
> Be speedily uprooted in our days.
> Let the Nazarenes [Christians] and the Minim [heretics] be destroyed in a moment
> And let them be blotted out of the Book of Life and not be inscribed together with the righteous.
> Blessed art thou, O Lord, who humblest the proud.[6]

Martyn argues that reciting the benediction divided the followers of Jesus from the synagogue. The threat of excommunication inhibited open confessions, and it was reinforced by the trial of, and death penalty for, preachers (16:2). Martyn sees these events reflected in what he calls "two-level" dramas about Jesus and about John's community. John 5, 7, and 9 are classic examples.

Phase 3 and version 2: Having experienced these events, especially expulsion from the synagogue, the gospel writer rewrote the signs gospel to address these new circumstances. This rewriting, in the late 80s C.E., employed two-level dramas that tell the community's own story under the guise of stories about Jesus. It introduced many of the gospel's distinctive features that we have previously noted.

Central are affirmations about Jesus: (1) One cannot follow Jesus and Moses. (2) Although Jesus is the prophet/messiah like Moses, the writer emphasizes that Moses bears witness to Jesus (5:45–46). (3) In contrast to Moses but reflecting the experience of hostility and alienation, Jesus is presented as the stranger from heaven, rejected by his own people (1:10–12). As the descending and ascending Son of Man, he is authorized to manifest God's authority and presence as judge. (4) The writer rejects the charge of ditheism in depicting Jesus' relationship with God in terms of Father and Son. (5) Whereas the signs gospel presented Jesus' resurrection from the dead as the greatest miracle, the gospel accounts for Jesus' death as an expression of the authorities' misunderstanding of Jesus' claims (ditheism).

The author also reinterpreted the signs gospel's claim that signs lead to faith. The author recognizes that although signs can lead to

faith (2:11), often they lead to unbelief (12:37). The gospel emphasizes believing Jesus' words.

Two other situations influenced the writing of the gospel: (1) Some
Jesus believers ("Crypto-Christians") remained in the synagogue.
The disapproving author heightened the dualism of being either
from above or from below. (2) Some believers had been scattered by
persecution (8:31–38). These "other sheep" (10:16) will be reunited
with John's community.

Raymond Brown

Brown's reconstruction includes not only John's gospel but also
subsequent developments in the three Johannine letters. We focus only
on Brown's work that concerned John's gospel. Brown proposed a process of development comprising five stages and three gospel versions.
There are significant similarities with Martyn's approach but also important differences:[7]

> Phase 1: An oral collection of accounts of Jesus' words and works,
> independent of the Synoptic Gospels and developed through preach-
> ing and teaching, presented Jesus as the Davidic Messiah. The key
> figure in this phase is John, son of Zebedee, the beloved disciple.[8]
> His group was located "in or near Palestine."

> Phase 2: Over several decades, this material was molded into the
> stories and discourses that became part of John's gospel. Oral
> preaching and teaching, shaped especially by one dominant preacher
> (a close disciple of John son of Zebedee), were significant influences.

> Phase 3 and version 1: This same person, a master preacher or evan-
> gelist, wrote a first version of the gospel, containing Jesus' words
> and works (not just signs as in Martyn's reconstruction), for a
> group now located in the Diaspora.

> Phase 4 and version 2 (by the same author): Changing circum-
> stances required additions and reworking: (1) A dispute with fol-
> lowers of John the Baptist who rejected Jesus and claimed John was
> God's envoy or Messiah required clarification of the Baptist's role in
> bearing witness to Jesus (1:19–34; 3:28). (2) The Jesus group was
> expelled from a synagogue after 70 C.E. (11:48) for confessing Jesus
> as Messiah, the one sent from God. Their more exalted claims for
> Jesus had come about because another group of antitemple Jews,
> along with Samaritan converts, had entered the community (John

2–4), bringing elevated claims about Jesus derived from Mosaic traditions. Jesus had seen God, come from God, and revealed God's will to people. These claims had led to charges that followers of Jesus had abandoned monotheism and adopted ditheism. (3) This second version had sharper polemic against those who had expelled the followers of Jesus. The authorities are children of the devil. Throughout, the gospel uses dualistic language to emphasize the division between believers and nonbelievers, life and death, light and darkness. (4) In this context of hostility and fear, this version emphasized realized eschatology, reassuring believers that Jesus' eschatological promises are realized in the present rather than awaited at his future return. Believers in Jesus are not condemned (3:17–21) but have already experienced the vindication of the judgment and have passed from death to eternal life (5:24). (5) John's community was also more open to Gentiles (12:20–23, 37–40). The author explains Jewish terms for Gentiles (1:38, 41, 42; 4:25; 9:7; 19:13, 17; 20:16, 24), emphasizes God's loving purposes for the world (3:16; 11:48–52), and affirms that people encounter God's purposes not by ethnicity but by God's actions (1:12; 3:3, 5). (6) A dispute with followers of Jesus who had not left the synagogue also resulted during this phase (12:42–43).

Phase 5 and the final redaction: Another author or redactor, belonging to the same group as the evangelist but probably after his death, added further material: (1) This material is identifiable by awkward intrusions (aporias) and duplications of existing material, as in 3:31–36, 6:51–58, and 12:44–50. (2) This redactor added a collection of Jesus' teaching to disciples in chapters 15–17, leaving in place the conclusion at 14:31 and doubling the content of chapter 14 in 16:4–33. (3) This redactor also added the Lazarus material and a new ending to Jesus' public ministry in chapters 11–12. This later addition accounts for the more neutral language of "the Jews" in chapters 11–12. (4) This redactor shifted the temple scene to chapter 2. (5) The redactor also heightened sacramental elements, emphasizing the Eucharist by adding 6:51–58 and possibly baptism by adding 3:5.

Comparisons between Martyn's and Brown's Approaches

Both reconstructions offer intriguing glimpses into possible versions of the gospel and into the changing circumstances of John's community, changes that might have shaped each version. Martyn and Brown admit the difficulty and elusiveness of what they have attempted. They acknowledge that their reconstructions are hypothetical and cannot be objectively verified, but these have received widespread support.[9]

Among the differences between the two attempts, Brown, in his first two phases, sees a much greater role for oral traditions. Martyn's first version of the gospel is essentially a collection of signs or miracle stories whereas Brown's version includes Jesus' words and works. Martyn pays little attention to authorship whereas Brown posits at least three significant figures: The apostle John, son of Zebedee, the beloved disciple, is responsible for the oral collection of phase one. His influence continues through two of his disciples, one responsible for the two written versions of phases 2–4 and another responsible for the further redaction and written version in phase 5. Brown also highlights the crucial influence of two groups that enter the community—Samaritans before the second version in phase 4 and then Gentiles before the final redaction—neither of which figures prominently in Martyn's reconstruction.

There are also similarities between the two reconstructions. Central to both is the expulsion of the Jesus group from a synagogue to form its own distinct and separate community. This event forms Martyn's phase 2 and Brown's phase 4. For both scholars, it is *the* key development that necessitates another written version of the gospel to address the new historical circumstances and new social location of John's community of believers, marked now by rejection, hostility, and persecution from the synagogue. And for both Martyn and Brown, this event of expulsion is attested in three key references—9:22, 12:42, and 16:2—in which the rare term ἀποσυνάγωγος (*aposynagōgos*, "put out of a synagogue") occurs.

Both see understandings of Jesus as being central to this expulsion. Martyn identifies these claims as centered on Jesus the Messiah. The synagogue regarded the Jesus group's claims as lacking support from the Scriptures, misleading the people, challenging the authority of Moses, and turning Jesus into a second god. The synagogue authorities used the Birkat ha-Minim to identify and expel believers (see Martyn's phase 2 above for its possible wording). Martyn argues that this benediction, part of a set of eighteen blessings, was created to reconstruct and unify Judaism after the fall of Jerusalem. He imagines that suspected believers were given leadership in reciting the Eighteen Benedictions in worship. Followers of Jesus would reveal themselves by stumbling over this twelfth benediction, unable to curse themselves. Martyn also sees attempts to try and execute those who preached about Jesus (16:2).

Brown also emphasizes the centrality of this expulsion, the role of Christology in this event, and the role of the Birkat ha-Minim in accomplishing it. But he differs from Martyn in what causes the separation. Brown complains that Martyn's scenario does not adequately explain how or why the synagogue authorities became so concerned about the Jesus group that they expelled them. In Martyn's reconstruction, believers in Jesus had been part of the synagogue for several decades before any action was taken against them. What happened to provoke the expulsion?

Brown addresses this inadequacy by arguing that new understandings of Jesus among believers account for the expulsion. Brown posits (appealing to John 4 and 8:48) that newcomers to the synagogue community, namely, antitemple Jews and Samaritans who were believers in Jesus, brought new understandings of Jesus.[10] These higher views were influenced not by understandings of Jesus as the Davidic Messiah (Brown's phase 3 and version 1 of the gospel) but by traditions that understood Moses as one who had ascended to God and revealed God and by expectations of a revealer-restorer Messiah (known as the *Taheb*). The Jesus group came to understand Jesus, not Moses, as the one who had seen God, who had been sent from God, and who had revealed God. The synagogue authorities found such claims to be blasphemy, as they threatened monotheism (5:18; 10:33; 19:7). These exalted claims and charges of ditheism were the catalysts for the expulsion. Subsequently the synagogue put to death those who promulgated such claims (16:2).

For Brown, a new written version of the gospel became necessary to address the new situation of confusion, hostility, and rejection (version 2). The existing traditions had to be reinterpreted and reasserted for changed circumstances. The new version affirms the new understandings of Jesus as sent from God to reveal God's purposes. Its dualistic language sharpens and confirms the theological and social division between believers and nonbelievers, children of God and children of the devil. It clarifies the hostile and hateful way of the world, deriving from its rejection of God's purposes. And it employs language of realized eschatology to assure readers that in these difficult times the present is significant and blessed as well as a time for faithfulness to God's purposes, whatever the cost. Since belonging to God's purposes is a matter not of ethnicity but of God's election and human response, Gentiles are welcome.

Evaluation: Questions and Issues

These fascinating reconstructions raise both literary and historical issues. Literary issues include questions on how the text of John is being read and interpreted, especially the relationship between what the text says and external events. Historical issues include the understanding of what was happening in the aftermath of Rome's destruction of Jerusalem in 70 C.E.

Literary Issues

First, those who think that attempts to reconstruct earlier forms of John's gospel are either impossible or illegitimate because of lack of data will never be convinced by any of these approaches, which are based on explaining the aporias. Do aporias, the difficulties or inconsistencies of sequence and content, provide a sufficient basis for positing different versions for changing circumstances? Perhaps they represent the inclusion of pieces of tradition added simply because of the passing of time. Perhaps the author thinks in paradoxical terms and structures his worldview on this basis.[11] Or perhaps the author is so intent on communicating his important message that smooth storytelling is not the greatest priority. Perhaps aporias are a rhetorical technique. Repetition of themes and motifs is a common literary device used to emphasize important material. As noted in chapter 6, above, in the ancient world, sublimity, obscurity, and solemnity were regarded as very appropriate for religious writing, expressive of religious mystery and exhibiting great literary skill in expressing profound subject matter. Thus, it is important to remember that multiple versions do not automatically or inevitably explain the so-called aporias. Aporias do not lead inevitably to theories of multiple versions.

Second, related to this concern is the question of how to read John, especially in assessing the relationship between the text and external events. For example, both Brown and Martyn appeal to 16:2 ("Indeed, an hour is coming when those who kill you will think that by doing so they are offering worship to God") as evidence for the trial and execution of those who preached the message about Jesus.[12] But their readiness to equate what the text says with actual events ignores a crucial factor about John's text, namely, that it is very polemical.

Luke Timothy Johnson has documented the standard polemical claims and language that Gentiles and Jews in the first-century world employed to speak about other Gentile and Jewish groups.[13] Opponents are described as liars and deceivers; blind; interested only in their own gain; hypocrites; immoral; savage; lovers of pleasure, money and glory; doers of violence; and killers of opponents. Charges that opponents initiate violence are evident, for instance, in Wis 14:22–29 (against Alexandrians), Josephus (against those urging war with Rome, including the

Sicarii, Idumeans, and Zealots [*J.W.* 5.399–402; 7.260–274]), and Philo (also against Alexandrians [*On the Embassy to Gaius* 120–131]). Such language and charges, marked by stereotypes, exaggeration, and blatant bias, signaled primarily not factual information but the existence of opponents. The attacks often had internal value, functioning to differentiate groups, to define the other negatively, and to secure one's own group's identity and way of life.

This stereotypical polemical context mandates great caution in interpreting the charges of killing in John 16:2 and the gospel's consistently hostile presentation of opponents. John continually presents Jewish authorities in these standard polemical terms, charging them with not understanding (8:43), being liars and murderers like their father the devil (8:44, 55), being blind (9:41), and being lovers of human glory (12:43). This is not objective, fair, and balanced writing based on extensive research and verifiable data. It is stereotypical polemic. In employing standard polemic, 16:2 certainly attests a perception of division between groups marked by significant hostility, but to conclude that it attests an actual practice of persecuting and executing Christian preachers is to conclude far too much.

Third, given this polemical atmosphere, we need to be careful in interpreting the references, in 9:22 and 12:42, to being put out of the synagogue as if they provide objective data for the formal expulsion that Martyn and Brown propose. (We will return to this issue below.)

We all know the experience of being involved in conflicts in which parties make exaggerated claims, misunderstand and misrepresent the statements of others, claim to be the victim of the others' words and actions, and report the conflict in a way that portrays themselves positively and the other very negatively. Such behaviors attest perceptions of conflict and hostility but often say little about the actual issues. There seems little doubt that 9:22 and 12:42 (along with 16:2) attest a perception of considerable conflict and hostility between two opposing groups. But the polemical tone presents great difficulty and requires great caution in reconstructing who initiated the conflict and what actually happened. Moreover, we have no records of the synagogue's side of the story.

The verses certainly attest the Jesus believers' sense of exclusion. But explaining how this sense came about is difficult. Martyn and Brown's claim of a formal action by the synagogue is one possibility among many. Certainly it is not the only possibility. Another scenario might posit a tense atmosphere of conflict over claims about Jesus in which some believers feel so uncomfortable and unwelcome that they withdraw voluntarily and then claim that they were expelled because their views were not accepted. Or a remark such as "We don't want people here who believe that sort of blasphemy" could be interpreted as "OK, leave" and experienced as "They are kicking us out." These hypothetical scenarios suggest the presence of hostility and separation, but they do not claim either expulsion or an active or formal means of accomplishing it. It is very difficult to reconstruct detailed historical events on the basis of polemical language.

Fourth, in his reconstruction, Brown places heavy emphasis on the role of Samaritan converts who bring more elevated understandings of Jesus that become the catalyst for the expulsion. But there are several difficult claims here. John's references to Samaritans may indicate some Samaritans among the Jesus believers (4:7, 9, 39–40; 8:48), but the gospel does not indicate that their entry brought new understandings about Jesus. The gospel's distinctive claims about Jesus do not require such an origin. We saw in the last chapter the importance of Jewish wisdom traditions, for example, as a likely source for shaping understandings of Jesus. But we do not know whether such thinking was well established or a new development introduced by a particular group.

Fifth, both Martyn and Brown use the synagogue separation verses (9:22; 12:42; 16:2) as significant points for their reconstructions. Both employ the strategy of a two-level reading—espoused, for example, in Martyn's discussion of John 9—whereby they read the gospel stories as referring to both the time of Jesus and the history of John's community. But Adele Reinhartz raises questions about this reading strategy and their inconsistent use of it.[14] When Reinhartz, for instance, applies this two-level reading strategy to John 11–12, she finds two more possible models of relationship between Jesus believers and the synagogue community that need to be set alongside Martyn and Brown's expulsion model. In the story of Mary and Martha in John 11–12, these two believer friends of Jesus receive comfort from Jews who are not identified as believers (cf. 11:45) but who join them in their house and share their grief and weeping at Lazarus's death (11:19, 31, 33). This model suggests caring coexistence.

In 12:11 Reinhartz finds a third model. The verse notes that on account of Lazarus' revival, the authorities are concerned that "many of the Jews were deserting and were believing in Jesus." This is a model of freely chosen separation whereby some leave the synagogue (?) and join the Jesus believers. The application of the two-level-drama reading strategy in fact yields three contradictory models: expulsion, cooperation, and freely chosen separation! What to do with these three models? Reinhartz argues that they cannot be reconciled. Her work suggests that this reading strategy is not helpful in trying to identify the changing historical-social circumstances that might have produced different versions of the gospel.

Sixth, a further factor can be added to this mix. Chapter 5, above, noted the gospel's pervasive use of dualistic language, which creates in the text a very sharp division between believers and nonbelievers. How does such entexting function for John's readers? Does it reinforce a social division that has already taken place, as Martyn and Brown would argue, or does it try to create a social division where no such division already exists? Perhaps the dualistic language reflects the author's attempt to create and/or impose both the awareness of a distinct identity and the experience of social separation. This possibility reminds us that we have to be cautious in trying to posit the historical contexts behind polemical and dualistic texts.

Historical Issues

In addition to these six literary issues, six historical considerations raise questions about aspects of Martyn and Brown's proposals. These issues concern the claim of a formal expulsion, that the Birkat ha-Minim was the means of formally identifying and expelling Jesus believers, thereby bringing about the separation of the two groups.[15]

First, Martyn makes much of John 9 as a two-level drama, but that chapter does not depict a formal confession and expulsion. The parents of the healed blind man are frightened to give *any* information that might link them to Jesus (9:20–23). Any sort of association, rather than a formal confession, is in view. Their son is identified as Jesus' disciple in 9:28 although he has not made a formal confession. He is driven out in 9:34, *before* he makes the confession of 9:38. Such details do not suggest any formal proceedings. Neither do 12:42 and 16:2.

Second, John 9 presents a situation in which the healed man is physically driven out of the synagogue. It does not present a situation in which he is cursed, does not concern a worship setting, and does not mention any sort of prayer, let alone one that resembles the Birkat ha-Minim. Nor does it have the blind man lead worship in the synagogue, the expulsion situation imagined by Martyn.

Third, the Birkat ha-Minim does not mention physical expulsion from a synagogue, the situation of 9:34. It does place an eschatological curse on heretics, but there is no reference to synagogues or physical expulsion.

Fourth, scholars have questioned whether the Yavneh gathering of rabbis formulated, distributed, and enforced a blessing against heretics/Christians in synagogues in the manner suggested by Martyn and Brown. There is some doubt about the dating of the Birkat, whether it was created by the time John was written or whether it developed over a lengthy period in subsequent decades.[16] There is also considerable debate about its actual wording and whether Christians were particularly in view.[17] Some have concluded that there is simply no evidence for the late-first-century practice of synagogues cursing Christians in prayers or for the Yavneh gathering as an authorized body issuing decrees to regulate all synagogue practices.[18]

Fifth, Martyn and Brown imagine that suspected Jesus believers were invited to lead the recitation of the Birkat in worship and were revealed by their inability to curse themselves. But this scenario is hardly convincing and seems somewhat at odds with both scholars' reconstructions. According to both, members of the Jesus group had existed for decades in the synagogue. They even had their own book, the first version of the gospel, and they were engaged in mission or evangelistic activity in recruiting more believers. For both scholars, there had been arguments among synagogue members about the claims concerning Jesus' identity. In such contexts, it seems likely that Jesus believers would be well known. It is, then, difficult to imagine that they needed flushing out or that, in a context of disputes, they would be entrusted with leadership in worship.

Sixth, centuries later, fourth-century Christian writers attest the presence of Christians in synagogue communities.[19]

These literary and historical considerations thus raise important concerns about central aspects of Martyn and Brown's proposals, in summary:

- John is a polemical text, marked by hostility, exaggeration, and a one-sided perspective.

- It is difficult to move from references such as 9:22, 12:42, and 16:2 to reconstruct precisely the circumstances influencing the text.

- The claims of expulsion derive from use of the two-level reading strategy. But a consistent application of this strategy produces at least two more models. The three models—expulsion, cooperation, freely chosen separation—cannot be readily reconciled.

- Various questions arise concerning claims about the existence, wording, meaning, and function of the Birkat ha-Minim as the means of effecting the expulsion and about its relevance to scenarios such as John 9.

These concerns do not completely dismiss Martyn and Brown's proposals. It remains possible that the gospel's aporias arise from mul-

tiple versions of the gospel. Studies of the Synoptic Gospels show the redaction or editing of accounts about Jesus whereby earlier versions (e.g.,
Mark) are reworked or redacted to address new and changing situations.[20] That John's gospel underwent a similar process is quite likely. It
is also quite likely that understandings of Jesus among John's believers
developed through the first century and that the circumstances and situations of their lives also changed. Both factors readily suggest an interpretive process including several versions of the gospel, redacted by
either the same author or several authors to address changing circumstances. The discussion above, however, alerts us to the great difficulty
of reconstructing those gospel versions in any detail and of delineating
the changing circumstances with significant confidence. Both tasks may
simply be beyond the data that we have.

This caution does not mean, however, that we have no sense of the
circumstances for which the (almost?) final version of John's gospel interpreted the story of Jesus. We noted above a strong perception that the
Jesus believers were alienated from the synagogue in circumstances of
conflict and hostility. How does such a perception arise if Martyn and
Brown's proposal of a formal expulsion is not entirely convincing?

One view suggests that the Jesus believers were part of a synagogue
community but the gospel's author wanted them to separate and to stay
away from the synagogue.[21] According to this reading, the gospel's author sees profound incompatibilities between Jesus believers and nonbelievers. He writes to help his group understand these incompatibilities
so that they will physically and socially separate themselves. To accomplish this separation, he tells the story of Jesus' rejection by hostile,
nonunderstanding, and violent authorities. He uses strongly dualistic
language to reveal the existence of two groups (believers/nonbelievers)
with vastly different evaluations of Jesus that reflect their different and
contrasting origins (God/the devil), allegiances (truth/falseness), and
identities (children of God/children of the devil). He also includes the
references to expulsion from the synagogue to show them as hostile, rejecting places and to reveal the logical (but not historical) consequences
of the vastly different and incompatible realities. The author is deeply
disturbed by the group's ongoing association with the synagogue. He
writes to reveal the "true" state of things to his group so that, troubled
and convinced by new understanding of the "real" state of affairs, they
will withdraw from the synagogue. It is the gospel's author who is
having the crisis, so this view suggests, not the group of Jesus believers.

A second explanation for the sense of alienation and hostility noted
above is that conflict could have arisen between the Jesus group and
the rest of a synagogue community over claims about Jesus. Elevated

tensions may have made things too uncomfortable for some of the Jesus group, or they may have decided that they did not want to associate with a synagogue community that resisted their claims. They voluntarily withdrew but, in pain and anger, understood their withdrawal as a forced separation. They experienced it as an expulsion and feared further, even violent, consequences. These perceptions would be reflected in the three key texts (9:22; 12:42; 16:2).

Is either of these scenarios more convincing than the other? It is difficult to decide, but the second seems more plausible. There is evidence for historical pressures on both the Jesus group and its opponents in post-70 Judaism, suggesting that conflict rather than peaceful coexistence between the two was likely. Lawrence Schiffman has shown that after Jerusalem and the temple had been destroyed in 70, pressures toward unity increased within the considerably diverse Judaism of the first century.[22] Increased unity in practices and understandings was seen as desirable especially after the disunity that, some thought, had contributed significantly to Rome's triumph in 70.

At the same time, forces in Christian groups worked against this unity. One was the growing numbers of Gentiles. Another was the increasingly elevated and exclusive claims about Jesus, which were shaped by wisdom traditions. In the post-70 context, John's gospel claims Jesus as the only reliable revealer of God's works, words, and will because he has come from God (4:34; 5:19–24; 14:6–11). It asserts that with the demise of the temple, Jesus is the one who provides atonement for sin (1:29, 35). In the community of believers in Jesus, God's presence is encountered through the Paraclete (14:25–26; 15:26). Only Jesus provides access to God's life in the new age (3:16; 14:6). Either one believes Jesus and encounters God's purposes, life, atonement, and presence, or one faces condemnation and exclusion (3:18–20; 8:42–47). Such exalted and exclusive claims regarding Jesus hardly allowed room for dialogue or even the tolerance of other ways of encountering God. Conflict and separation seem inevitable. John may well interpret earlier traditions about Jesus to address such a context by blaming the synagogue and presenting the separation as expulsion. In such a context, however, it is difficult to reconstruct earlier versions of the gospel.

The Gospel's Resistance to Rome's World

One final aspect of the circumstances for which John interprets the Jesus traditions should be mentioned. With attention on conflicts between John's community and a synagogue, it is easy to forget that these believers lived in a larger world that knew Rome's harsh rule on a daily basis.[23] Rome's destruction of Jerusalem and its temple in 70 freshly demonstrated Rome's apparently invincible power to all inhabitants of the Roman world. Claims that the gods, especially Jupiter, had chosen Rome to order the world seemed vindicated.[24] Rome's military seemed invincible. Its way of ordering the world, in which an elite of 2 to 3 percent of the population benefited, at the expense of the rest, from the control of land and resources (produce and labor) through taxes, tributes, and rents seemed never-ending. Roman propaganda declared Rome to be *Roma aeterna* ("eternal Rome") or *urbs aeterna* ("eternal city"), an *imperium sine fine* ("empire without end").[25]

This divinely sanctioned, never-ending, militarily-protected order in perpetuity meant much misery and deprivation for most people. Roman "justice" was experienced as injustice; Roman rule, as exploitation, Roman "peace," as brokenness. It included widespread poverty, subsistence living, an inadequate food supply because of taxes paid in kind, inadequate nutrition, overwork, anxiety, disease, indebtedness, social dislocation through the loss of land or the inability to support a household, urban squalor and overcrowding, societal conflicts, ethnic tensions, and war. Claims of *Roma aeterna* proclaimed the eternal existence of Rome's destructive hierarchical social experience as the way of ordering the world.

In such a context, John's gospel can be understood to contest this vision of human society. In telling the story of the crucifixion of Jesus at the hands of Rome and its Jerusalem allies, it narrates Jesus' challenge to this order. Rome crucified those who threatened its interests. The gospel narrates Jesus' judgment on the temple, the center of power for Rome's Jerusalem allies (2:13–22). The chief priest, Caiaphas, refers to the threat of Rome's destruction of the city and temple as a rationale for destroying Jesus (11:47–53). But ironically, John suggests, instead of keeping the city safe, their rejection of Jesus brings judgment on the city in the events of 70. Jesus' resurrection shows that the worst that Rome and its allies can do, namely, putting the revealer and agent of God's purposes to death, cannot thwart God's purposes because God raises him from the death that they impose (chs. 20–21).

Throughout, Jesus has revealed God's purposes, which concern not eternal Rome but eternal life, or "life of the age" (see ch. 5, above) (3:16; 11:25–26; 20:30–31). This transformed age comprises, as in various forms of Jewish eschatological thinking, the still future establishment of God's good and just purposes, which is marked by the end of tyranny, sin, and death (the rejecting "world") and evidenced in human wholeness/ health and abundant food and resources. As noted previously, Jesus' miracles of supplying abundant wine and food (2:1–11; 6:1–14) and of transforming sickness to wholeness (4:46–54; 5:1–16; 9:1–18) are signs of the wholeness, abundance, and the triumph of life over death and sin that mark "life of the age." Eternal life is to know God (17:3), a societal life in which God's good and just purposes are established.

We have also noted that Jesus' ministry reveals God's life-giving purposes for all people, including those marginalized by the hierarchical imperial social structure. The low-status poor, lacking power, honor, and resources, such as the man who has been sick for thirty-eight years (5:1–9) and the man born blind (9:1–8), are healed and restored to society. A child (4:46–54), a woman and a Samaritan (ch. 4), low-status Galileans (ch. 6), and those who habitually ignore the law (7:49) are caught up in God's purposes, which offer a vastly different social vision and experience. Karris argues that the inclusion of such people in John's community and God's purposes may have been a source of offense to the synagogue leadership and a factor in the growing tension between the two groups.[26]

John thus interprets the traditions about Jesus in relation to Rome's world. That "world" is shown to be contrary to and resistant to God's life-giving and just purposes (see ch. 5, above). Rome's world is revealed to be under judgment. The gospel also reveals to the community of Jesus believers that it participates in and anticipates a vastly different reality, namely, the very life of God (5:24; 17:3). This alternative community, or countercommunity, this antisociety reflected in, and shaped by, the gospel's antilanguage,[27] is commissioned to continue to do the works Jesus did (14:12–17), to reveal God's life-giving purposes even though it will be tough and resisted work (15:18–25).

Notes

1. Bultmann, *Gospel of John,* 6–7, 10–12, and passim; Smith, *Composition and Order,* 213–38.

2. Bultmann, *Gospel of John,* viii–xi, 10–11; Brown, *Introduction to the Gospel,* 42–46.

3. Emphasized by Anderson, *Christology.*

4. Among others, Ashton, *Understanding,* 160–204; Painter, *Quest for the Messiah,* 61–87; Culpepper, *Gospel and Letters,* 39–61 (incorporating 1–3 John).

5. J. L. Martyn, *History and Theology in the Fourth Gospel* (3d ed.; Louisville: Westminster John Knox, 2003); "Source Criticism and Religionsgeschichte in the Fourth Gospel," in *The Interpretation of John* (ed. J. Ashton; Philadelphia: Fortress, 1968), 99–121; "Glimpses into the History of the Johannine Community," in *The Gospel of John in Christian History* (New York: Paulist, 1979), 90–121. Martyn seems to suggest (*History and Theology,* 73 n. 100) that the community may have been located in Alexandria.

6. Martyn, *History and Theology*, 62–63. The brackets indicate Martyn's explanations.

7. Brown presents somewhat different versions of his scheme. I am conflating Brown, *Gospel according to John*, 1:xxxiv–xl, xcviii–cii, and passim; *The Community of the Beloved Disciple* (Mahwah, N.J.: Paulist, 1979), passim, esp. 166–67. In his *Introduction to the Gospel*, 58–89, Brown collapses five stages into three, although the three seem to contain the five. For a discussion, see F. Moloney, "Raymond Brown's New *Introduction to the Gospel of John*: A Presentation—and Some Questions," *CBQ* 65 (2003): 1–21, here 3–5.

8. On the relationship between the gospel's author, John son of Zebedee, and "the beloved disciple," see ch. 9, below.

9. For Martyn, see D. M. Smith, "The Contribution of J. Louis Martyn to the Understanding of the Gospel of John," in *The Conversation Continues: Studies in Paul and John in Honor of J. Louis Martyn* (ed. R. Fortna and B. R. Gaventa; Nashville: Abingdon, 1990), 275–94; also in *History and Theology*, 1–23; for Brown, see Moloney, "Raymond Brown's New *Introduction*." For support, see Rensberger, *Johannine Faith*, 22; W. Meeks, "Breaking Away: Three New Testament Pictures of Christianity's Separation from the Jewish Communities," in *"To See Ourselves as Others See Us": Christians, Jews, "Others" in Late Antiquity* (ed. J. Neusner and E. S. Frerichs; Chico, Calif.: Scholars Press, 1985), 93–115, here 102.

10. Brown, *Community*, 34–54; W. Meeks, *The Prophet-King: Moses Traditions and the Johannine Christology* (Novum Testamentum Supplements 14; Leiden: Brill, 1967), 318–19.

11. Emphasized by Anderson, *Christology*.

12. Martyn, *History and Theology*, 72–83; Brown, *Community*, 41–43.

13. Johnson, "New Testament's Anti-Jewish Slander."

14. Reinhartz, *Befriending*, 37–53.

15. See also W. Horbury, "The Benediction of the *minim* and Early Jewish-Christian Controversy," *Journal of Theological Studies* 38 (1982): 19–61.

16. Meeks, "Man from Heaven," 55 n. 40.

17. Various forms of the Birkat exist. The form that Martyn cites includes a double referent (Notzrim/Nazarenes and Minim) in which the first term is likely a much later addition to refer to Christians. R. Kimmelman ("Birkat ha-Minim and the Lack of Evidence for an Anti-Christian Jewish Prayer in Late Antiquity," in *Jewish and Christian Self-Definition* [ed. E. P. Sanders, A. I. Baumgarten, and A. Mendelson; 3 vols.; Philadelphia: Fortress, 1980–1982], 2:226–44) argues that in early rabbinic literature (the Tannaitic literature) *minim* refers to deviant Jews and can refer to Jewish Christians but is not directed specifically against them or against Gentiles (pp. 228–32); also S. Katz, "Issues in the Separation of Judaism and Christianity after 70 C.E.: A Reconsideration," *JBL* 103 (1984): 43–76, here 64–74; P. van der Horst, "The Birkat ha-Minim in Recent Research," *ExpTim* 105 (1994): 363–68, here 367.

18. Kimmelman, "Birkat ha-Minim."

19. Ibid., 238–40. L. Schiffman ("At the Crossroads: Tannaitic Perspectives on the Jewish-Christian Schism," in *Jewish and Christian Self-Definition* [ed. E. P. Sanders, A. I. Baumgarten, and A. Mendelson; 3 vols.; Philadelphia: Fortress, 1980–1982], 2:115–56, here 149–55) emphasizes a general concern with strengthening unity post 70. Van der Horst ("Birkat ha-Minim," 368) concurs,

arguing that it was "never intended to throw Christians out of the synagogues ... [but it] served to strengthen the bonds of unity within the nation."

20. Carter, *Matthew: Storyteller,* ch. 4.

21. Kimmelman, "Birkat ha-Minim," 234–35.

22. Schiffman, "At the Crossroads."

23. Cassidy, *John's Gospel;* Rensberger, *Johannine Faith;* Carter, *Pontius Pilate.*

24. For elaboration, see W. Carter, *Matthew and Empire: Initial Explorations* (Harrisburg, Pa.: Trinity Press International, 2001). For further discussion, see W. Carter, *John and Empire* (Harrisburg, Pa.: Trinity Press International, forthcoming).

25. So Livy, 4.4.4; 28.28.11; Tibullus, 2.5.23; Ovid, *Fasti,* 3.72, Virgil, *Aen.* 1.279–283.

26. Karris, *Jesus,* 102–7.

27. For explanation, see ch. 5 n. 2, above.

PART THREE

JOHN: EVANGELIST

CHAPTER 9

John the Evangelist: Author and "Author-ity"

Our discussion of the likely interpretive work that produced the gospel (ch. 7, above) and of the ongoing interpretive work that led to multiple versions of it for changing circumstances (ch. 8, above) has raised the question of the identity and role of John whose name is associated with the gospel. The previous two chapters have alerted us to some of the complexity of the issue and to the need for a flexible understanding of authorship that includes the possibility of multiple authors or editors (redactors) and for defining the author as the one whose ideas are expressed in the gospel (its "author-ity"), distinct from the actual writer or writers.[1] This chapter investigates some of the claims about the identity, geographical location, date, and cultural environment of these authors/editors. I will suggest that

- we do not have enough evidence to conclude who the gospel's author or authors were;

- the apostle John may well have been associated with the development and proclamation of the early traditions about Jesus that play a significant role in the later gospel, but the apostle John did not write the gospel;

- we do not know where the author/s (and writer/s-editor/s-redactor/s) lived;

- we can know something about the cultural contexts in which the author/s lived;

- he (or she?) was perhaps a hellenistic Jew;

- whoever was responsible for the gospel's final form probably worked in the 90s C.E.

The Gospel according to John

The gospel does not explicitly identify its author.[2] This claim sounds strange because, after all, we know that the gospel is identified as "the gospel according to John" and throughout we have referred to this John as its author.

The matter, however, is more complex. The earliest manuscript evidence for "According to John" as the gospel's title appears in two papyri, one ($\mathfrak{P}^{66}$) dating from around 200 and the other ($\mathfrak{P}^{75}$) dating from the third century. It seems to have been added to the gospel late in the second century. Not only does this "According to" statement not tell us who John is (and John was a common name in the first and second centuries); in addition, this earliest evidence for linking the name John to this gospel does not appear until seventy to one hundred years after the gospel's (almost?) final form.

Irenaeus, the bishop of Lugdunum (Lyon) in Gaul, writing about 180 C.E., reports that a gnostic writer, Ptolemy, a disciple of Valentinus, offered an interpretation of the gospel's prologue, which Ptolemy ascribes to "John, disciple of the Lord" (*Haer.* 1.8.5). Another gnostic writer, Heracleon, who wrote the first commentary on the gospel, likewise attributed it to John "disciple of the Lord" (Origen, *Commentarii in evangelium Joannis* 6.3).[3] Irenaeus attacks these gnostic readings of the gospel for various reasons, but he, too, identifies its author as John: "Then John the disciple of the Lord, who also had rested on his breast/ chest, himself published a gospel while he dwelt at Ephesus in Asia" (*Haer.* 3.1.1).

The image of John resting on Jesus' breast or chest, an image of intimate relationship,[4] appears in John 13:23: "One of his disciples—the one whom Jesus loved—was reclining next to [lying close to the breast/ chest of] him." But although Irenaeus, perhaps reflecting gnostic claims, identifies this loved disciple as John, John's gospel does not do so. Irenaeus, not the gospel, supplies the name of John to identify this "loved disciple."[5] And he does not indicate which John this would be. A reasonable guess is that he means John the son of Zebedee, but Irenaeus does not explicitly say so; another John could be in view. And there is a time gap of nearly one hundred years between the likely time of writing and this first linkage of the gospel with a figure called John, probably John the son of Zebedee.

Author, or Authors and Editors?

The gospel, however, undermines the claim that John the son of Zebedee was the gospel's author, in the following ways:[6]

1. Nowhere in the gospel is a disciple by the name of John mentioned. There are nineteen references to John the Baptist and four references to Peter's father ("son of John" 1:42; 21:15–17), but no disciple is explicitly identified as John. The "sons of Zebedee" are mentioned only once, in 21:2, and there they are identified by a father-son relationship, not by name. It is only from the other gospels that we know their names to be James and John (Mark 1:19; Matt 4:21; Luke 5:10).

2. Whereas in the Synoptics John the son of Zebedee was a Galilean fisherman (Mark 1:16–20; Matt 27:55–56), the Gospel of John focuses much more on Jerusalem than on Galilee (Jesus spends only 1:43–2:12; 4:1–3, 43–54; 6:1–7:9 in Galilee). John has no fishing scenes until chapter 21, which seems to have been added by a later editor (see its likely original ending in 20:30–31).

3. The Synoptics identify three events in which Peter, James, and John are specially associated with Jesus (the healing of Jairus's daughter; the transfiguration; the garden of Gethsemane). But John's gospel does not single out these three disciples, does not mention James the brother of John, and does not include these events (Gethsemane is not identified, and there is no struggle when Jesus is arrested in 18:1–11).

4. Other inconsistencies with the Synoptics include these: John the son of Zebedee desires to incinerate the Samaritan village in Luke 9:54, whereas John's gospel presents Samaritans positively (John 4); exorcisms with which John is especially associated in the Synoptics are missing in John's gospel;[7] and all the disciples flee from Jesus after his arrest in the Synoptics (Mark 14:50) whereas the beloved disciple in John remains at the cross (John 19:25–27).

5. Mark 10:39 records a prophecy from Jesus that the sons of Zebedee would share Jesus' fate. James dies as a martyr in Acts 12:2, but no first-century text records John's martyrdom. A fifth-century tradition from Philip of Side claims that John was martyred at the same time as James. Would Mark 10:39 be

included in a gospel written about 70 C.E. if Jesus' words had not already come true? Was John son of Zebedee dead long before the Gospel of John was written?

These factors make it most unlikely that John the son of Zebedee is the gospel's author, as later traditions claim. Perhaps John's modesty meant that he did not actively promote himself in the story. But this argument comes up short if one identifies the beloved disciple as John, who is always boasting of his special relationship with Jesus.

Moreover, when the gospel does refer to its writing, it does so in plural terms. In 21:24–25, at the gospel's conclusion, we find these claims:

> This is *the disciple* who is testifying to these things and has written them [or "who has had them written"],[8] and *we* know that *his* testimony is true. But there are also many other things that Jesus did; if every one of them were written down, *I* suppose that the world itself could not contain the books that would be written.

These two concluding verses seem to identify three parties involved in producing the gospel: "the disciple"/"his," "we," and "I."

1. The "disciple who . . . has written them [or 'had them written']" is difficult to identify with any certainty. Following 21:20–23, it likely points to the mysterious and unnamed "disciple whom Jesus loved" mentioned in those verses, but it may instead begin a separate and concluding section that refers to another disciple. Moreover, what exactly has this disciple written (or had written)? Does "these things" refer just to chapter 21, which seems to have been added to an earlier version, or to an earlier version of the whole gospel? Further, the declaration that "we know that his testimony is true" does not indicate whether he is an eyewitness or is passing on material from others.

2. "We" indicates a confessing group. Similar confessions appear in 1:14 ("we have seen his glory") and 3:11 ("we speak of what we know"). This group might comprise several authors engaged in writing the gospel (one of whom is "I"), or a group of disciples who knew Jesus (the Twelve do not figure prominently in John), or the Johannine school or community, wherever this community was located (see below).[9] The gospel speaks the community's confession. Does it suggest a committee effort in its composition?

3. "I" has added at least the last two verses, perhaps even all of chapter 21, since an earlier version of the gospel seems to have ended in 20:30–31. Some have suggested that this redactor added other material throughout the gospel (such as 19:35). If this is so, the gospel's earlier version would not have contained an eyewitness claim.

These verses suggest that we have a source ("the disciple"), an author or authors ("we" the evangelist), and an editor, or redactor ("I"). If "the disciple" is identified as the "beloved disciple," who has written (or has had written) and been a source for part of, or an earlier version of, the gospel, what can we know about this figure?

The "Disciple Whom Jesus Loved"

The "disciple whom Jesus loved" appears six times:

- 13:23–26: Leaning on Jesus' chest at the last meal, this disciple, at Peter's urging, asks Jesus about the one who will betray Jesus.

- 19:25–27: At the cross Jesus gives his mother to this disciple as his own mother.

- 20:2–10: This disciple, hearing from Mary Magdalene that Jesus' body is not in the tomb, races Peter to the tomb.

- 21:7: While fishing with Peter, this disciple recognizes the risen Jesus.

- 21:20–23: Peter asks Jesus about this disciple's destiny. Jesus' answer seems to have caused confusion that this disciple would not die before Jesus returned. The explanation suggests he died before the redactor ("I") added the last part of the gospel.

- 21:24: The redactor affirms this disciple as the reliable source of the gospel's material.

The beloved disciple enjoys a special relationship with Jesus, is prominent at crucial points in the story (the Last Supper, the crucifixion, the empty tomb, the resurrection appearances of Jesus), and is presented as a perceptive witness who has insight into the events and Jesus' significance (20:8–9; 21:7).[10] Clearly, he has an authoritative and central role. But strangely, he does not appear until chapter 13 and is not identified with any of the events or disciples that appear in the first twelve chapters. In chapter 21 Peter goes fishing with Thomas, Nathanael, the sons of Zebedee, and two unidentified disciples (21:2). One of these six (not Peter), it seems, is identified as the beloved disciple five verses later, when he recognizes the risen Jesus (21:7). But the gospel does not say which individual this is. Nor does it give any indication earlier that the beloved disciple might be a fisherman or come from Galilee.

Following Irenaeus, some scholars have identified the beloved disciple as John the son of Zebedee.[11] The possibility is kept open by the reference to the "sons of Zebedee" in the list of disciples in 21:2; one of those listed seems to be identified as the beloved disciple in 21:7. This position is also aided by the linkage of the beloved disciple with Peter in four of the six references. The pairing of Peter and John is evident on a few occasions in the other gospels (e.g., Matt 17:1) and in Acts (e.g., Acts 3:1–11).

But there are difficulties with identifying the beloved disciple as John the son of Zebedee:

1. The absence of any references to the beloved disciple in Jesus' public ministry in the first twelve chapters and the absence of John the fisherman from Galilee from the gospel's narrative speak against the beloved disciple being this person (Mark 1:16–20 par.; Matt 27:55–56).

2. Along similar lines, the association of the beloved disciple only with Jerusalem poses a difficulty.

3. If the beloved disciple were the gospel's writer, it would seem to be less than appropriate for the gospel's author to draw attention to his special relationship and identity as the one Jesus loved.

4. Some scholars have identified as the beloved disciple the un-named disciple with Peter in 18:15. But it is difficult to explain how a Galilean fisherman would be known to the elite high priest in Jerusalem.[12]

5. Against claims of a special link between Peter and John is the ob-servation that the gospel does not support this association. As we have noted, John is not named in the gospel. The only named disciples with which Peter is associated (apart from Thomas, Nathanael, and the unnamed sons of Zebedee listed in 21:2) are his brother Andrew (1:40–44; 6:8) and Mary Magdalene (20:1), neither of whom is listed in 21:2.

Does the gospel offer any other possible contenders for identifying the beloved disciple? [13] Some have suggested Lazarus.[14] He is identified as being loved by Jesus (11:3, 5, 36). He appears in John 11, two chapters before the first reference to the beloved disciple in 13:23–26. He lives in Bethany of Judea. The rumor of 21:23 that the beloved disciple would not die might be related to Lazarus being raised from the dead. But the case is hardly conclusive. The whole world is said to be loved in 3:16. In 12:9, when Lazarus is again mentioned after the raising, he is described not as "the disciple whom Jesus loved" but as "Lazarus, whom he [Jesus] had raised from the dead." And the gospel does not explicitly identify Lazarus as the beloved disciple. Moreover, Mary and Martha are also said to be loved by Jesus in 11:5.

Some have suggested that the quest to identify a historical person is not only impossible but misdirected. The figure, so the argument goes, is symbolic and representational, not historical.[15] His importance is literary, as a figure in the story. He represents ideal disciples, in intimate relation with Jesus, faithful to him (unlike the betrayer), attentive to Jesus' teaching, exercising care for Jesus' family, focused on the cross and empty tomb, able to recognize and serve the risen Jesus. Certainly the beloved disciple exhibits these traits of discipleship. But the insistence on his role as an authoritative witness to parts of Jesus' ministry, together with the references to his death (21:20–23), suggests some historical, as well as literary, identity, even if this identity remains elusive for us.

Second- and Third-Century Sources about the Gospel

Where the gospel is imprecise and/or uninformative about its authorship, second- and third-century writers fill in the gaps.[16] Notably, they specify the identity of the author and of the beloved disciples as John the disciple of Jesus (probably referring to the son of Zebedee) and link the gospel with Ephesus. In making these claims, do they offer historical information, or are their concerns elsewhere?

As noted, the earliest links of the gospel with the name John come from some mid-second-century gnostic writers. Since our source for information about their views is Irenaeus, we are limited by what he cites and by his bias against them. But the claim of John's authorship of the gospel is one item on which he finds agreement with them. In Irenaeus, writing about 180 C.E., about a decade after them, this John seems to have become the son of Zebedee, although not explicitly identified as such.[17] And about the same time (ca. 180–200 C.E.), the Muratorian Canon identifies "John, one of the disciples," as the gospel's writer, though without specifying which John.

How does Irenaeus know John is the gospel's author? Does he simply take over this claim from the gnostic writers? Or does he have other information? He mentions two figures who he claims had some links with John but neither of whom attests the gospel being written by John. One of these figures is Papias. Earlier in the second century, Papias had written expositions of Jesus' teaching. His writings, however, survive only in quotations from later writers. Irenaeus describes Papias as "a hearer of John and a companion of Polycarp" (*Haer.* 5.33.4; also Eusebius, *Hist. eccl.* 3.39.1). But Papias himself says that he did not know John,[18] and Irenaeus does not claim that Papias attests John as the writer of the gospel in Ephesus.

The fourth-century writer Eusebius also quotes Papias. According to Eusebius, Papias claims to have inquired from those who had "followed the presbyters" about "the words of the presbyters" or disciples. He identifies the presbyters as Andrew, Peter, Philip, Thomas, James, John, and Matthew. He then goes on to mention another John, saying that he also inquired what "Aristion and the presbyter John, the disciples of the Lord, were saying" (Eusebius, *Hist. eccl.* 3.39.2–4). Papias thus mentions two groups of disciples and two Johns without linking either John to the writing of the gospel. Not only does Papias not identify John the son of Zebedee as the gospel's author; he muddies the waters by introducing the name of another John, John the Elder, who some have suggested might be the gospel's author.

The second figure whom Irenaeus mentions is Polycarp, bishop of Smyrna. Irenaeus claims to have learned much from Polycarp when Irenaeus was a boy. He remembers Polycarp's "discourses which he made to the people, how he reported his intercourse with John and with the others who had seen the Lord, how he remembered their words" (Irenaeus, *Letter to Florinus*, quoted by Eusebius, *Hist. eccl.* 5.20.4–8). Irenaeus suggests an authoritative chain spanning nearly a century from John to Polycarp to himself. But Irenaeus does not actually say that Polycarp attests John's writing of the gospel. Polycarp wrote a letter to the church at Philippi and did not mention John. And a later biography of Polycarp by Pionius does not mention Polycarp knowing John.

It seems, then, that it was not until the mid- to late second century that some gnostic writings, around the time of Irenaeus and the Muratorian canon, identified the gospel's author as a disciple, John, probably the son of Zebedee. This identification was made even though there is little historical evidence for it and though the beloved disciple is unlikely to have been John the son of Zebedee, as we have already seen.

Some scholars have suggested that Irenaeus misidentified the author, mistakenly confusing him with the son of Zebedee instead of the actual author, another John, perhaps either John Mark or John the Elder, mentioned by Papias.[19] But there is no compelling information linking these Johns to the gospel. More likely, the claim that John the son of Zebedee wrote the gospel emerged out of a context of disputes among various groups.[20] These groups viewed the gospel as useful for supporting the practices and understandings that they were advocating. For example, this gospel figured in:

- the Quartodeciman controversy in Asia, over whether to observe Easter as a Christian Passover precisely on the fourteenth of Nisan or on the following Sunday;

- the Montanist controversy, over the role of the Spirit in Christian life and communities;

- the controversy with the Alogi, who denied the roles of the Logos and the Spirit, with one writer, Gaius, rejecting John's authorship partly on the basis of the gospel's order of events and omission of key incidents (when compared with the Synoptics) and attributing it to the gnostic Cerinthus;

- the controversies with gnostics over knowledge of God and cosmic, rather than salvation-historical, views of salvation.

In disputes, the authority of those to whom one appeals matters. As noted, it is in the context of gnostic claims and Irenaeus's counterclaims that the link with John the son of Zebedee emerges most clearly. Attributing authorship of the gospel to a disciple of Jesus brought "author-ity" and legitimation to the various claims that diverse groups wanted to make on the basis of the Gospel according to John.

An Arbitrary Choice or Historical Memory?

Although the evidence points to this mid-to-late-second-century link between the gospel and John, there remains the question of why John's name should emerge as the "author-ity" or "author-ization" for this gospel. Why not Andrew or Peter or Nathanael or Mary Magdalene if it was primarily a matter of finding someone who had been associated with Jesus to provide authority for the gospel?

This question suggests that linking John with the gospel was not an arbitrary choice as some have suggested. Rather, it suggests that the disciple John, son of Zebedee, had some connection with the gospel's origin.[21] What this connection might be cannot be established with any certainty, and so we can only speculate. Perhaps John was influential in collecting and preaching the initial material about Jesus (sayings and signs) that later developed into the gospel. Perhaps John was significant in giving a collection of material some of the distinctive theological flavor that marks the gospel. Perhaps John was an important teacher and preacher in the church from which the gospel would later emerge. Or perhaps John was associated with the figure known as the beloved disciple.

Any of these scenarios could readily include loyal disciples of John, especially the so-called beloved disciple, who honored his memory and continued his work with the later writing of (several versions of?) the gospel. Various traditions from the late second century on (including the Muratorian Fragment and Clement of Alexandria) attest involvement of disciples of John in the gospel's origin. They thereby also ensured that John's name would come to be linked with the gospel in the second century. We simply cannot determine which of these, or other, scenarios might be the most accurate, but they do provide possible explanations for the gospel's association with John the disciple of Jesus.

Is an Author and Audience Profile Possible?

If we cannot know the author's (or authors') name(s) with any certainty, can we know anything else about the gospel's author(s), the one(s) responsible for most of the written gospel as we have it, and/or its editor(s)? In addressing such a question, we have to interpret clues from the gospel. And can we know anything about those for whom they wrote? When we look for clues from the gospel about authors, we should be aware that a writing reveals something about the audience for whom it is written. An author, for example, is not going to use a language or employ cultural traditions that are inaccessible to an audience, but will shape the communication in ways that are appropriate to the intended audience. While focusing below on an author profile, we are simultaneously identifying some features of the community for whom the gospel was written.

Gender

The name John implies a male author. But if the name is attached to the gospel later in the second century, the possibility remains that a woman was involved in its writing. Moreover, in debating the possible identity of the beloved disciple, to whom is attributed an important role in the gospel's origin (21:24–25), scholars have often observed that Lazarus is said to be loved by Jesus (11:3, 5, 36), as already mentioned. But they have often overlooked a similar description for Mary and Martha: "Jesus loved Martha and her sister and Lazarus" (11:5). Could Mary or Martha be the beloved disciple? Mary Magdalene plays a crucial role in encountering and proclaiming the risen Jesus in chapter 20. Could she be a significant force in the gospel's origin? We have observed important roles for women in the gospel: preaching the good news (4:28–30, 39), witnessing the crucifixion (19:25–27), and encountering and proclaiming the risen Jesus (20:1–18). Such references may point to a community in which women had valued leadership roles. It would be quite consistent with such roles for a woman to be involved in the gospel's composition.[22] But in the final analysis, no evidence exists to determine the author's (or authors') gender.

Date of Writing

Several factors suggest that the final form of the gospel was probably completed in the 90s C.E.[23] It had to have been written by about 130, since the earliest manuscript evidence for the gospel, a papyrus fragment of 18:31–33, 37–38 ($\mathfrak{P}^{52}$), dates from about 125. The writings of Ignatius (ca. 110) and Justin Martyr (ca. 135) may echo John in several expressions, but the evidence is not especially convincing.[24]

If John knew Mark, as some suggest (see the discussion in ch. 7, above), 70 C.E., the approximate time when Mark is written, provides the earliest date. The reference in John 21:18–19 to Peter's crucifixion, perhaps taking place in the 60s, also points to this time. More helpful are the references in 2:13–22 and 11:48–50 to Rome's destruction of Jerusalem and the temple in 70. By claiming Jesus to be the definitive revealer of God's purposes, the gospel addresses issues posed by the loss of the temple in this post-70 period (the revelation of God's will, God's presence, atonement).[25] The struggle with a synagogue community over these claims also points to a post-70 era with its growing consolidation among Jewish groups (9:22; 12:42; 16:2). The death of the beloved disciple (21:22–23) may also have been a catalyst for (the final form of?) the gospel. The 90s seems, then, to allow a reasonable period of time for the developing gospel tradition to be expressed in the gospel's final form.[26]

Where Did the Author/Writer Live?

Several places have been suggested for the writer's and audience's residence. The explanations of Jewish terms and customs, together with the inclusion of Gentiles (7:35–36; 11:51–52; 12:19, 32), suggests a non-Palestinian context at least for the final form(s).[27]

Antioch or Syria has been suggested, but there is little compatibility between John and the Gospel of Matthew, which likely originated from Antioch.[28] And as noted above, Ignatius, leader of the church in Antioch about 110, certainly does not draw on John with any frequency, if at all. These observations do not preclude a place of origin elsewhere in Syria, but the gospel's importance suggests its likely link with a significant center.

As also mentioned, Irenaeus claims that John wrote in Ephesus in the Roman province of Asia (*Haer.* 3.1.1), and Ephesus has continued to receive considerable support.[29] But in addition to the problem of the late-second-century linkage of John with the gospel, there is little early evidence for John having lived or written in Ephesus. No New Testament writings link John with Ephesus; both Acts 20 and the deutero-pauline letter to the Ephesians are silent on John. Ignatius writes to Ephesus but does not mention John, and Papias does not link John to Ephesus. Justin Martyr, writing at Ephesus about 135 C.E., mentions John as having lived there but does not mention that he wrote a gospel (*Dialogue with Trypho* 81.4). The *Acts of John,* from perhaps "the second half of the second century,"[30] works very hard to establish John as the one who brings the Christian message to Ephesus, but it does not mention his writing a gospel there.

Alexandria is another contender.[31] With at least a million Jews according to Philo (*Against Flaccus* 43), interaction with a synagogue community was likely. We have seen the importance of wisdom traditions and of dualistic formulations for the gospel; these traditions and ways of thinking were strong in Alexandria, with writings such as Wisdom of Solomon and those of Philo (see further below). The distance of Alexandria from centers such as Antioch, Asia Minor, and Rome (with which the Synoptic Gospels are associated) may explain somewhat the distinctive telling of the Jesus story. The earliest papyrus of the gospel comes from Egypt ($\mathfrak{P}^{52}$), and Egyptian gnostics such as Valentinus clearly valued the gospel. If John's inclusion of Samaritans among believers in Jesus reflects any information about the gospel's readers (John 4)—and it is a debatable proposition—it may be important to note there is some evidence for Samaritans in Alexandria.[32]

None of these possibilities is immediately compelling, and none determines the interpretation of the gospel. Tradition favors Ephesus, while a number of factors could support Alexandria.

Multicultural Context

The issue of location raises the question of the various cultural contexts that might influence the author(s) and hearers of the story. The gospel reflects a multicultural world; its author(s) and audience live in the interplay of the Jewish, Hellenistic, and Roman worlds.[33]

Jewish Culture

In making its central claim that Jesus is the definitive revealer of God's life-giving purposes, the gospel draws upon and engages numerous Jewish traditions and institutions. The opening verses evoke the Genesis creation accounts to declare that "all things came into being through him" (1:3). The Scriptures (5:39; see the discussion in ch. 7, above) and Moses (5:45–47) are claimed to bear witness to Jesus, who is their definitive interpreter (8:17–18). The author draws on traditions about a Messiah or Christ to present Jesus as the one commissioned to be God's agent or Son to reveal God's purposes in Jesus' life-giving works and words (3:16–21; 7:25–44). In a context of numerous claims for heavenly revealers of God's purposes, Jesus outreveals all of them.[34] Whereas they ascend for a brief glimpse of the heavens and then descend, he was in the beginning in intimate relationship with God (1:1, 18). Descending from God in heaven, Jesus is sent to speak of the One whom he has seen, heard, and knows (1:18; 5:19–20, 30; 8:28, 38). He condemns the center of power, the unjust temple (2:13–22), claims to reinterpret the Sabbath, rituals, and festivals (2:1–12; 5:1–18; 7:37–39; ch. 9; 10:22–39), and offers forgiveness for sin (1:29, 36). He constantly attacks the Jerusalem-based elite, whose vision of society is at odds with Jesus' revelation of God's life-giving purposes (chs. 5–12). Consistent with the promise to Abraham to bless all the nations of the earth (Gen 12:1–3; John 8:39–59), he demonstrates that those purposes embrace women and Samaritans (John 4), the physically damaged and the poor (5:1–16; 9:1–8), and Jews and Gentiles (7:35–36; 11:51–52; 12:19, 32).[35] Loyalty to Jesus means clashes with synagogue leaders and separation (9:22–34).

This attests the gospel's critical engagement with important issues of Jewish identity and practice and with central Jewish institutions and authoritative figures. It exhibits the gospel's claim that the means of encountering God's life-giving purposes are found only in Jesus and his interpretation of the temple, law, Scriptures, and acts of worship. It addresses central issues of the post-70 world, after Rome had destroyed Jerusalem and its temple—issues of knowing God's purposes and will, encountering God's presence, and experiencing atonement—by pointing to Jesus, the revealer of God's purposes.

Scholars have also noted parallels with the Dead Sea Scrolls, discovered at Qumran in the late 1940s.[36] Especially significant have been a

dualistic way of framing the world and dualistic vocabulary that resemble John's: truth and falsehood, life and death, light and dark, God
and the devil. The Scrolls also share John's emphasis on knowing
God and on commitment to a community marked by love for one another (13:34–35; 15:12). Yet obvious differences between John and
Qumran should not be overlooked. Whereas John is focused on Jesus,
the Qumran material focuses, for example, on the law and the temple.
Scholars try to account for these similarities and differences in various
and much debated ways. Some suggest quite specific connections. Was
one of the key voices in the formation of the traditions about Jesus that
make up the gospel a member of the Qumran community? Did some
followers of John the Baptist, influenced by Qumran thinking, join the
movement? Others suggest more generic or indirect influence. Was such
thinking in the air as part of a broader cultural matrix, and do the similarities between John and Qumran attest this pervasive way of thinking?
More recent contributions have played down claims of direct influence.[37] In the final analysis, we do not know for sure. But the similarities
reinforce the notion that author(s) and audience were familiar with
diverse Jewish traditions.

Hellenistic Influence

Hellenism was not a cultural context from which Judaism was separated. The gospel, even as it engaged Jewish issues, was written in Greek,
and so its author(s) and audience experienced at least that much Hellenistic influence. Many Jews lived outside Judea and were familiar with,
and influenced by, Hellenistic philosophical and cultural traditions.
Such influence, for example, on wisdom traditions is evident in the Wisdom of Solomon.[38] Wisdom writings form part of the diverse cultural
phenomenon known as Hellenistic Judaism. Several scholars have suggested that the author(s) of John employed language ("life," "light,"
"truth") and ideas (rebirth, descending and ascending redeemer figures,
mystic knowledge of God, immortality) familiar to the Hellenistic world
in order to gain a hearing for the gospel.[39] At least two possible points
of contact between the gospel and Hellenistic traditions have been
suggested.

The writings of Philo, an educated Jewish leader in Alexandria and
representative of Hellenistic Judaism who died in 50 C.E., form one suggested point of contact. In his interpretation of Scripture, Philo is especially indebted to Plato and the interpretation in middle Platonism,
although Stoic and Pythagorean ideas also appear. A number of similarities between Philo and John's gospel can be noted.[40] Both use the no-

tions of the *logos,* or word, as a revealer of God and of a heavenly man as
well as the symbols of light, water, and shepherd. For both, knowing
God is paramount and constitutes eternal life. God reveals himself in the
Scriptures, notably, for Philo, through Moses. To accept this revelation
through faith and love is to become a child of God.

Although they share some similarities of language and theme, there
are also major differences, notably the gospel's christocentric focus. The
logos, for Philo, is immanent in creation and is not a human being or
even a personal guide and companion. By contrast, for the gospel, the
Word becomes flesh in the person of Jesus (1:14). Likewise John's man
from heaven lives not, as for Philo, as the *nous,* or mind, in all people but
as a human being among humans, where he is crucified and raised. Nor
does John's gospel evidence the comprehensive philosophical framework evident in Philo or engage in the extensive allegorical reading of
Scripture evident in Philo. Any literary dependence is difficult to establish, but the affinities may result from a common cultural milieu that included scriptural material, especially wisdom traditions.[41]

A second point of contact is the suggestion that John's author(s)/
editor(s) were influenced by the philosophical religious traditions that
would be recorded in the second-to-third-century writings called the
Hermetica.[42] This collection centered on the Egyptian teacher Hermes
Trismegistus, who was deified as the god Thoth. Again there are certain
similar words ("light," "life") and themes (knowing God; revealed
knowledge; rebirth) but quite different frameworks and worldviews.
The dating of the Hermetica to the time after John's gospel also
poses problems. The most sustainable conclusion seems to be that the
similarities attest some of the vocabulary and concerns of a larger cultural milieu.

Roman Imperial Power

Investigating possible cultural influences on John's author(s) and
audience, scholars have emphasized religious and intellectual matters
and frequently neglected the sociopolitical and economic context of the
Roman Empire. John's gospel derives from a world dominated by
Roman power exercised through a hierarchical social structure and economic (land ownership, taxation), military, social (alliances with local
elites, patronage), ideological (imperial theology and cult), rhetorical,
and judicial means.[43] The temple-based Jerusalem elite, allied with
Rome and its representative, the governor Pontius Pilate, embody this
power structure in the crucifixion of Jesus. Roman power is clearly
evident in other ways in the gospel:

1. The gospel contains references to the fall of Jerusalem and its temple in 70 C.E. at the hands of Rome (2:13–22; 11:48). The latter verse describes well-known imperial realities. If the Jerusalem leaders, who exercise power in alliance and compliance with Rome, do not bring Jesus under control (some think that he is king of the Jews, 6:15), they will lose this power and their positions of wealth and prestige, and Rome will exercise military retaliation by destroying "both our holy place and our nation."

2. The gospel tells the story of Jesus' crucifixion, a distinctly Roman form of execution reserved for lowly ranked provincials and those who challenge Roman power. Pilate executes Jesus after taunting his allies, the Jerusalem leaders, and eliciting from them a stunning confession that renounces all covenant commitments with the God of Israel when they declare, "We have no king but the emperor" (19:15).

3. The gospel engages in theological analysis of the social order, which rejects and crucifies Jesus, God's anointed agent. The gospel styles it as "the world," the domain of humans created and loved by God (1:10a–b; 3:16) but rejecting God's purposes of life for all people (1:10c). This world has a "ruler" (12:31; 14:30; 16:11), usually identified as Satan or the devil; thus, Rome's world manifests the devil's purposes, not God's. The same language, "rulers," is also used for the elite, the Jerusalem-based, Rome-allied leaders who oppose Jesus (3:1; 7:26, 48; 12:42). They work with Pilate to execute him, suggesting an alliance between Pilate, the Jerusalem leaders, and the devil against God's anointed. Jesus calls them children of the devil in 8:44. And in 19:11 Jesus tells Pilate that Pilate has no power over him, just as he declares in 14:30 that the ruler of the world has no power over him.

4. The gospel depicts the disastrous results of Rome's rule in the poor and the physically broken.[44] In a society in which elite practices ensure that 97 percent of the people know degrees of poverty as their daily reality, begging is inevitable (9:8), hunger is common (6:1–14), disease and physical brokenness are rife (4:46–54; 5:1–15, esp. 5:3; 6:2; 9:1–7; ch. 11), and the sharing of resources through almsgiving is a basic survival strategy (12:5–8; 13:29). Practices and attitudes elevate the elite and demean the nonelite, whether by gender and ethnicity (4:9) or by status (7:49, the ignorant crowds are cursed; 9:34, the elite resent that

the healed blind beggar is teaching them). These are the everyday manifestations of Rome's power structures, and the gospel presents them as contrary to God's purposes.

5. The gospel offers God's alternative to the hierarchical, unjust order enforced by eternal Rome. As noted in chapter 5, above, the gospel proclaims eternal life, or "life of the age," a life centered on knowing God (17:3). Death and sin are no more, and God's purposes transform Rome's present existence, which is marked by scarcity and injustice for most. The actions of Jesus in healing and providing abundant food and wine anticipate this just and blessed existence.

The author(s)/editor(s) are very aware of this Roman world and of the challenge that Jesus presents to it. It is part of the complex, multicultural world in which they live and to which they attempt to address the good news.

Socioeconomic Status

If the author(s) wrote the gospel themselves, their literacy suggests their higher socioeconomic status. The highest concentration of literacy skills was found in about 15 percent of urban males, including professional scribes, though some slaves also had such skills.[45] If the gospel was dictated, resources, perhaps from a wealthier, higher-status group patron, would be needed to finance the writing. John's audience would, in all likelihood, comprise a cross-section of the population, reflecting a few of the elite and the extensive range of poor, low-status, and powerless people who constituted most of the population.

Ethnicity

The ethnicity of those involved in its writing is, given the intermixing of Jewish, Hellenistic, and Roman worlds, difficult to determine. The earliest forms of the tradition could well have been shaped by a Palestinian Jew, with the later author(s) more likely being Hellenistic Jews.

Conclusion

This chapter has made the following points: The gospel does not identify an author. Several figures may have been involved in writing several versions of the gospel. There is no prominence for, or special link with, the disciple John in the gospel. The author is conventionally understood to be a male, but there is no evidence for the author's gender. The title "According to John" is at the earliest a late-second-century addition. An unnamed, elusive figure called the beloved disciple plays a crucial role in author-izing or being an author-ity for the developing traditions. And second- and third-century traditions author-ized the gospel by linking it with "John, the disciple of Jesus," likely the son of Zebedee, a link that may reflect his strategic role in the origins and/or shaping of the traditions that inform the later gospel.

Concerning the author(s) and editor(s) involved in the writing of the gospel, we have only limited clues about their gender, the date of writing, the location, their socioeconomic status, ethnicity, and the precise nature of their interactions with Jewish, Hellenistic, and Roman cultures.

Notes

1. Brown, *Introduction to the Gospel*, 189–91, clarifies the distinction between "author" and "writer."

2. For good discussions with differing conclusions, see Barrett, *John*, 83–114; Brown, *Gospel according to John* 1:lxxxvii–civ; *Introduction to the Gospel*, 189–219; Culpepper, *Gospel and Letters*, 29–37.

3. For a discussion, see E. Pagels, *The Johannine Gospel in Gnostic Exegesis: Heracleon's Commentary on John* (Nashville: Abingdon, 1973).

4. The same language and image appear in 1:18 to denote the close relationship between Jesus (Son) and God (Father).

5. *Acts of John* 89–90, from about the same time as Irenaeus (B. Ehrman, *Lost Scriptures: Books That Did Not Make It into the New Testament* [Oxford: Oxford University Press, 2003], 94), links John, Jesus' breast, and being loved by Jesus.

6. P. Parker, "John the Son of Zebedee and the Fourth Gospel," *JBL* 81 (1962): 35–43.

7. See Matt 9:32; 12:22; Mark 1:23, 32; 5:1; 7:24; 9:17; Luke 11:14.

8. The verb can indicate one's own writing or one's dictation; cf. 1 Cor 4:13, 14:37, 16:21, which indicates that the letter was dictated, although Paul claims to have written it.

9. On a Johannine school, see R. A. Culpepper, *The Johannine School: An Evaluation of the Johannine-School Hypothesis Based on an Investigation of the Nature of Ancient Schools* (Missoula, Mont.: Scholars Press, 1975).

10. R. Bauckham, "The Beloved Disciple as Ideal Author" *JSNT* 49 (1993): 21–44, here 36–38.

11. E.g., Brown, *Gospel according to John*, 1:xciii–xcviii.

12. Acts 4:13 identifies John as an "uneducated and ordinary" man. Some have concluded that he was not literate enough to write the gospel, but the conclusion does not follow, given the practices of dictation and the availability of educated scribes. The question is not, "Could John have written the gospel?" but, "Do we have any reliable historical evidence that he did?"

13. Bauckham, "Beloved Disciple," identifies the beloved disciple and the author as John the Elder. J. H. Charlesworth (*The Beloved Disciple: Whose Witness Validates the Gospel of John?* [Valley Forge, Pa.: Trinity Press International, 1995]) surveys twenty-two options (pp. 127–224) before adding a twenty-third, namely, Thomas (pp. 225–87). R. A. Culpepper (*John, the Son of Zebedee: The Life of a Legend* [Columbia: University of South Carolina Press, 1994], 72–88) considers ten diverse possibilities, including references to individuals and to larger entities: the apostle John, Lazarus, John Mark, Matthias, the rich young ruler, Paul, Benjamin, Gentile Christianity, an itinerant prophetic community, the elder who wrote 2–3 John.

14. F. Filson, "Who Was the Beloved Disciple?" *JBL* 68 (1949): 83–88; M. W. G. Stibbe, *John as Storyteller* (Cambridge: Cambridge University Press, 1992), 77–81, with John the Elder as author.

15. Bultmann (*Gospel of John*, 483–85) offers an allegorical reading. Peter (and Mary in 19:26–27) represents Jewish Christendom; John represents the Gentile Christendom of the evangelist. Schneiders ("'Because of the Woman's Testimony . . .'") argues that the beloved disciple is "a literary device (a textual paradigm) and a pluralistic historical reality. . . . [T]he textual paradigm is derived from real disciples in whom it is realized in diverse ways" (pp. 526–27).

16. For discussions, see Culpepper, *John, the Son of Zebedee*, 107–38; J. N. Sanders, *The Fourth Gospel in the Early Church* (Cambridge: Cambridge University Press, 1943).

17. Irenaeus explicitly refers to John son of Zebedee three times (*Haer.* 1.21.2; 3.12.5; 3.12.15) without linking him to the gospel.

18. As Eusebius, *Hist. eccl.* 3.39.1–2, points out in correcting Irenaeus.

19. For arguments, see Brown, *Gospel according to John*, 1:xc–xcii. Hengel (*Johannine Question*, 74–135) advocates John the Elder. For an interesting discussion on John Mark, see P. Parker, "John and John Mark," *JBL* 79 (1960): 97–110.

20. For various perspectives, see Sanders, *Fourth Gospel*; J. J. Gunther, "Early Identification of Authorship of the Johannine Writings," *Journal of Ecclesiastical History* 31 (1980): 403–27.

21. I am indebted to the discussion in Brown, *Gospel according to John*, 1:xcviii–cii.

22. Ringe (*Wisdom's Friends*, 17) addresses Jesus' identification of the beloved disciple as "son" in 19:26 by arguing that the term denotes more the well-recognized role of caring for the mother of a dying friend than specifying gender and that a male term for a female referent may have enhanced the gospel's credibility in an increasingly patriarchal church.

23. Among others, see Brown, *Introduction to the Gospel*, 206–15.

24. Barrett (*John*, 92–94) concludes that Ignatius did not know John but that Justin may have. Sanders (*Fourth Gospel*, 12–32) reaches similar conclusions.

25. Carter, "Prologue."

26. J. A. T. Robinson (*The Priority of John* [Oak Park, Ill.: Meyer-Stone, 1985], 67–93; *Redating the New Testament* [London: SCM, 1976], 254–311) suggests a much earlier date for a first (50–55 C.E.) and second (ca. 65 C.E.) edition.

27. Brown, *Introduction to the Gospel*, 199–206. On Jewish terms and customs, J. J. Gunther ("The Alexandrian Gospel and Letters of John," *CBQ* 41 [1979]: 581–603, here 582) identifies "Rabbi" (1:38), "Rabbouni" (20:16),

"Messiah" (1:41), "Cephas" (1:42), and "Siloam" (9:7); customs include purification (2:6), nonassociation with Samaritans (4:9), festivals (5:1; 6:4; 7:2), and burial (19:40).

28. Carter, *Matthew and the Margins,* 15–16.

29. E.g., Brown, *Introduction to the Gospel,* 204–6; S. van Tilborg, *Reading John in Ephesus* (Leiden: Brill, 1996).

30. Ehrman, *Lost Scriptures,* 94.

31. Gunther, "Alexandrian Gospel"; Ringe, *Wisdom's Friends,* 13–14.

32. E. Schürer, *History of the Jewish People in the Age of Jesus Christ (175 B.C.–A.D. 135)* (rev. and ed. G. Vermes, F. Millar, and M. Goodman; 3 vols. in 4; Edinburgh: T&T Clark, 1973–1987), vol. 3, part 1, pp. 42, 49, 59–60.

33. Discussion of Bultmann's dubious claims about gnostic and Mandaean influences is omitted here. For discussions, see Dodd, *Interpretation,* 97–130; Brown, *Gospel according to John,* 1:lii–lvi; Brown, *Introduction to the Gospel,* 115–50.

34. Carter, "Prologue."

35. K.-J. Kuschel, *Abraham: Sign of Hope for Jews, Christians, and Moslems* (New York: Continuum, 1995); J. Siker, *Disinheriting the Jews: Abraham in Early Christian Literature* (Louisville: Westminster John Knox, 1991).

36. J. H. Charlesworth, ed., *John and the Dead Sea Scrolls* (New York: Crossroad, 1990).

37. R. Bauckham, "Qumran and the Fourth Gospel: Is There a Connection?" in *The Scrolls and the Scriptures: Fifty Years After* (ed. S. Porter and C. Evans; Sheffield, Eng.: Sheffield Academic Press, 1997), 267–79; D. Aune, "Dualism in the Fourth Gospel and the Dead Sea Scrolls: A Reassessment of the Problem," in *Neotestimentica et philonica: Studies in Honor of Peder Borgen* (ed. D. Aune, T. Seland, and J. H. Ulrichsen; Leiden: Brill, 2003), 281–303.

38. J. J. Collins, *Between Athens and Jerusalem: Jewish Identity in the Hellenistic Diaspora* (New York: Crossroad, 1986); D. J. Harrington, *Invitation to the Apocrypha* (Grand Rapids: Eerdmans, 1999), 55–77.

39. See the summary in Gunther, "Alexandrian Gospel," 583–84; Barrett, *John,* 101; Dodd, *Interpretation,* 8–9.

40. Dodd, *Interpretation,* 54–73; Gunther, "Alexandrian Gospel," 584–88.

41. R. McL. Wilson, "Philo and the Fourth Gospel," *ExpT* 65 (1953–1954): 47–49; Brown, *Gospel according to John,* 1:lvii–lviii, 519–25.

42. See Dodd, *Interpretation,* 10–53, esp. 34–35, for linguistic similarities; Brown, *Gospel according to John,* 1:lviii–lix.

43. R. J. Cassidy, *Christians and Roman Rule in the New Testament: New Perspectives* (New York: Crossroad, 2001), 37–50; *John's Gospel;* Carter, *Matthew and Empire,* 9–53; R. Horsley, ed., *Paul and the Roman Imperial Order* (Harrisburg, Pa.: Trinity Press International, 2004), 1–23; Van den Heever, "Finding Data."

44. Karris, *Jesus.*

45. Dewey, "Gospel of John," 240, citing W. V. Harris, *Ancient Literacy* (Cambridge: Harvard University Press, 1989), 267.

CHAPTER 10

The Good News according to John

We have employed three perspectives to examine John's gospel. Part 1 has viewed it as a story narrated; part 2, as traditions interpreted; and part 3, as good news proclaimed. We have referred to the gospel's author, represented by the name John, as storyteller, interpreter, and evangelist (recognizing that these singular terms may refer to several figures). The term "evangelist" derives from the Greek word for "bringing good news" and signifies one who proclaims good news. This final chapter addresses the question "What is John's good news?" Or taking the gospel's title and employing the double meaning (noted in ch. 1, above) of "gospel" as both message and medium, it asks, "What is the gospel according to John?" The one-sentence answer, to be developed in this chapter, is as follows:

> The good news according to John is that Jesus is the definitive revealer of God's life-giving purposes and that his mission continues in and through the alternative community, the church, an antisociety that is sustained by the Spirit, or Paraclete, in a hostile world until God's purposes are established in full.

This chapter elaborates this summary of the good news according to John.[1] At times, it points back to the material of previous chapters rather than repeat all the elements of those discussions. It begins with Jesus' identity and mission (to use conventional theological terms, Christology and soteriology). That discussion requires that we articulate God's revealed purposes (theology and eschatology) and the sinful context that necessitates such a revelation (hamartiology). Then we consider the consequences of Jesus' mission—the creation of a community, the church, that entrusts itself to God's purposes (ecclesiology). This community is sustained and guided in those purposes by the Spirit (pneumatology) until the completion of God's purposes (eschatology). The postscript will consider briefly some of the implications of these claims for contemporary readers of John in a complex, multireligious world.

Christology: Jesus the Revealer of God's Life-Giving Purposes

Central to John's gospel is the claim that Jesus is the definitive revealer of God's life-giving purposes (1:18; 20:30–31). The gospel attests that such a claim is by no means obvious and is, indeed, controversial for several reasons. First, various Hebrew traditions recognized that God had previously revealed God's purposes. Creation and Abraham are two examples, as is the exodus from slavery in Egypt, for Moses receives a revelation of God's purposes (the Decalogue or Ten Commandments) on Mount Sinai. Subsequent prophets, such as Isaiah, attest God's just purposes. And Lady Wisdom works among humans summoning them to encounter God's ways. Thus, Jesus is not the first revealer of God's purposes. Why should he have primacy of place?

Second, in the first century C.E., and especially in the post-70 context, Jewish groups pointed to various figures who, either by visions or by ascents and journeys into the heavens, received revelations of God's purposes, revelations that some of them brought back to earth. Such figures include Enoch, Abraham, Adam, Isaiah, and Moses.[2] Jesus, then, is not the only figure whom groups claim to be the revealer of God's purposes. Why should he be the definitive revealer (1:18)?

Third, Roman propaganda proclaimed that the world was blessed by Rome's reign. Imperial theology declared that the gods, including Jupiter, had chosen Rome and its emperor to be the means by which the gods' will was accomplished among humans and their blessings revealed. Roman power, so it claimed, had divine sanction. Hierarchical Roman society, profoundly destructive for much of the population, reflected the gods' purposes. In presenting Jesus as the revealer of God's purposes, the gospel contests Rome's version of what a divinely sanctioned human society might look like. What ensures that Jesus' revelation is right?

How does John's gospel negotiate such claims and address these questions? It cannot afford to ignore them. In presenting Jesus as the definitive revealer, the gospel must establish what is so compelling about Jesus.

Origin, Identity, Agency

The gospel focuses attention heavily on Jesus' origins with God. It opens, as we have seen, with the words "In the beginning," which evoke the creation story (Gen 1:1). But unlike Genesis, the beginning to which the gospel refers is not the creation of heaven and earth but the timeless "beginning" of the existence of "the Word" in intimate relationship with God before creation: "In the beginning was the Word, and the Word was with God, and the Word was God." The Word exists before creation "with" God, a preposition that literally means in Greek "toward" God. The image is of the Word turned toward God in intimate, face-to face relationship "with" God.[3] John 1:18 confirms this intimacy with its reference to being "close to the Father's heart [in the bosom of the Father]."

The Word, however, exists not only pre-creation and in intimate relationship with God. The Word is God (1:1), and creation comes into being through the Word (1:2–3). This claim of being God is puzzling (it is repeated in 20:28). The Word seems to be both a separate, independent being yet is God. How to explain this? Does this mean that there are two Gods? The gospel strongly denies the charge of ditheism when Jesus' opponents make the claim on two occasions (5:18; 10:33). It upholds Israel's traditional affirmation that "the LORD is our God, the LORD alone" (Deut 6:4).

Contemporary Christian readers might solve the dilemma by pointing to the Christian understanding of the Trinity. But in the late first century, such an understanding did not exist. God was not understood as a triune being whose three persons share the same essence or being. This trinitarian understanding would emerge in the subsequent centuries, partly as readers wrestled with the gospel's difficult claims.

John instead settles for the paradox that the Word is both identical with God yet a separate entity. The two are connected in that the Word is God's self-revelation. We have noticed already that such a paradox is evident in Israel's wisdom traditions (Prov 8), where Wisdom exists before creation in intimate relationship with God before creation yet is an agent of creation and revealer of God's purposes among humans (see ch. 7, above). Jesus is Wisdom for John. As such, the choice of the image of the Word in these opening verses, whatever its possible affinities with Hellenistic and/or Jewish contexts, conveys the very basic notion of communication.[4] The Word, like Wisdom, is the revelation or self-manifestation of God.

The Word's pre-creation, relational existence with God as God is foundational for the gospel's revelation. Since the Word was with God in the beginning before all else, in exclusive relationship with God (John 1:1, 18), the Word's revelation of God has temporal priority over that of creation or particular events or persons. Moreover, the Word was in intimate relationship with God, and so, qualitatively, the Word's revelation surpasses all other claims of revelation by showing them to be partial and inferior at best. The gospel does not deny some revelation to Abraham (8:56), Moses (5:45–47), Isaiah (12:41), or the Scriptures (5:39). It claims, however, that they point to Jesus. No one else has "seen God" (1:18).

The Word becomes flesh (1:14) and dwells among humans in the person of Jesus. What is true for the Word is true for Jesus. Jesus is in intimate relationship with God, one with God (10:30). As wisdom, he is God in that he is the self-expression of God, the communication or revelation of God's purposes.[5] He is God made visible (12:45; 14:9), made audible (12:49; 14:10), made knowable (1:18; 14:7). He reveals what he has heard from God (8:26, 29), and what he has seen God doing (5:19–20). The emphasis on Jesus' origin frames his revelation as definitive.

So too does John's emphasis on Jesus' identity and role. He is the revealer of God's purposes because God commissions him to be:

1. John identifies Jesus as the Christ (the Greek term) or the Messiah (the Hebrew term, 1:17, 41). Recent scholarship has emphasized that expectations about a Messiah in the first century were neither uniform nor universal.[6] Not all Jews were waiting for a Messiah, and not all Jews had a checklist of features by which they could readily identify the Messiah. Among the minority who were looking for a Messiah, expectations were quite diverse. The gospel reflects some of this debate.[7]

   The basic meaning of the term "Messiah" or "Christ" is "anointed." To be anointed or "christed" is to be commissioned or legitimized to perform a particular role, usually an act of service for God. A king is anointed to exercise rule on God's behalf (Ps 2:7). A priest is anointed for priestly duties (Lev 4:3). Cyrus the Persian is commissioned to let God's people return to their land from exile in Babylon in the sixth century B.C.E. (Isa 44:28–45:1). Jesus is commissioned or anointed to reveal God's life-giving purposes. He is the agent of God's purposes.

2. The gospel also identifies Jesus as "the Son" (seventeen times), the "Son of God" (eight times), "Son of Man" (thirteen times), and "only Son of God" (four times). The adjective "only" (*monogenēs*, μονογενής), occurring in John 1:14, 18; 3:16, 18, under-

lines Jesus' one-of-a-kind role as revealer. The image of "Son" emphasizes both intimacy with God (1:18) and Jesus' special role as the commissioned agent and revealer of God's purposes. Although the Father is greater than the Son (14:28), the Father loves the Son and reveals all things to him (3:35; 5:20). The Father commissions or authorizes the Son to give life and to judge (5:21–22). The Son is dependent on, and subordinate to, the Father, doing the Father's will and works (5:30, 36), obedient to the Father's will (6:38; 12:49–50), revealing the Father's words and what he has heard from God (8:26, 28, 40; 17:8, 14). In the sense that Jesus performs the Father's purposes and will, God and Jesus are one (10:30).

In Israel's traditions, to be a son of God is to be in special or intimate relation with God and to be God's agent. Israel's kings are God's sons, chosen and loved by God to represent God's just reign among humans (Ps 2:7–11; 72). Israel is the "son" or "child" of God, chosen to be in special relationship with God as God's people, who manifest God's purposes among the nations (Hos 11:1–2).

In John's gospel, John the Baptist, Nathanael, Martha, Jesus, and the gospel itself bear witness that Jesus is Son of God (John 1:34, 49; 10:36; 11:27; 20:31). In the context of the term's previous uses and the gospel's claims, "Son of God" denotes Jesus' intimate relationship with God and his God-given commission to manifest life. In 11:27 Martha uses this title as a synonym for "Messiah," a term that designates commissioning. In 19:7 the Jerusalem elite put Jesus to death for claiming to be Son of God, the agent of God's purposes that clearly counter and resist the unjust social structure that the elite maintain. Acknowledgment of Jesus' identity and role as God's Son means participation in God's life-giving purposes, which he manifests (5:25). Refusal to acknowledge means exclusion from these purposes (3:18).

The other "son" title, "Son of Man," also emphasizes Jesus' manifestation of God's purposes. The term appears in Dan 7:13 as part of a vision in which this figure is the agent of God's reign, ending previous unjust human empires and establishing God's rule forever. In John, the term emphasizes Jesus' role as revealer of God's purposes (1:51). This role includes his descent from heaven and his lifting up on the cross in death, resurrection, and ascension (3:13–14; 6:62), vindication from judgment (5:27), and his enabling participation in the life of God's new age both now (6:27, 53; 9:35–39) and in its future establishment (5:27). The remaining uses of "Son of Man" are especially associated with Jesus' death and resurrection.[8] His resurrection reveals the limits of Rome's power and its subjection to God's purposes in the vindication of Jesus as God's agent (see further below).

3. God's commissioning of Jesus as the agent of God's life-giving purposes is also seen in the gospel's pervasive use of two verbs for "send."[9] Repeatedly John presents God as sending Jesus (5:36; 7:29; 17:18, 21, 23, 25), and Jesus as the one sent by God (5:38; 6:29). The sending of Jesus denotes God's authorizing of Jesus' mission. Jesus does not come "on my own" but because God "sent me" (8:42) to accomplish God's purposes (4:34; 5:30).

But the "sending" verbs also describe Jesus' mission as revealing God's saving purposes. God sends Jesus (a) not to condemn the world but that the world might be saved through him (3:17); (b) to utter the words of God (3:34; 7:16; 12:49); and (c) to work the works of the One who sent him (9:4). Accordingly, the recognition of Jesus as the one sent by God is crucial for participating in life with God (5:24; 17:3). Refusal to recognize this origin and legitimization is designated as opposition to God's purposes (10:36).

4. Further verbs underline Jesus' origin from God and commissioning by God: those of descending[10] from heaven (3:13; 6:33, 38, 41, 51) and coming from God (3:2; 8:42; 16:27; 17:8) or from heaven (3:31).[11] Heaven is the abode of God, and so it functions as a synonym for God.

5. The English prepositions "of," "from," and "with" denote Jesus' identity as God's agent originating from, and authorized by, God. He is the "Lamb of God" (1:29, 36), "Son of God" (1:49, etc.), "the bread of God" (6:33), the "Holy One of God" (6:69). Different Greek constructions translated into English with the preposition "from" denote that he is from above (3:31; 8:23) and from God (6:46; 8:42; 9:33; 16:27, 30). God is *with* him (3:2; 8:29).

By means of these key titles, verbs, and other constructions, the gospel establishes Jesus' origin, special identity, and definitive agency in revealing God's purposes. What are these purposes? What does Jesus reveal? How does he do this revealing work?

Revealing the Life-Giving Purposes of God

The gospel declares that God's purposes comprise "life," or "eternal" or "agely" life, or "life of the age" (20:30–31) (see ch. 5, above):

- Revealing this life denotes Jesus' mission (10:10) and identity (11:25–26; 14:6).

- "Agely" or eschatological life concerns both quantity and quality of life. It consists of life in relationship to God (17:3), free of all sin and death (5:24).

- This claim of never-ending life has a polemical edge. It counters Rome's claims to be the "eternal city." God's life-giving purposes will prevail, ending Rome's oppressive empire.

- Such eschatological life includes new physical life. It is somatic, with renewed bodies (resurrection, 5:24–29; the healing of Lazarus, ch. 11).

- Eschatological life is social, including transformed relationships of love and service among those who participate in God's purposes (13:13–17, 13:34–35).

- This life is known in part in the present (5:24) and will be fully established in God's future at Jesus' return (14:3, 18, 28).

How does Jesus reveal this life? He manifests it in his words, works, and death and resurrection.

Jesus' *words* announce God's life-giving purposes (8:27, 29), enabling people to pass from death to a judgment-free life of knowing God (5:24). But what does this life look like? Jesus' "I am" sayings employ predicates from everyday life ("bread," "gate," "shepherd," "vine") (see ch. 6, above). The predicates frequently evoke Hebrew Bible accounts in which God rescues the people from tyranny and from everything (including sociopolitical, material, and physical conditions) that is contrary to God's life-giving purposes (bread, Exod 16; light, Ps 27:1; shepherd [contrast the bad shepherds of Ezek 34, who deprive the people of resources necessary for life and who rule harshly]). The predicates identify aspects of the blessed life that God intends for all people as descendants of Abraham (cf. Gen 12:1–3; John 8:31–58).

"I am" statements that do not have predicates ("I am"; John 8:24, 28, 58; 13:19) underline the authority with which Jesus' words reveal God's purposes. Such statements in the Hebrew Bible denote God's self-revelation (Exod 3:14). John's use of "I am" without a predicate emphasizes Jesus' divine authority as a participant in the very life of God. This revelation can be overwhelming. When Judas comes to the garden to arrest Jesus with a band of Roman soldiers and temple police (John 18:3), Jesus identifies himself with these words, "I am" (18:5). John 18:6 repeats Jesus' declaration and comments that those who come to arrest him "stepped back and fell to the ground." His revelation momentarily overwhelms these enemies before they persevere with their plans to destroy him.[12]

Jesus' *works* also reveal the life that God intends for all people (see chs. 3 and 5, above). Framed by prophetic and apocalyptic traditions, Jesus' healings and his supplying of abundant wine and food depict and anticipate the transformed life, which differs so greatly from present life under Roman rule. God's purposes are contrary to "normal" life, the harsh near-subsistence that results in so much suffering and death for so many in Rome's empire. God's life is marked by justice that ensures access to abundant resources for all and enables wholeness and health. In line with such a vision, Jesus attacks the Jerusalem temple and its governing elite for reducing "my Father's house" to a "marketplace [house for trade]," one defined and owned by their economic, social, and political purposes rather than by God's just purposes (2:13–22).

Jesus' *death, resurrection, and ascension,* viewed by John as one event, similarly reveal God's life-giving purposes.[13] The cross is profoundly ironic. Although the governing elite, the alliance of Roman power represented by Pilate and the Jerusalem leaders, think that they have eliminated Jesus as a challenge to their power and social structure, they have in fact provided a stage that reveals the triumph of God's purposes.

1. Their actions in crucifying God's commissioned agent of revelation, the one sent from God and in intimate relation with God, reveal the depth of their opposition to God's purposes and the length to which they will go to maintain their corrupt status quo.

2. Although they think they are in control, John repeatedly shows God's will being carried out. The gospel refers to Jesus' "hour," an image that denotes, among other things, the time for Jesus' death as appointed by God (12:23, 27; 13:1; 17:1).[14] Accordingly, when it is not his hour, they cannot arrest him (7:30; 8:20), and other attempts to arrest or kill him are unsuccessful (5:18; 7:19; 8:59; 10:31–39). Jesus allows himself to be arrested (18:1–11) and reminds Pilate that the governor has no power except what God allows him to exercise (19:11). Jesus gives himself to die,

laying down his life not as the victory of the elite but as a death "for," "on behalf of," "for the benefit of" others (10:15–18; 11:50–52), including Gentiles (11:48–53). He dies as a martyr to liberate his people.[15] His death provides the opportunity to participate in God's "agely" life (12:24), in relationship with God (17:3).[16] John reveals his death to be subject to God's timing and authority, not to those of the political rulers.

3. While they mock Jesus as the treasonous, defeated, and executed "King of the Jews" (18:33–40; 19:1–3, 14–16, 19–22, Pilate's trilingual notice on the cross), they unwittingly proclaim Jesus' rightful identity. He is king, an agent of God's sovereignty over the world (see the vision of the king as agent of God's rule in Ps 72). The gospel identifies Jesus' death as a lifting up (John 3:14; 8:28; 12:32, 34). The verb not only denotes Jesus' physical elevation in being strung up on the cross (as Moses raised up the serpent, Num 21:8–9) but also his resurrection and ascension as he returns or departs to God (John 13:1–3; 16:7; 20:17). Moreover, in the Septuagint (the Greek translation of the Hebrew Bible), the verb translated "lifting up" frequently denotes God's elevation of people to positions of power and rule or to social honor and safety from enemies (Ps 3:3; 9:14).[17] In lifting up Jesus on the cross, they unwittingly enthrone him as king, vindicated by God in the resurrection and ascension. In crucifying him, they reveal their own resistance to God's purposes and their own loyalty to Rome and Caesar. Appropriately, they declare their loyalty to Caesar as emperor (John 19:15).

4. Jesus' resurrection and ascension reveal the limit of the elite's power. The apparently invincible alliance of the Roman and Jerusalem governing elite has done its utmost to protect its social structure from God's life-giving purposes revealed in Jesus. They have crucified him. But their power is not sufficient to keep him dead. In raising Jesus, God exposes the limits of their power, overpowering with life-giving power the death that they effect. This act displays Jesus' (15:13) and God's love for the world (3:16) in that Jesus' resurrection anticipates the general resurrection, the transformation of all things according to God's purposes, when "all who are in their graves will hear his voice and will come out" to a resurrection either of life or of condemnation (5:29). God's power is expressed as love that draws people to Jesus (12:32).

5. This death, resurrection, and ascension, then, constitute Jesus' glorification. Throughout his ministry, Jesus has revealed God's "glory," a term that in the Hebrew Bible denotes the revelation of God's presence and purposes (Exod 16:10; 24:16). Disciples discern "glory," God's presence and purposes, in Jesus' actions or signs (John 1:14; 2:11). In speaking of this cluster of crucifixion, resurrection, and ascension as Jesus' glorification (7:39; 12:16, 23; 17:1, 5), the gospel manifests God's glorification (13:31–32), the revelation of God's life-giving purposes and presence.

John's gospel provides no description of Jesus' ascension as does Luke-Acts. At the end of Luke's gospel, Jesus is "carried up into heaven" (Luke 24:50–51). In Acts 1:9–10 the description is more detailed: "he was lifted up, and a cloud took him out of their sight. While he was going and they were gazing up toward heaven . . ." John's attention is on the significance of the event. It is Jesus' vindication, his return to the Father (John 20:17), the revelation of the triumph of God's life-giving purposes.

6. The Passover setting for Jesus' ministry and death (2:13; 6:4; 11:55) underlines the quality of God's purposes for life. Jesus dies at the time of the slaughter of the lambs for Passover (19:14). He is the lamb of God who takes away the sin of the world (1:29, 36). The link with Passover shows that these sins are not just personal and "spiritual" but communal and structural, embracing all that resists God's purposes, including oppression in all its forms. Passover celebrates the liberation of God's people from tyranny and slavery in Egypt. It celebrates a way of life free of such oppressive rule and structures. Rome, knowing the potential danger of Passover as a festival of liberation, deployed troops in Jerusalem "to watch the people and repress any insurrectionary movements" (Josephus, *J.W.* 5.244; also 2.224; 1.88; *Ant.* 20.106). By linking Jesus with Passover, John evokes and depicts God's life-giving purposes as saving the world from such realities and establishing "agely" life, free from every form of sin and death.

7. Jesus' ascension is not the end of his revelatory work. God's purposes are encountered in the present. This "agely" life is experienced now in part as freedom (8:32) from death and judgment (3:18; 5:24). But the gospel does not announce the end of sin in the present, and it anticipates the still future establishment of life in all its fullness.[18] Bodily resurrection (5:28–29; 6:39–40, 54),

eternal life (12:25), and judgment (12:48) remain as future events, part of a Jewish eschatological cluster that denotes God's transformation of the world. John suggests that God's intervention will occur through Jesus' return (14:2–3, 28). Until then the Spirit abides with disciples (16:7). As is typical in some Jewish eschatological expectations, tribulation and opposition to representatives of God's purposes mark this intervening time (15:18–23).

Why Is Revelation Necessary? Sin, Satan, Ioudaioi/"the Jews," the World

Jesus' revelation of God's life-giving purposes is necessary because the world is contrary to God's purposes but does not seem to know it. Jesus constantly confronts humans with God's purposes for human life. He reveals the slavery of humans to sin as a controlling and ruling power (8:34). Such sin means alienation from God for all human beings ("No one comes to the Father," 14:6b)[19] and the creation of forms of human interaction and social structures that fail to manifest God's life-giving purposes (15:22). Jesus' works, such as his healings and feedings, his death and resurrection, exacerbate sin in that some witness them but reject them as revelations of God's purposes (15:24). Fundamentally, sin means not to believe in, or entrust oneself to, Jesus as the one commissioned by God to reveal God's purposes (16:8–9). This is "the world" (see ch. 5, above), which does not know its Creator (1:10).

This nonfulfillment of God's purposes is not just a matter of individual sins and societal imperfections. It is cosmic. John depicts a dualism in which the devil, or Satan, opposes God's purposes (see ch. 5, above). This cosmic struggle, however, does not take place away from humans. The devil is "the ruler of this world" (12:31; 14:30; 16:11). Satan has human agents who carry out its aim of opposing God's purposes, notably the Rome-allied societal, political, and religious Jerusalem elite (8:44, "the Jews"; see ch. 4, above) or rulers (3:1; 19:11) and disciples such as Judas (13:2, 27). Their lived commitments to the devil's purposes constitute their opposition to God, expressed not only in killing Jesus as God's agent but also in structuring and ruling over society in a way that is not life-giving but is marked by falseness and destruction (lies and murder, 8:44–46). Sin and death are inevitably linked (8:21, 24). We have seen how destructive Rome's socioeconomic order, sanctioned by claims of divine blessing and military might, was for most of the population.

This is the gospel's revelation about its contemporary Roman order. Its analysis of, and verdict on, its social context are that it is contrary to God's purposes. It is diabolical, in the control of Satan. Thus, the gospel reveals sin to be not only individual but systemic, not only personal but also political, social, economic, and religious. Accordingly, the divine life or salvation that the gospel reveals embraces all these dimensions.

Sin does not, however, have the final word. There is freedom from its slavery (8:34–36). Jesus takes away the sin of the world (1:29) in revealing and enacting God's life-giving power of love. Sin and death remain the way of the world unless one believes in Jesus as the one commissioned by God to reveal the Creator's purposes for human life (8:24). What does such believing or entrusting entail?

Human Believing/Entrusting

Nearly one hundred times, John designates believing/entrusting as the means by which humans respond positively to and accept Jesus' revelation. To entrust oneself to Jesus' revelation of God's purposes is to attach or commit oneself to it, thereby actively participating in God's life-giving purposes (3:16; 20:30–31). Such believing/entrusting includes the following (see ch. 5, above):

- the transfer from the realm of Satan, death, darkness, and sin to that of God;

- a personal and dynamic commitment or allegiance to Jesus;

- an identity ("one who believes/entrusts") that constitutes an ongoing way of life;

- a lived commitment expressed in appropriate actions;

- insight into Jesus' origin, identity, authority, mission, and relationship with God as revealer of God's life-giving purposes;

- a revelation of one's origin and identity as being from/of God as one of the "children of God" (1:12–13; 8:44);

- membership in a community of other believers, distinct from those who do not believe.

Synonyms such as "sees," "hears," "knows," "comes to" in John's gospel emphasize these dimensions. Not to believe denotes the rejection of all such claims and commitments.

How does this believing/entrusting response come about? John recognizes both human and divine roles.

1. Divine roles: God is actively at work to bring people into a believing/entrusting relationship with God (3:16). God gives power to become God's children (1:12–13), gives believers to Jesus (6:39, 65), and draws people (6:44). Jesus calls (10:3) and chooses believers (15:16).

2. Human roles: John both commands (8:24; 14:1, 11) and solicits (12:44; 20:30–31) believing/entrusting. The language of "everyone who believes"/"whoever believes" (3:16, 36) and the assurance that Jesus rejects no one who "comes" to him (6:37) indicate the opportunity for anyone to choose to believe. But humans must do the discerning work of "hearing" and "knowing" Jesus' voice (10:3–5). "Comes to me," a synonym for "believes me"/"entrusts oneself to me," expresses insight and active commitment (6:35, 37). John even recognizes that disciples can "unbelieve" by not persevering in allegiance to Jesus (6:66–69).

The exact nature of the interaction between God's role and the person's is difficult to determine. The gospel's presentation of Jesus' signs and the place they play in faith poses the difficulty. Some find Jesus' words to be sufficient without any signs (4:42), a position commended to the gospel's readers (20:29). Some see Jesus' actions, discern God's purposes and Jesus' identity in them, and entrust themselves to Jesus (2:11; 4:46–54). Others discern something of God's purposes but do not adequately understand Jesus' identity or mission (6:14; 2:23–25). Yet others witness miracles but discern nothing of God's purposes (12:37).

True to the paradoxical nature of much of the gospel's presentation, both God's and the person's roles have to be held together. John recognizes that God actively seeks to encounter humans regardless of human interest. This initiative demonstrates God's love (3:16), or what writers such as Paul would call grace. It places humans in a "crisis of decision" as to whether they will embrace God's purposes. Whatever response humans make determines their identity (child of God or child of the devil), reveals their origins (from above or from below), locates them socially ("children" in or against John's community), and determines whether they know life or death. A positive acceptance seems to require some openness to the possibility of God's intervention in revealing God's life-giving purposes for the world.

The Community of Disciples: The Church and the Spirit

Consistent with God's purpose that humans live in community (Gen 2:18–25), Jesus' revelatory work creates not just individual believers but a community of disciples, the church.[20] John 13–17, Jesus' farewell address to the disciples, emphasizes Jesus' absence and so highlights important aspects of ecclesial existence until he returns to establish God's purposes. One of the dominant features of this group's identity is its identity as an alternative community, a countercommunity or antisociety, committed to God's life-giving purposes—a minority community at odds with, and subversive of, its society's commitments and structures.[21]

God's power creates "children of God," differentiated from the larger, rejecting world by their allegiance to Jesus (1:12–13). Believing/entrusting is personal, social, and antisocietal. The language of "children" is multivalent: (1) As covenant language, it locates disciples of Jesus in the much larger context of God's relationship with God's people. (2) Although the gospel uses different Greek words for believers as children and Jesus as Son, the familial images draw the two ideas together, so that Jesus is recognized as drawing believers into his relationship with God. John emphasizes an interdependent relationship and a mutual indwelling between Jesus and believers (14:20; 15:1–7; 17:21, 26). (3) In the first-century world, with its high infant mortality rates, children were loved but were regarded as vulnerable. They were also regarded as marginal and threatening to the elite (male-dominated) social order until they were mature enough to take their allotted places.[22] As children of God shaped by, and obedient to, Jesus' teaching and commandments (14:15, 18–24), John's community knows vulnerability and marginality. Believers are out of step with a world that rejects the revealer of God's purposes (1:10). They are warned of hostility from a hateful world (15:18–25). Just as Jesus was rejected and crucified by the power group, disciples can expect similar persecution (15:20).

The community of believers lives in the presence of the Spirit, or Paraclete, in the absence of Jesus (14:16, 26): (1) On his ascension, Jesus gives the Spirit (7:37–39) or, more accurately, asks God to do so (14:16, 26; 15:26). (2) The Spirit brings birth from above and life to believers whereby they enter and live in God's reign (3:5–8; 6:63). That is, the Spirit makes available the eschatological benefits of believing in Jesus' revelation. (3) With Jesus' departure and ascension to God, the Spirit is his successor ("another Advocate [Paraclete]," 14:16), manifesting his presence and continuing his work among disciples (16:7). Three passages in chapters 13–17 identify the Spirit as the Paraclete (14:15–17, 26; 15:26–27; 16:7–14). This image is multivalent. "Paraclete" was "a word of general meaning which could appear in legal contexts, and when it did the *paraklētos* was a supporter or sponsor." This patron figure provided support and advice in various contexts, including making "a great person favourable to a suppliant."[23] Others have suggested that John's image is informed by traditions about heavenly angelic and wisdom figures who mediate the divine will.[24] (4) The Paraclete is identified as the Spirit of truth (14:17), an agent of God acting in faithfulness to God's salvific and life-giving commitments to bless all the families of the earth (see ch. 5, above). The Paraclete guides believers in these purposes (16:13). (5) The Paraclete has particular functions concerning disciples. The Spirit remains with disciples (14:17), teaches them (14:26; 16:14), reminds them of Jesus' teaching (14:26; see 2:22; 12:16), announces the future (16:13), bears witness to Jesus (15:26), and glorifies Jesus (16:14). In these tasks the Spirit is seen to guide the community in (re)interpreting and understanding Jesus' revelation in new circumstances and through the passing of time. (6) In performing these roles among disciples, the Paraclete distinguishes disciples from the world that rejects the Spirit (14:17), confirming the rightness of their commitment while showing the world to be wrong about sin, justice, and judgment (16:8–11).

The community of believers lives in and manifests God's love for the world (3:16) and for the Son (3:35). Jesus reveals this love for disciples and forms the basis for the community (15:9, 12–17; 17:26), whereby interactions among disciples enable one another to encounter God's loving purposes (13:34–35). The community is unified in its participation in the love and life that God and Jesus share (17:21, 23, 26). Some scholars see Jesus' entrusting of his mother to the beloved disciple as constituting a community of love (19:26–27). Along with practices of love, service, as demonstrated in Jesus' washing of the disciples' feet, marks the community (13:12–17). This life of mutual service, which seeks the good of the other, renounces, subverts, and challenges the "power over" model of domination that marks hierarchical Roman society. God's life-giving purposes create alternative forms, counterforms, of societal interaction in this alternative community.

The community is commissioned to continue Jesus' mission of revealing God's life-giving purposes.[25] As the Father has sent Jesus, so he sends disciples (17:18; 20:21). The Spirit empowers this mission (20:22), which consists of bearing witness to Jesus as the revealer of God (15:27) and doing the works that Jesus does, and even greater or more of them, since there are more believers (14:12; the fruit of 15:5): revealing God's life-giving purposes, confronting the unjust and death-bringing ways of the ruling elite (2:13–22), bringing wholeness/healing and abundance (6:1–14), effecting forgiveness or release (20:23), and announcing God's loving purposes. This life-giving work of justice causes the same backlash as Jesus' mission (15:18–16:4).

Consistent with this identity is the inclusive nature of the community of believers. The gospel narrates the inclusion of a wide range of believing persons embraced by God's purposes: Jews, Samaritans, Gentiles, the poor, the physically damaged, women, men.

This identity and way of life are sustained through prayer. Immediately following Jesus' word that believers continue his mission, he instructs disciples to ask for anything in his name (14:13–14). This difficult countercultural way of life can only be sustained by abiding or remaining in relationship with Jesus as branches draw life from a vine (15:1–8). In this relationship, mission and life-giving acts (15:5) go hand in hand with prayer (15:7; 16:23–24). Jesus prays for the faithful mission of the community (17:9–19) and for its continuing unified life (17:20–26).

The Community and Sacraments

Does John's gospel uphold the celebration of sacraments? This is a much debated question.[26] John does not provide explicit accounts of the institution of baptism and the Eucharist or the Last Supper as do the Synoptic Gospels.[27] John the Baptist does not baptize Jesus, although John does report the descent of the Spirit on Jesus, something that the Synoptics link to Jesus' baptism (1:29–34). Nor is it clear that Jesus baptizes; he does in 3:22 but does not in 4:2. Jesus has a last meal with his disciples in chapter 13, but it is not a Passover meal as in the Synoptics, and Jesus gives no instructions for its continuing observation. Rather, he washes the disciples' feet and instructs them on life in his absence until his return.

These omissions could suggest that sacraments do not matter for this gospel. But the issue is more complicated. John contains texts that can be interpreted as evoking or pointing to the sacraments. For example, some scholars have seen the turning of water into wine in 2:1–11 as denoting the Eucharist, the mention of water in 3:5 ("without being born of water and the Spirit") as a reference to baptism, the feeding of the crowd in 6:1–14 as a reference to the Eucharist (the word "Eucharist" is derived from the Greek verb for "giving thanks," which appears in 6:11), as is the material later in the chapter about eating Jesus' flesh and drinking Jesus' blood (6:51–58). Some have seen further references to the Eucharist in the foot washing of chapter 13 and in 15:1–6 (the vine and branches).[28] Many have seen 19:34 (the water and blood from Jesus' side) as linking both baptism and the Eucharist to Jesus' death. Thus, some have argued that John assumes the institution of the sacraments and is much more interested in emphasizing their significance for initiating and sustaining believers in Jesus.

Although these passages can be read as referring to the sacraments, readings that do not recognize such references are also quite possible. The wine in chapter 2, for example, and the feeding in 6:1–14 reveal God's purposes for abundant fertility. The water in 3:5 refers either to the womb or to sperm or to the Spirit. The eating and drinking of chapter 6 metaphorically depict believing in Jesus. Chapters 13 (service) and 15 (close relationship, fruitful discipleship) describe aspects of the life God expects from believers. The water and blood of 19:34 signify that Jesus is dead. Accordingly, some have interpreted John as being either opposed to sacraments or not interested in them.

Scholars also argue over the possibility that only some of these references indicate sacraments. Probably 3:5, 6:51–58, and 19:34 would receive the most support as referring to sacraments. The scenes in chapters 2, 13, and 15 would receive less. Scholars who see a limited number of references to sacraments have to account for the existence of these few references and the lack of institution narratives. Explanations positing the addition of references are often linked to the approaches (discussed in ch. 8, above) about multiple versions for the gospel that developed as the circumstances of readers changed. These are some of the options:

- An earlier version of this gospel, opposed to sacraments, omitted references to them, but a redactor, upset by the omissions, added the references in 3:5 and 6:51–58 to make it more acceptable to other Christian communities (Bultmann).

- The additions were friendly amendments added to make explicit what was implicit in earlier versions.

- The additions were critical amendments added to correct what were regarded as wrong ideas.

- The first version of this gospel emerged from a community and author who did not know about the sacraments, but as the gospel was used by other Christians, references to sacraments were needed and added.

- The first version, not concerned with sacraments for whatever reason (ignorance? opposition?), was created before the fight with a synagogue community. If John's community separated to form its own community, sacraments then became important as the new community defined its boundaries and reinforced its identity.

- The inclusion of minimal references to sacraments reflects a compromise for a dispute within John's community between those who emphasized them and those who valued them little.

Ultimately, we do not know if any of these theories is correct. Nor does the gospel give us clear clues for whether the texts discussed above refer to baptism and the Eucharist. Rather, interpreters of John often seem to reflect their own ecclesial commitments in making decisions about whether texts refer to sacraments. Interpreters from ecclesial traditions that do not emphasize sacraments tend not to find references to sacraments. On the other hand, those from ecclesial traditions that emphasize sacraments tend to find them in John. Raymond Brown, for example, discusses the work of some Catholic interpreters who have seen twenty-five references in the gospel to five of the church's sacraments (matrimony, extreme unction, penance, baptism, the Eucharist), three of which an interpreter belonging to the Protestant tradition is very unlikely to identify.[29] Brown, a Catholic, offers two criteria for determining sacraments: textual indicators and evidence from early church traditions. But the former are often quite subjective, and the latter often reflect the ecclesial commitments and the catechetical and/or liturgical interests of the interpreters.

Ethics

Some have questioned the helpfulness of John's gospel in providing ethical guidance.[30] Compared with the Synoptics (e.g., the Sermon on the Mount, Matt 5–7), it offers relatively little explicit moral instruction and few models. Its emphasis on God's work in drawing people to believing/entrusting relationship could even be understood as minimizing ethical commitment.

Yet our discussion of the church noted some central aspects of ethical living that John requires of disciples.[31] Believers in Jesus are to live lives based on, and expressive of, Jesus' revelation of God's life-giving purposes, which confront the societally normative structures and ways of being and provide different forms of societal interaction. They are to do the "greater works" (14:12) and bear the fruit (15:1–6) that embody God's purposes of abundant life for all people. Like Jesus, they proclaim, challenge, heal, and feed, actions that confront a status quo contrary to God's purposes and enact transformation and justice expressive of God's life-giving purposes until Jesus returns to establish these purposes in full. We have noted the commands to love and to serve as important and challenging elements of such a way of life (John 13), and the inevitable backlash of hate and resistance that comes from those defending their interests of power and status (15:18–27).

Conclusion

The good news according to John is that Jesus is the definitive revealer of God's life-giving purposes, whose mission continues in and through the alternative community, the church, an antisociety that is sustained by the Spirit, or Paraclete, in a hostile world until God's purposes are established in full.

Notes

1. For discussions, see Bultmann, *Theology,* 2:3–92; Brown, *Gospel according to John,* 1:cv–cxxviii; Ladd, *Theology,* 213–308; Kysar, *John: The Maverick Gospel;* Ashton, *Understanding;* G. Beasley-Murray, *Gospel of Life: Theology in the Fourth Gospel* (Peabody, Mass.: Hendrickson, 1991); D. M. Smith, *The Theology of the Gospel of John* (Cambridge: Cambridge University Press, 1995); Culpepper, *Gospel and Letters,* 87–105; D. Rensberger, "The Messiah Who Has Come into the World: The Message of the Gospel of John," in *Jesus and the Johannine Tradition* (ed. R. Fortna and T. Thatcher; Louisville: Westminster John Knox, 2001), 15–23; Brown, *Introduction to the Gospel,* 220–77.

2. Carter, "Prologue," 43–44.

3. Moloney (*John,* 33, 42) translates, "turned toward God."

4. Brown (*Gospel according to John,* 1:519–24) considers affinities with Greek philosophical thought (Heraclitus, the Stoics, Philo, and Hermetic, Mandaean, and gnostic literature, in which "the word" often has some role in expressing divine purposes in creation) as well as with Jewish traditions (the efficacious word of the Lord, wisdom, speculation on the law, and the use of the Aramaic word for "word" [*memra*] in the Targumim).

5. Later affirmations such as that of the Council of Chalcedon in 451 C.E. would recast these understandings in terms of shared being or ontology. See T. Pollard, "The Exegesis of John 10:30 in the Early Trinitarian Controversies," *NTS* 3 (1956–57): 334–49.

6. See M. de Jonge, "The Messiah," *ABD* 4:777–88; Charlesworth, ed., *The Messiah;* Nickelsburg, *Ancient Judaism,* 89–117.

7. John 1:19–28, not John; 4:25–29, the Samaritan revealer; 7:25–31, unknown origin; worker of signs; 7:40–44, origin from Galilee? from David and

Bethlehem? 9:22, expulsion from the synagogue; 10:24, uncertainty; 12:34, remains forever.

8. John 8:28; 12:23, 34; 13:31–32.

9. Ἀποστέλλω, *apostellō;* πέμπω, *pempō.*

10. Καταβαίνω, *katabainō.*

11. Ἔρχομαι, *erchomai.*

12. Sometimes such falling down denotes openness to God's revelation (Ezek 1:28). Other instances of God resisting enemies include 2 Kgs 1:9–14 and Ps 27:2.

13. See ch. 3, above. D. Senior, *The Passion of Jesus in the Gospel of John* (Collegeville, Minn.: Liturgical, 1991); M. de Boer, *Johannine Perspectives on the Death of Jesus* (Kampen, Neth.: Kok, 1996).

14. "Hour" also denotes significant times when Jesus' life affects disciples. Some "hours" denote what will happen after his resurrection (4:21; 16:2, 25[?]) and at the final establishment of God's purposes (5:28–29). Others denote something already happening in anticipation of its still future full experience (4:23; 5:25; 16:32).

15. L. Schottroff, "Important Aspects of the Gospel for the Future," in *Readers and Readings of the Fourth Gospel* (vol. 1 of *What Is John?* ed. F. F. Segovia; SBLSymS 3; Atlanta: Scholars Press, 1996), 205–10, here 208.

16. G. O'Day, "Johannine Theology as Sectarian Theology," ibid., 199–203.

17. Abraham, Gen 24:35; Isaac, Gen 26:13; Joshua, Josh 3:7; Saul, 1 Sam 10:23–24; David, 2 Sam 22:49 (over enemies); 1 Chr 17:17.

18. As noted in ch. 8, above, scholars have sought to explain these emphases on the present and the future in John's eschatology as resulting from the work of different writers and redactors in creating different versions of the gospel. Although reflection on the origin of this paradox is appropriate, it is important to observe the existence of both elements in the final form of the gospel and the interaction between the two. See N. Dahl, " 'Do Not Wonder!' John 5:28–29 and Johannine Eschatology Once More," in *The Conversation Continues: Studies in Paul and John in Honor of J. Louis Martyn* (ed. R. Fortna and B. Gaventa; Nashville: Abingdon, 1990), 322–36; Brown, *Introduction to the Gospel,* 234–48.

19. Emphasized by C. Koester, "Jesus the Way, the Cross, and the World according to the Gospel of John," *WW* 21 (2001): 360–69.

20. Some scholars have seen John's gospel in very individualistic terms, as lacking an ecclesiology. For a pervasive ecclesiology, see A. Correll, *Consummatum est: Eschatology and Church in the Gospel of St John* (London: SPCK, 1958); Rensberger, *Johannine Faith,* passim.

21. See ch. 5 n. 2.

22. W. Carter, *Households and Discipleship: A Study of Matthew 19–20* (JSNTSup 103; Sheffield, Eng.: Sheffield Academic Press, 1994), 90–114.

23. K. Grayston, "The Meaning of PARAKLĒTOS," *JSNT* 13 (1981): 67–82, here 74–75.

24. Brown, *Gospel according to John* 2:1135–44; G. M. Burge (*The Anointed Community* [Grand Rapids: Eerdmans, 1987], 10–31) provides a helpful summary of options, but he misleadingly argues for *paraklētos* as a "forensic term evolving out of the Jewish juridical scene" (p. 208). See J. Ashton, "Paraclete," *ABD* 5:152–54.

25. E.g., A. J. Köstenberger, *The Mission of Jesus and the Disciples according to the Fourth Gospel with Implications for the Fourth Gospel's Purposes and the*

Mission of the Contemporary Church (Grand Rapids: Eerdmans, 1998); J. Nissen, "Mission in the Fourth Gospel: Historical and Hermeneutical Perspectives," in *New Readings in John: Literary and Theological Perspectives from the Scandinavian Conference on the Fourth Gospel, Arhus, 1997* (ed. J. Nissen and S. Pedersen; JSNTSup 182; Sheffield, Eng.: Sheffield Academic Press, 1999), 213–31; T. Okure, *The Johannine Approach to Mission: A Contextual Study of John 4:1–42* (Wissenschaftliche Untersuchungen zum Neuen Testament 31; Tübingen: J. C. B. Mohr [Paul Siebeck], 1988).

26. In addition to appropriate sections in the discussions cited in n. 1, above, see Rensberger, *Johannine Faith*, 64–86.

27. For Jesus' baptism, Mark 1:9–11; Matt 3:13–17; Luke 3:21–22; for the Last Supper, Mark 14:22–25; Matt 26:26–29; Luke 22:14–23.

28. See, e.g., Thomas, *Footwashing*, who concludes that baptism and the Eucharist were practiced as sacraments (p. 177), as was foot washing, which replaces the institution of the Eucharist in John 13 (177–85).

29. R. Brown, "The Johannine Sacramentary," 51–76, here 75–76; "The Eucharist and Baptism in John," 77–95, in *New Testament Essays* (New York: Paulist, 1965).

30. See the helpful discussion of W. Meeks, "The Ethics of the Fourth Evangelist," in *Exploring the Gospel of John: In Honor of D. Moody Smith* (ed. R. A. Culpepper and C. C. Black; Louisville: Westminster John Knox, 1996), 317–26; J. Nissen, "Community and Ethics in the Gospel of John," in *New Readings in John: Literary and Theological Perspectives from the Scandinavian Conference on the Fourth Gospel, Arhus, 1997* (ed. J. Nissen and S. Pedersen; JSNTSup 182; Sheffield, Eng.: Sheffield Academic Press, 1999), 194–212.

31. Engaging some of the challenges of these guidelines is D. M. Smith, "Ethics and the Interpretation of the Gospel," in *Word, Theology, and Community in John* (ed. J. Painter, R. A. Culpepper, and F. F. Segovia; St. Louis: Chalice, 2002), 109–22.

Postscript: Good News? Reading John Today in Our Multireligious World

The three parts of this book have engaged John's gospel as a narrative (chs. 1–6), interpreted by several authors for changing circumstances (chs. 7–8), and announcing the good news according to John, namely, Jesus' revelation of God's life-giving purposes (chs. 9–10). Reading John's narrative, however, is an ongoing interpretive task that engages the narrative and its good news in ever-changing and new circumstances. Does this text, almost two thousand years old, have anything of significance to say to contemporary readers? What is the good news according to John for the twenty-first century?

Most readers of John today are members of Christian faith communities. We read this gospel as part of our canon, as a definitive text. We hear it preached;[1] we study it in bible studies and retreats.[2] We give this text power as a privileged and authoritative text to shape how we think about the world that we inhabit, about God's purposes and presence in, or absence from, this world, and about how we live our daily lives. We give it power to shape our understanding and practice of Christian existence.[3] This starting point, however, does not excuse us from the task of thinking hard about how we read and about the meanings that we create in reading this gospel. Indeed, John's authoritative status requires that we think critically and in an informed way about the implications of reading and living this gospel today in a multireligious world.

This postscript identifies six issues that seem especially relevant to evaluating our readings in our complex and multireligious world. It poses some of these issues in antithetical relationship and others in complementary relationship. This discussion is by no means comprehensive. Rather, it invites the reader to reflect further on these topics, to identify further issues, and to explore their implications for contemporary living.

Individual and Communal Readings

John has long been interpreted as assisting individual Christians in their relationship with Jesus. Numerous sermons have been preached on Jesus as "my good shepherd," who knows me and whose voice I should know (John 10). Many Christians have found in 15:1–7, the passage about the vine and the branches, encouragement to attend carefully to their individual relationship with God so as to abide or remain in God, to have God's words abide in them, and to bear fruit in daily living. For millennia Christians have engaged in numerous spiritual practices such as prayer, Bible study, the study of other writings, acts of charity and justice, and fasting to nurture their relationship with God.

But although we often conceive of Christian existence in individual terms, it is important to note that John's gospel often presents it in communal terms; together, Christians nurture relationship with God. We miss this communal casting of Christian existence for several reasons. The very individualistic orientation of our own society and church life shapes our reading. Moreover, the English language is unable to distinguish between the second-person singular and plural pronouns ("you"). Thus, although John often uses plural language, we tend to understand "you" in singular terms. John 15:2 refers to "every branch" in the singular, but 15:3, when it addresses "you" ("You have already been made clean"), uses the plural pronoun "you" to refer to the community of believers. And John 15:4, when it instructs, "Abide in me as I abide in you," uses a plural form of the verb, "you [all] abide," and the plural pronoun "in you [all]" to describe a communal Christian existence. Although John often writes in the plural, in the communal sense, we often hear the singular, the individual sense.

This emphasis on the communal is important for several reasons. John's gospel highlights the inclusive quality of the community of believers. The community constituted by this gospel embraces those usually marginalized by the ruling power group—women, the poor, the physically damaged, Samaritans, those despised by the elite as ignorant of the law. The community thereby embodies, or incarnates, God's radical, inclusive, and comprehensive love for the world (3:16), love that confronts and challenges the world's commitments and structures and offers it an alternative. Contemporary Christian living, shaped by John, must bear this mark.

Moreover, as we have seen, John envisages Christian living as a mission existence. Christians do not live for their own individual comfort or personal satisfaction; they live to continue the mission of Jesus (14:12; 20:21). In a world that is presented as often resisting God's purposes even with violence (15:18, 20; 16:2), only a community can sustain and engage such a mission. There the love of God can be revealed in relationships and acts of justice and service.

Spiritual and Social

This communal emphasis matters for a further reason. We have seen that in John's gospel God's life-giving purposes revealed by Jesus embrace the physical (healing the sick, feeding the hungry) and the social (the socioeconomic role of the temple; the unjust distribution of resources making people sick). That is, this gospel is fundamentally concerned to show that the oppression effected through the structures and personnel of the Roman empire and their allies in a provincial center, Jerusalem, is contrary to God's purposes. These unjust structures and sinful realities constitute "the world" that God loves and seeks to transform. Believers in Jesus continue his mission to establish God's just and life-giving purposes, which embrace all of society and all of life.[4]

Christians have often thought of Christian existence in very "spiritual" or otherworldly terms, as focusing almost exclusively on one's own relationship with God. But for John's gospel, eternal, or "agely" (see ch. 5, above) life, life that encounters God and enacts God's purposes (17:3), entails, as we have seen, participation in God's purposes for all creation now as God redeems or saves the world to be what God created it to be. Jesus' healings and feedings signify that God's purposes embrace the flourishing of all creation and people. Hence, the sort of Christian existence that John's gospel commends means participation in a mission community that performs the "greater works" of transforming justice and thereby continuing Jesus' life-giving mission (14:12; 20:21).

David Rensberger, making the same point, comments that, for John, one knows God by "seeing and contemplating Jesus' deeds of self-giving love that reveal God, and by sharing in them in order to go where Jesus has gone, to be where Jesus is." Deeds of self-giving love not only mean love for other disciples but also engagement in a "struggle against a world that refuses to know God. . . . Acts of love that resist the world's values involve the individual believer and the believing community in downward mobility, in a self-lowering that disregards self-interest and status in the sight of the world and finds joy in service to others and in identification with those whom the world despises."[5]

Affirmation and Action

John 20 concludes with a declaration of this gospel's purpose: "These are written so that you may come to believe that Jesus is the Messiah, the Son of God, and that through believing you may have life in his name" (20:31). As in several other statements, here to "believe/entrust" means giving assent to certain understandings about Jesus especially. Clearly, right thinking about Jesus matters very much. We have asked what it means to affirm that Jesus is the Christ. It is a declaration (among others) that affirms Jesus to be commissioned or anointed by God to carry out God's purposes, notably, the revelation of God's life-giving purposes for the world. We have also explored John's claims about Jesus being the Son of God. To be the Son means to be in intimate relationship with God and to be an agent, a representative, a revealer, of God's life-giving purposes. This gospel wants its readers to gain proper intellectual understanding about Jesus' origin, identity, role, mission, and destiny. And through the millennia, John has been a constant source of affirmations for central understandings of the Christian faith.

But given this postscript's first two observations, about engaging John's gospel in our multireligious world, it is clear that affirmations without actions mean nothing. To believe/entrust oneself to Jesus as the Christ and Son, the agent of God's life-giving purposes, means not only intellectual agreement with such claims but active participation in these purposes. For John's gospel, Christian existence continues Jesus' mission and comprises numerous comparable acts of giving life. Christian existence, for this gospel, entails both affirmations and actions.

Sectarian or Transsectarian Christian Existence?

The heading of this section is borrowed from a short but insightful essay written by Robert Kysar, an astute and wise interpreter of John's gospel.[6] Kysar notes that especially in the North American scene (but one could extend his observation to numerous parts of the world), the church increasingly occupies a minority and marginal location in a multireligious society (this is what he means by "sectarian"). He wonders how John's gospel, reflecting a somewhat similar situation of a minority community feeling under siege and employing an us-against-them dualism throughout, might function to sanction and empower contemporary faith communities.

Kysar suggests that the challenge is to interpret John so as to "appropriate the *best* of that sectarian strain . . . without succumbing to what I take to be the *worst* of such a perspective."[7] Among the latter qualities, he identifies this gospel's hostility and hatred toward opponents, including its depiction of them as demonic. Among the former (or transsectarian) qualities, he identifies its focus on God's love for the world and the church's mission to the world. Christian communal existence is not retreat from the world. Kysar suggests that our reading of John will need to be "critical," in the sense of discerning what will guide Christian practice. I would add that this gospel, even at times despite itself, provides the central criterion by which we might do this discernment. Consistent with its central theological and christological affirmations, what manifests God's life-giving, loving, and liberating purposes should guide our thinking and shape our practices. This gospel offers, then, both an affirmation of the distinctive identity of the Christian community and an active embracing of the world so as to manifest God's love and life.

Ambiguous and/or Absolute Truth Claims

Another issue relevant to reading John in today's complex world concerns our understanding of the truth of its message. The pairing in this section's heading likewise comes from Kysar's essay. One of his concerns is how John's gospel might "continue to function in a revelatory way."[8] He notes the ever-expanding role of the media, especially visual media, in reshaping language and consciousness. "Controlling and fundamental images," multivalent graphics, ambiguities, diverse points of view, and information overload are important elements of the contemporary, media-dominated context in which readers engage John's gospel.

I would add that one effect of these developments is the greater consumerist mentality evident in being able to select sources of information according to one's own preferences. The effect of such selectivity is, paradoxically, to confirm the pervasiveness of spin, the ambiguity of human experience, and the relativity of human claims. Kysar suggests that in such a context, John's images and paradoxical language (the Word became flesh; present and future eschatology; divine drawing and human response-ability) may become more important than John's propositions. Increased attention to John's multivalent images and symbols will inevitably result in understandings that are more ambiguous. In such a context, it will be increasingly difficult to assert a monolithic meaning, and increasingly necessary to recognize diversity in interpretations of John's gospel. Such a situation will pose significant challenges to members of the Christian tradition because we have often shown that we do not cope well with such diversity.

Exclusive or Inclusive Claims and Practices?

In such contexts, what role will John's gospel play in shaping the church's engagement with the world? Of immediate relevance to interpreting John in a multireligious world are its exclusivist claims that God can be encountered only through Jesus: "I am the way, and the truth, and the life. No one comes to the Father except through me" (14:6; see also 6:44–45, 53; 15:6).

And as much as this gospel is often identified as the gospel of love, its commands to love concern disciples (13:34–35; 15:12), not neighbors or enemies, unlike, for example, Matthew (Matt 5:38–48; 22:37–39). Does John's gospel disqualify all other religious experiences and traditions in asserting its own? Does it require isolation from the world rather than engagement with it?[9] These apparent claims of religious exclusivity also create divisions among Christians. Some Christians read them with great discomfort and cannot find them to be normative for their practice. Others find such exclusivist claims to be a nonnegotiable element of faith. Mutual despising and judging often result.

How did John's exclusivist claims arise? It is helpful to recall that this gospel likely originated in contexts of considerable dispute with others in a synagogue community over claims about Jesus (chs. 8–9, above). In this polemical context, with John's community feeling overpowered and marginalized, John's gospel adopts polemical language and form, consistent with its times,[10] to assert strongly its claims that the revelation of God's purposes is found definitively in Jesus. In doing so, it reinterprets Jewish traditions and observances and, at its lowest and most hateful point, denigrates the Jerusalem leaders as children of the devil (8:44). John's horizons are certainly not our great world religions of Islam, Hinduism, or Buddhism but a very local dispute with another group in the same Jewish tradition about how God is encountered. John's concern is to celebrate the revelation in Jesus to which the community has committed itself and which constitutes its distinctive identity.[11]

This much is clear. But the claim that there were no broader horizons for John is debatable. We have seen his denunciation of the Roman empire and its Jerusalem allies, an empire that claimed sanction from the gods, especially Jupiter. It is not a big step from the immediate polemic of 14:6 to understanding the nonvalidity of other religious claims in this gospel's own world. But whatever *John's* horizons, for contemporary Christians, diverse religious expressions exist all around us, in our cities and suburbs, on television, and throughout the world. And there is little doubt that this gospel's negative presentation of the Jerusalem leaders has long transcended its specific and limited context of origin to feed a long and despicable tradition of anti-Jewish sentiment and action by Christians.[12] Does John compel us to adopt an absolutely intolerant stance that will not recognize any authentic experience of God, however named, apart from Jesus?

Some Christians would answer "yes" to this question. But there are indications that we may have here another of John's paradoxes, holding together two apparently contradictory notions. Alan Culpepper notes the claims of John's opening verses, which frame the rest of the gospel.[13] Drawing on wisdom traditions, the prologue affirms that the Word is active throughout all creation, manifesting the life and light of God to people (1:4–5). The Word is an agent of God's love for the world (3:16). Indeed, the Word becomes flesh (1:14), but as wisdom traditions recognize, the Word's revelatory activity is not restricted to one place, time, or person. It pervades the created realm. The prologue declares that "the true light, which enlightens everyone, was coming into the world" (1:9). This verse affirms God's activity in drawing all people to Godself. We can reasonably elaborate the revealing Word's activity to embrace diverse cultures, religious traditions, and human history. Within such a huge framework, John's gospel concerns itself with one particular revelation and means of encounter with God.

The "both/and" of this gospel's affirmations, God's worldwide activity as well as the revelation in and through Jesus and his followers, means that there is no surrender of the Christian claim that, *for us,* God's life-giving purposes are encountered through Jesus the Christ, the Son of God. Nor is there any reason to abandon the commission from Jesus to continue his mission of manifesting God's purposes. These are central aspects of our Christian identity and practice.

But the "both/and" of this gospel's affirmations does significantly affect how we conduct ourselves and our mission in God's world. If God is at work in diverse ways to draw the world to Godself, Christians cannot make triumphalist and exclusive claims about our role or affirmations. John is quite clear that the task of judgment belongs not to believers but to Jesus (5:22). And it certainly provides no mandate for explicit hatred toward Jews or members of any religious group. Nor does it sanction attitudes that consider all non-Christian religious experience as illegitimate.

Rather, using John's gospel as a guide, we will view our Christian identity and task faithfully and with humility. And drawing on this gospel's revelation of God's life-giving purposes, we will look for other expressions of God's life-giving purposes throughout our world. We will participate in partnership with such expressions, resisting all that is contrary to God's purposes, seeking to transform all that bears the mark of sin and death, manifesting God's life for God's world.

Notes

1. R. Kysar, *Preaching John* (Minneapolis: Fortress, 2002); G. O'Day, "John's Voice and the Church's Preaching," *WW* 21 (2001): 394–403.

2. S. Schneiders, *Written That You May Believe: Encountering Jesus in the Fourth Gospel* (New York: Crossroad, 1999); D. Rensberger, "Spirituality and Christology in Johannine Sectarianism," in *Word, Theology, and Community in John* (ed. J. Painter, R. A. Culpepper, and F. F. Segovia; St. Louis: Chalice, 2002), 173–88.

3. J. Beutler ("Faith and Confession: The Purpose of John," in *Word, Theology, and Community in John* [ed. J. Painter, R. A. Culpepper, and F. F. Segovia; St. Louis: Chalice, 2002], 19–31) argues that the gospel deepens faith and encourages open confession despite the social consequences.

4. B. N. Y. Vaughan, "Sermons in John and the Problem of Justice," *Theology* 102 (1999): 186–94.

5. Rensberger, "Spirituality and Christology," 185–86.

6. R. Kysar, "Coming Hermeneutical Earthquake in Johannine Interpretation," in *Readers and Readings of the Fourth Gospel* (vol. 1 of *What Is John?* ed. F. F. Segovia; SBLSymS 3. Atlanta: Scholars Press, 1996), 185–89.

7. Ibid., 186.

8. Ibid., 187.

9. F. F. Segovia, "The Gospel at the Close of the Century: Engagement from the Diaspora," in *Readers and Readings of the Fourth Gospel* (vol. 1 of *What Is John?* ed. F. F. Segovia; SBLSymS 3; Atlanta: Scholars Press, 1996), 211–16.

10. Johnson, "New Testament's Anti-Jewish Slander."

11. O'Day, the section "Reflections on John 14:1–11," in "Gospel of John," 9:743–45.

12. The literature is extensive. See, e.g., Bieringer, Pollefeyt, and Vandecasteele-Vanneuville, eds., *Anti-Judaism;* R. A. Culpepper, "The Gospel of John as a Document of Faith in a Pluralistic Culture," in *Readers and Readings of the Fourth Gospel* (vol. 1 of *What Is John?* ed. F. F. Segovia; SBLSymS 3; Atlanta: Scholars Press, 1996), 107–27, here 112–16; R. A. Culpepper, "Inclusivism and Exclusivism in the Fourth Gospel," in *Word, Theology, and Community in John* (ed. J. Painter, R. A. Culpepper, and F. F. Segovia; St. Louis: Chalice, 2002), 85–108.

13. Culpepper, "Gospel of John as a Document," 121–25.

Bibliography

Abrams, M. H. *A Glossary of Literary Terms*. 3d ed. New York: Holt, Reinhart & Winston, 1971.

Achtemeier, P. J. "*Omne verbum sonat:* The New Testament and the Oral Environment of Late Western Antiquity." *Journal of Biblical Literature* 109 (1990): 3–27.

Albright, W. F. "Recent Discoveries in Palestine and the Gospel of St. John." Pages 153–71 in *The Background of the New Testament and Its Eschatology*. Edited by W. D. Davies and D. Daube. Cambridge: Cambridge University Press, 1956.

Anderson, P. N. *The Christology of the Fourth Gospel: Its Unity and Disunity in the Light of John 6*. Valley Forge, Pa.: Trinity Press International, 1996.

Aristotle, "On the Art of Poetry." Pages 29–75 in T. S. Dorsch, *Classical Literary Criticism: Aristotle, Horace, Longinus*. Baltimore: Penguin, 1965.

Ashton, J. A. "Paraclete." Pages 152–54 in *The Anchor Bible Dictionary*. 5 vols. Edited by D. N. Freedman. New York: Doubleday, 1992.

———. *Studying John: Approaches to the Fourth Gospel*. Oxford: Clarendon, 1994.

———. *Understanding the Fourth Gospel*. Oxford: Clarendon, 1991.

Ashton, J. A., ed. *The Interpretation of John*. Philadelphia: Fortress, 1986.

Attridge, H. "Genre Bending in the Fourth Gospel." *Journal of Biblical Literature* 121 (2002): 3–21.

Aune, D. "Dualism in the Fourth Gospel and the Dead Sea Scrolls: A Reassessment of the Problem." Pages 281–303 in *Neotestimentica et philonica: Studies in Honor of Peder Borgen*. Edited by D. Aune, T. Seland, and J. H. Ulrichsen. Leiden: Brill, 2003.

————. "Gospels, Literary Genre of," Pages 204–6 in *The Westminster Dictionary of New Testament and Early Christian Literature and Rhetoric.* Louisville: Westminster John Knox, 2003.

————. *The New Testament in Its Literary Environment.* Philadelphia: Westminster, 1987.

Bacon, B. W. *The Fourth Gospel in Research and Debate.* New York: Moffat, Yard, 1910.

Ball, D. *"I Am" in John's Gospel: Literary Function, Background, and Theological Implications.* Journal for the Study of the New Testament: Supplement Series 124. Sheffield, Eng.: Sheffield Academic Press, 1996.

Barrett, C. K. "Christocentric or Theocentric? Observations on the Theological Method of the Fourth Gospel." Pages 1–18 in *New Testament Essays.* Philadelphia: Westminster, 1982.

————. "'The Father Is Greater than I,' John 14:28: Subordinationist Christology in the New Testament." Pages 19–36 in *New Testament Essays.* Philadelphia: Westminster, 1982.

————. *The Gospel according to St. John.* London: SPCK, 1955.

————. *The New Testament Background: Selected Documents.* London: SPCK, 1980.

Bauckham, R. "The Beloved Disciple as Ideal Author." *Journal for the Study of the New Testament* 49 (1993): 21–44.

————. "Qumran and the Fourth Gospel: Is There a Connection?" Pages 267–79 in *The Scrolls and the Scriptures: Fifty Years After.* Edited by S. Porter and C. Evans. Sheffield, Eng.: Sheffield Academic Press, 1997.

Beasley-Murray, G. *Gospel of Life: Theology in the Fourth Gospel.* Peabody, Mass.: Hendrickson, 1991.

————. *John.* Word Biblical Commentary 36. Waco, Tex.: Word, 1986.

Beirne, M. M. *Women and Men in the Fourth Gospel: A Genuine Discipleship of Equals.* Journal for the Study of the New Testament: Supplement Series 242. Sheffield, Eng.: Sheffield Academic Press, 2003.

Beutler, J. "Faith and Confession: The Purpose of John." Pages 19–31 in *Word, Theology, and Community in John.* Edited by J. Painter, R. A. Culpepper, and F. F. Segovia. St. Louis: Chalice, 2002.

————. "The Use of 'Scripture' in the Gospel of John." Pages 147–62 in *Exploring the Gospel of John: In Honor of D. Moody Smith.* Edited by R. A. Culpepper and C. C. Black. Louisville: Westminster John Knox, 1996.

Bieringer, R., D. Pollefeyt, and F. Vandecasteele-Vanneuville, eds. *Anti-Judaism and the Fourth Gospel.* Louisville: Westminster John Knox, 2001.

Black, C. C. "'The Words That You Gave to Me I Have Given to Them':
The Grandeur of Johannine Rhetoric." Pages 220–39 in *Exploring
the Gospel of John: In Honor of D. Moody Smith*. Edited by R. A.
Culpepper and C. C. Black. Louisville: Westminster John Knox,
1996.

Blomberg, C. L. *The Historical Reliability of John's Gospel: Issues and
Commentary*. Downers Grove, Ill.: InterVarsity, 2001.

Boer, M. de. "The Depiction of 'The Jews' in John's Gospel: Matters of Be-
havior and Identity." Pages 141–57 in *Anti-Judaism and the Fourth
Gospel*. Edited by R. Bieringer, D. Pollefeyt, and F. Vandecasteele-
Vanneuville. Louisville: Westminster John Knox, 2001.

———. *Johannine Perspectives on the Death of Jesus*. Kampen, Neth.:
Kok, 1996.

Borgen, P. *Bread from Heaven*. Leiden: Brill, 1965.

———. "God's Agent in the Fourth Gospel." Pages 67–78 in *The Interpretation of John*. Edited by J. A. Ashton. Philadelphia: Fortress,
1986.

———. *Philo, John, and Paul: New Perspectives on Judaism and Early
Christianity*. Atlanta: Scholars Press, 1987.

Brodie, T. *The Quest for the Origin of John's Gospel: A Source-Oriented
Approach*. New York: Oxford University Press, 1993.

Broer, I. "Knowledge of Palestine in the Fourth Gospel?" Pages 83–90 in
Jesus in Johannine Tradition. Edited by R. T. Fortna and T. Thatcher.
Louisville: Westminster John Knox, 2001.

Brown, R. *The Community of the Beloved Disciple*. Mahwah, N.J.: Paulist,
1979.

———. "The Eucharist and Baptism in John." Pages 77–95 in *New Testament Essays*. New York: Paulist, 1965.

———. *The Gospel according to John*. 2 vols. Anchor Bible 29, 29A. New
York: Doubleday, 1966–1970.

———. *The Gospel of John*. Philadelphia: Westminster, 1971.

———. "The Gospels (Form)." Pages 86–92 in vol. 1 of *Twentieth Century Theology in the Making*. Edited by J. Pelikan. 3 vols. London:
Collins/Fontana, 1969–1970.

———. "The History of Religions Background of the Prologue to the
Gospel of John." Pages 18–35 in *The Interpretation of John*. Edited
by J. A. Ashton. Philadelphia: Fortress, 1986.

———. *An Introduction to the Gospel of John*. Edited by F. Moloney.
New York: Doubleday, 2003.

———. "The Johannine Sacramentary." Pages 51–76 in *New Testament
Essays*. New York: Paulist, 1965.

———. *Theology of the New Testament*. Vol 2. London: SCM, 1955.

Bultmann, R. *The Gospel of John.* Philadelphia: Westminster Press, 1971.

———. "The Gospels (Form)." Pages 86–92 in volume 1 of *Twentieth Century Theology in the Making.* Edited by J. Pelikan. London: Collins/Fontana, 1969.

———. "The History of Religions Background of the Prologue to the Gospel of John." Pages 18–35 in *The Interpretation of John.* Edited by J. A. Ashton. Philadelphia: Fortress, 1986.

———. *Theology of the New Testament.* Vol 2. London: SCM, 1955.

Burge, G. M. *The Anointed Community.* Grand Rapids: Eerdmans, 1987.

Burney, C. F. *The Aramaic Origin of the Fourth Gospel.* Oxford: Clarendon, 1922.

Burridge, R. A. *What Are the Gospels? A Comparison with Graeco-Roman Biography.* Society for New Testament Studies Monograph Series 70. Cambridge: Cambridge University Press, 1992.

Carson, D. A. "John and the Johannine Epistles." Pages 245–64 in *It Is Written: Scripture Citing Scripture.* Edited by D. A. Carson and H. G. M. Williamson. Cambridge: Cambridge University Press, 1988.

Carter, W. *Households and Discipleship: A Study of Matthew 19–20.* Journal for the Study of the New Testament: Supplement Series 103. Sheffield, Eng.: Sheffield Academic Press, 1994.

———. *John and Empire.* Harrisburg, Pa.: Trinity Press International, forthcoming.

———. *Matthew: Storyteller, Interpreter, Evangelist.* Rev. ed. Peabody, Mass.: Hendrickson, 2004.

———. *Matthew and Empire: Initial Explorations.* Harrisburg, Pa.: Trinity Press International, 2001.

———. *Matthew and the Margins: A Sociopolitical and Religious Reading.* Maryknoll, N.Y.: Orbis, 2000.

———. *Pontius Pilate: Portraits of a Roman Governor.* Collegeville, Minn.: Liturgical, 2003.

———. "The Prologue and John's Gospel: Function, Symbol, and the Definitive Word." *Journal for the Study of the New Testament* 39 (1990): 35–58.

Cassem, N. H. "A Grammatical and Contextual Inventory of the Use of κόσμος in the Johannine Corpus with Some Implications for a Johannine Cosmic Theology." *New Testament Studies* 19 (1972–1973): 81–91.

Cassidy, R. J. *Christians and Roman Rule in the New Testament: New Perspectives.* New York: Crossroad, 2001.

———. *John's Gospel in New Perspective: Christology and the Realities of Roman Power.* Maryknoll, N.Y.: Orbis, 1992.

Charlesworth, J. H. *The Beloved Disciple: Whose Witness Validates the Gospel of John?* Valley Forge, Pa.: Trinity Press International, 1995.

Charlesworth, J. H., ed. *John and the Dead Sea Scrolls.* New York: Crossroad, 1990.

———. *The Messiah: Developments in Earliest Judaism and Christianity.* Minneapolis: Fortress, 1992.

Chatman, S. *Story and Discourse: Narrative Structure in Narrative and Film.* Ithaca, N.Y.: Cornell University Press, 1978.

Clark-Soles, J. *Scripture Cannot Be Broken: The Social Function of the Use of Scripture in the Fourth Gospel.* Leiden: Brill, 2003.

Cohen, S. J. D. *The Beginning of Jewishness: Boundaries, Varieties, Uncertainties.* Berkeley: University of California Press, 1999.

Collins, J. J. *The Apocalyptic Imagination: An Introduction to the Jewish Matrix of Christianity.* New York: Crossroad, 1984.

———. *Between Athens and Jerusalem: Jewish Identity in the Hellenistic Diaspora.* New York: Crossroad, 1986.

Coloe, M. *God Dwells with Us: Temple Symbolism in the Fourth Gospel.* Collegeville, Minn.: Liturgical, 2001.

Conway, C. *Men and Women in the Fourth Gospel: Gender and Johannine Characterization.* Society of Biblical Literature Dissertation Series 167. Atlanta: Society of Biblical Literature, 1999.

Correll, A. *Consummatum est: Eschatology and Church in the Gospel of St John.* London: SPCK, 1958.

Crane, S. "The Concept of Plot." Pages 233–43 in *Approaches to the Novel.* Edited by R. Scholes. Rev. ed. San Francisco: Chandler, 1966.

Crenshaw, J. L. "Theodicy." Pages 444–47 in *The Anchor Bible Dictionary.* 5 vols. Edited by D. N. Freedman. New York: Doubleday, 1992.

Culpepper, R. A. *Anatomy of the Fourth Gospel: A Study in Literary Design.* Philadelphia: Fortress, 1983.

———. *The Gospel and Letters of John.* Interpreting Biblical Texts. Nashville: Abingdon, 1998.

———. "The Gospel of John as a Document of Faith in a Pluralistic Culture." Pages 107–27 in *Readers and Readings of the Fourth Gospel.* Vol. 1 of *What Is John?* Edited by F. F. Segovia. Society of Biblical Literature Symposium Series 3. Atlanta: Scholars Press, 1996.

———. "Inclusivism and Exclusivism in the Fourth Gospel." Pages 85–108 in *Word, Theology, and Community in John.* Edited by J. Painter, R. A. Culpepper, and F. F. Segovia. St. Louis: Chalice, 2002.

———. *The Johannine School: An Evaluation of the Johannine-School Hypothesis Based on an Investigation of the Nature of Ancient Schools.* Missoula, Mont.: Scholars Press, 1975.

————. *John, the Son of Zebedee: The Life of a Legend.* Columbia: University of South Carolina Press, 1994.

————. "The Origin of the 'Amen, Amen' Sayings in the Gospel of John." Pages 253–62 in *Jesus in Johannine Tradition.* Edited by R. T. Fortna and T. Thatcher. Louisville: Westminster John Knox, 2001.

————. "Reading Johannine Irony." Pages 193–207 in *Exploring the Gospel of John: In Honor of D. Moody Smith.* Edited by R. A. Culpepper and C. C. Black. Louisville: Westminster John Knox, 1996.

Culpepper, R. A., and C. C. Black, eds. *Exploring the Gospel of John: In Honor of D. Moody Smith.* Louisville: Westminster John Knox, 1996.

Dahl, N. "'Do Not Wonder!' John 5:28–29 and Johannine Eschatology Once More." Pages 322–36 in *The Conversation Continues: Studies in Paul and John in Honor of J. Louis Martyn.* Edited by R. Fortna and B. Gaventa. Nashville: Abingdon, 1990.

D'Angelo, M. "Abba and 'Father': Imperial Theology and the Jesus Traditions." *Journal of Biblical Literature* 111 (1992): 611–30.

Darr, J. *On Character Building: The Reader and the Rhetoric of Characterization in Luke–Acts.* Louisville: Westminster John Knox, 1992.

Davies, M. *Rhetoric and Reference in the Fourth Gospel.* Journal for the Study of the New Testament: Supplement Series 69. Sheffield, Eng.: JSOT Press, 1992.

Davies, W. D., and D. Daube, eds. *The Background of the New Testament and Its Eschatology.* Cambridge: Cambridge University Press, 1956.

Deissmann, A. *Light from the Ancient East.* New York: Hodder & Stoughton, 1911.

Dewey, J. "The Gospel of John in Its Oral-Written Media World." Pages 239–52 in *Jesus in Johannine Tradition.* Edited by R. T. Fortna and T. Thatcher. Louisville: Westminster John Knox, 2001.

Dodd, C. H. *Historical Tradition in the Fourth Gospel.* Cambridge: Cambridge University Press, 1963.

————. *The Interpretation of the Fourth Gospel.* Cambridge: Cambridge University Press, 1953.

Duke, P. *Irony in the Fourth Gospel.* Atlanta: John Knox, 1985.

Egan, K. "What Is a Plot?" *New Literary History* 9 (1978): 455–73.

Ehrman, B. *Lost Scriptures: Books That Did Not Make It into the New Testament.* Oxford: Oxford University Press, 2003.

Fehribach, A. *The Women in the Life of the Bridegroom: A Feminist Historical-Literary Analysis of the Female Characters in the Fourth Gospel.* Collegeville, Minn.: Liturgical, 1998.

Filson, F. "Who Was the Beloved Disciple?" *Journal of Biblical Literature* 68 (1949): 83–88.

Fortna, R. *The Fourth Gospel and Its Predecessor.* Philadelphia: Fortress, 1988.

————. *The Gospel of Signs: A Reconstruction of the Narrative Underlying the Fourth Gospel.* Cambridge: Cambridge University Press, 1970.

Fortna, R. T., and T. Thatcher, eds. *Jesus in Johannine Tradition.* Louisville: Westminster John Knox, 2001.

Foster, E. M. *Aspects of the Novel.* New York: Penguin Books, 1962.

Franklin, L. "There's More Than One Text in This Class: John's Evoking of the Intertext of Isaiah in John 1:23's Citation of Isaiah 40:3." Paper presented at the annual meeting of the Central States Region of the Society of Biblical Literature. St. Louis, April 2002.

Freed, E. D. *Old Testament Quotations in the Gospel of John.* Leiden: Brill, 1965.

————. "Variations in the Language and Thought of John." *Zeitschrift für die neutestamentliche Wissenschaft* 55 (1964): 167–97.

Frye, N. *Anatomy of Criticism.* Princeton, N.J.: Princeton University Press, 1971.

Funk, R. *The Acts of Jesus: The Search for the Authentic Deeds of Jesus.* San Francisco: HarperSanFrancisco, 1998.

————. *The Five Gospels: What Did Jesus Really Say?* New York: Polebridge, 1993.

Gardner-Smith, P. *Saint John and the Synoptic Gospel.* Cambridge: Cambridge University Press, 1938.

Garnsey, P. *Food and Society in Classical Antiquity.* Cambridge: Cambridge University Press, 1999.

Gaventa, B. "The Archive of Excess: John 21 and the Problem of Narrative Closure." Pages 240–52 in *Exploring the Gospel of John: In Honor of D. Moody Smith.* Edited by R. A. Culpepper and C. C. Black. Louisville: Westminster John Knox, 1996.

Gill, C. "Character-Development in Plutarch and Tacitus." *Classical Quarterly* 33 (1983): 469–87.

————. "The Character-Personality Distinction." Pages 1–31 in *Character and Individuality in Greek Literature.* Edited by C. R. Pelling. Oxford: Oxford University Press, 1990.

Goodwin, C. "How Did John Treat His Sources?" *Journal of Biblical Literature* 73 (1954): 61–75.

Grayston, K. "The Meaning of PARAKLĒTOS." *Journal for the Study of the New Testament* 13 (1981): 67–82.

Greimas, A. J. *Sémantique structurale.* Paris: Larousse, 1966.

Grigsby, B. H. "The Cross as an Expiatory Sacrifice in the Fourth Gospel." *Journal for the Study of the New Testament* 15 (1982): 51–80.

Gunther, J. J. "The Alexandrian Gospel and Letters of John." *Catholic Biblical Quarterly* 41 (1979): 581–603.

———. "Early Identification of Authorship of the Johannine Writings." *Journal of Ecclesiastical History* 31 (1980): 403–27.

Halliday, M. A. K. "Antilanguages." *American Anthropologist* 78 (1976): 570–84.

Hanson, A. T. *The Prophetic Gospel: A Study in John and the Old Testament.* Edinburgh: T&T Clark, 1991.

Hanson, K. C., and D. E. Oakman, *Palestine in the Time of Jesus.* Minneapolis: Fortress, 1998.

Harner, P. B. *The "I Am" of the Fourth Gospel.* Philadelphia: Fortress, 1970.

Harrington, D. J. *Invitation to the Apocrypha.* Grand Rapids: Eerdmans, 1999.

Harris, W. V. *Ancient Literacy.* Cambridge: Harvard University Press, 1989.

Hedrick, C. "The Four/Thirty-Four Gospels: Diversity and Division among the Earliest Christians." *Bible Review* 18 (June 2002): 20–31, 46–47.

———. "Vestigial Scenes in John, or Settings without Dramatization— and Why?" Paper presented at the annual meeting of the Central States Region of the Society of Biblical Literature. St. Louis, April 2004.

Hengel, M. *The Johannine Question.* Philadelphia: Trinity Press International, 1989.

Hochman, B. *Character in Literature.* Ithaca, N.Y.: Cornell University Press, 1985.

Horbury, W. "The Benediction of the *minim* and Early Jewish-Christian Controversy." *Journal of Theological Studies* 38 (1982): 19–61.

Horsley, R., ed. *Paul and the Roman Imperial Order.* Harrisburg, Pa.: Trinity Press International, 2004.

Horst, P. van der. "The Birkat ha-Minim in Recent Research." *Expository Times* 105 (1994): 363–68.

Howard-Brooks, W. *Becoming Children of God: John's Gospel and Radical Discipleship.* Maryknoll, N.Y.: Orbis, 1995.

Jeremias, J. *The Rediscovery of Bethesda.* Louisville: John Knox, 1966.

Johnson, L. T. "The New Testament's Anti-Jewish Slander and the Conventions of Ancient Polemic." *Journal of Biblical Literature* 108 (1989): 419–41.

Jonge, M. de. "The Messiah." Pages 777–88 in *The Anchor Bible Dictionary.* 5 vols. Edited by D. N. Freedman. New York: Doubleday, 1992.

Jonge, M. de, et al., eds. *L'Évangile de Jean: Sources, Rédaction, Théologie.* Bibliotheca ephemeridum theologicarum lovaniensium 44. Gembloux, Belgium: J. Duculot, 1977.

Karris, R. J. *Jesus and the Marginalized in John's Gospel.* Collegeville, Minn.: Liturgical, 1990.

Katz, S. "Issues in the Separation of Judaism and Christianity after 70 C.E.: A Reconsideration." *Journal of Biblical Literature* 103 (1984): 43–76.

Keck, L. "Derivation as Destiny: 'Of-ness' in Johannine Christology, Anthropology, and Soteriology." Pages 274–88 in *Exploring the Gospel of John: In Honor of D. Moody Smith.* Edited by A. Culpepper and C. C. Black. Louisville: Westminster John Knox, 1996.

Kim, S.-J. "The Johannine Jesus and Its Sociopolitical Context." *Yonsei Review of Theology and Culture* 6 (2001): 209–21.

Kimmelman, R. "Birkat ha-Minim and the Lack of Evidence for an Anti-Christian Jewish Prayer in Late Antiquity." Pages 226–44 in vol. 2 of *Jewish and Christian Self-Definition.* Edited by E. P. Sanders, A. I. Baumgarten, and A. Mendelson. 3 vols. Philadelphia: Fortress, 1980–1982.

Kittel, G. and G. Friedrich, eds. *Theological Dictionary of the New Testament.* Translated by G. W. Bromiley. 10 vols. Grand Rapids: Eerdmans, 1964–1967.

Klassen, W. "Judas Iscariot." Pages 1091–92 in *The Anchor Bible Dictionary.* 5 vols. Edited by D. N. Freedman. New York: Doubleday, 1992.

Koester, C. "Comedy, Humor, and the Gospel of John." Pages 123–41 in *Word, Theology, and Community in John.* Edited by J. Painter, R. A. Culpepper, and F. F. Segovia. St. Louis: Chalice, 2002.

———. "Jesus the Way, the Cross, and the World according to the Gospel of John." *World and Word* 21 (2001): 360–69.

———. " 'The Savior of the World' (John 4:42)." *Journal of Biblical Literature* 109 (1990): 665–80.

———. *Symbolism in the Fourth Gospel: Meaning, Mystery, Community.* Minneapolis: Fortress, 1995.

Köstenberger, A. J. *The Mission of Jesus and the Disciples according to the Fourth Gospel with Implications for the Fourth Gospel's Purposes and the Mission of the Contemporary Church.* Grand Rapids: Eerdmans, 1998.

Kuschel, K.-J. *Abraham: Sign of Hope for Jews, Christians, and Moslems.* New York: Continuum, 1995.

Kysar, R. "Anti-Semitism and the Gospel of John." Pages 113–27 in *Anti-Semitism and Early Christianity: Issues of Polemic and Faith.* Edited by C. Evans and D. Hagner. Minneapolis: Fortress, 1993.

———. "Coming Hermeneutical Earthquake in Johannine Interpretation." Pages 185–89 in *Readers and Readings of the Fourth Gospel.* Vol. 1 of *What Is John?* Edited by F. F. Segovia. Society of Biblical Literature Symposium Series 3. Atlanta: Scholars Press, 1996.

———. *The Fourth Evangelist and His Gospel: An Examination of Contemporary Scholarship.* Minneapolis: Augsburg, 1975.

———. "The Fourth Gospel: A Report on Recent Research." *ANRW* 25.3:2389–480. Part 2, *Principat,* 25.3. Edited by H. Temporini and W. Haase. New York: de Gruyter, 1985.

———. "Johannine Metaphor—Meaning and Function: A Literary Case Study of John 10:1–8 [i.e., 10:1–18]." *Semeia* 53 (1991): 81–105.

———. *John.* Minneapolis: Augsburg, 1986.

———. *John: The Maverick Gospel.* Rev. ed. Louisville: Westminster John Knox, 1993.

———. "The Making of Metaphor: Another Reading of John 3:1–15." Pages 21–41 in *Readers and Readings of the Fourth Gospel.* Vol. 1 of *What Is John?* Edited by F. F. Segovia. Society of Biblical Studies Symposium Series 3. Atlanta: Scholars Press, 1996.

———. *Preaching John.* Minneapolis: Fortress, 2002.

Ladd, G. *A Theology of the New Testament.* Grand Rapids: Eerdmans, 1974.

Larsson, T. *God in the Fourth Gospel: A Hermeneutical Study of the History of Interpretations.* Coniectanea biblica: New Testament Series 35. Stockholm: Almqvist & Wiksell International, 2001.

Lee, D. "Beyond Suspicion? The Fatherhood of God in the Fourth Gospel." *Pacifica* 8 (1995): 140–54.

———. *Flesh and Glory: Symbolism, Gender, and Theology in the Gospel of John.* New York: Crossroad, 2002.

———. *The Symbolic Narratives of the Fourth Gospel: The Interplay of Form and Meaning.* Journal for the Study of the New Testament: Supplement Series 95. Sheffield, Eng.: Sheffield Academic Press, 1994.

Lenski, G. *Power and Privilege: A Theory of Social Stratification.* Chapel Hill: University of North Carolina Press, 1984.

Lincoln, A. *Truth on Trial: The Lawsuit Motif in the Fourth Gospel.* Peabody, Mass.: Hendrickson, 2000.

Lindars, B. "Discourse and Tradition: The Use of the Sayings of Jesus in the Discourses of the Fourth Gospel." *Journal for the Study of the New Testament* 13 (1981): 83–101.

———. *The Gospel of John.* New Century Bible Commentary. Grand Rapids: Eerdmans, 1972.

Louw, J. P. "On Johannine Style." *Neotestamentica* 20 (1986): 5–12.

Lowe, M. "Who Were the *Ioudaioi?*" *Novum Testamentum* 18 (1976): 102–7.

Maccini, R. *Her Testimony Is True: Women as Witnesses according to John.* Journal for the Study of the New Testament: Supplement Series 125. Sheffield, Eng.: Sheffield Academic Press, 1995.

MacMullen, R. *Roman Social Relations.* New Haven, Conn.: Yale University Press, 1974.

Malina, B. J. *The Gospel of John in Sociolinguistic Perspective.* Protocol of the Colloquy of the Center for Hermeneutical Studies in Hellenistic and Modern Culture 48. Berkeley, Calif.: Center for Hermeneutical Studies, 1985.

Martyn, J. L. "Glimpses into the History of the Johannine Community." Pages 90–121 in *The Gospel of John in Christian History.* New York: Paulist, 1979.

———. *History and Theology in the Fourth Gospel.* 3d ed. Louisville: Westminster John Knox, 2003.

———. "Source Criticism and Religionsgeschichte in the Fourth Gospel." Pages 99–121 in *The Interpretation of John.* Edited by J. Ashton. Philadelphia: Fortress, 1968.

Matson, M. "The Temple Incident: An Integral Element in the Fourth Gospel's Narrative." Pages 145–53 in *Jesus in Johannine Tradition.* Edited by R. Fortna and T. Thatcher. Louisville: Westminster John Knox, 2001.

Mead, A. H. "The *basilikos* in John 4:46–54." *Journal for the Study of the New Testament* 23 (1985): 69–72.

Meeks, W. "Breaking Away: Three New Testament Pictures of Christianity's Separation from the Jewish Communities." Pages 93–115 in *"To See Ourselves as Others See Us": Christians, Jews, "Others" in Late Antiquity.* Edited by J. Neusner and E. S. Frerichs. Chico, Calif.: Scholars Press, 1985.

———. "Equal to God." Pages 309–21 in *The Conversation Continues: Studies in Paul and John in Honor of J. Louis Martyn.* Edited by R. Fortna and B. Gaventa. Nashville: Abingdon, 1990.

———. "The Ethics of the Fourth Evangelist." Pages 317–26 in *Exploring the Gospel of John: In Honor of D. Moody Smith.* Edited by R. A. Culpepper and C. C. Black. Louisville: Westminster John Knox, 1996.

———. "The Man from Heaven in Johannine Sectarianism." *Journal of Biblical Literature* 91 (1972): 44–72. Repr. pages 67–78 in *The Interpretation of John.* Edited by J. A. Ashton. Philadelphia: Fortress, 1986.

————. *The Prophet-King: Moses Traditions and the Johannine Christology.* Novum Testamentum Supplements 14. Leiden: Brill, 1967.

Meyer, P. W. "The Presentation of God in the Fourth Gospel." Pages 255–73 in *Exploring the Gospel of John: In Honor of D. Moody Smith.* Edited by R. A. Culpepper and C. C. Black. Louisville: Westminster John Knox, 1996.

Moloney, F. "The Fourth Gospel and the Jesus of History." *New Testament Studies* 46 (2000): 42–58.

————. "The Function of John 13–17 within the Johannine Narrative." Pages 43–65 in *Literary and Social Readings of the Fourth Gospel.* Vol. 2 of *What Is John?* Edited by F. F. Segovia. Society of Biblical Literature Symposium Series 7. Atlanta: Scholars Press, 1998.

————. *The Gospel of John.* Sacra pagina 4. Collegeville, Minn.: Liturgical, 1998.

————. "The Gospel of John as Scripture." Pages 333–47 in *The Gospel of John: Text and Context.* Boston: Brill, 2005.

————. *The Johannine Son of Man.* Rome: Libreria Ateneo Salesiano, 1976.

————. "The Johannine Son of Man Revisited." Pages 177–202 in *The Christology and Theology of the Fourth Gospel: Essays by Members of the New Testament Studies Johannine Writings Seminar.* Edited by G. van Belle and J. van der Watt. Bibliotheca ephemeridum theologicarum lovaniensium. Leuven: Peeters, 2005.

————. "Raymond Brown's New *Introduction to the Gospel of John:* A Presentation—and Some Questions." *Catholic Biblical Quarterly* 65 (2003): 1–21.

Moore, S. *Literary Criticism of the Gospels.* New Haven, Conn.: Yale University Press, 1989.

Morrow, S. "Κόσμος in John." *Catholic Biblical Quarterly* 64 (2002): 90–102.

Motyer, S. *Your Father the Devil? A New Approach to John and "the Jews."* Carlisle, Eng.: Paternoster, 1997.

Neirynck, F. "John and the Synoptics." Pages 73–106 in *L'Évangile de Jean: Sources, Rédaction, Théologie.* Edited by M. de Jonge et al. Bibliotheca ephemeridum theologicarum lovaniensium 44. Gembloux, Belgium: J. Duculot, 1977.

————. "John and the Synoptics: The Empty Tomb Stories." *New Testament Studies* 30 (1984): 161–87.

Nelson, H. K. "Johannine Research." Pages 11–30 in *New Readings in John: Literary and Theological Perspectives from the Scandinavian Conference on the Fourth Gospel, Arhus, 1997.* Edited by J. Nissen and S. Pedersen. Journal for the Study of the New Testament: Supplement Series 182. Sheffield, Eng.: Sheffield Academic Press, 1999.

Neyrey, J. *An Ideology of Revolt: John's Christology in Social-Science Perspective.* Philadelphia: Fortress, 1988.

Nicholson, G. *Death as Departure: The Johannine Descent-Ascent Schema.* Society of Biblical Literature Dissertation Series 63. Chico, Calif.: Scholars Press, 1983.

Nickelsburg, G. W. E. *Ancient Judaism and Christian Origins: Diversity, Continuity, and Transformation.* Minneapolis: Fortress, 2003.

Nicol, W. *The sēmeia in the Fourth Gospel.* Leiden: Brill, 1972.

Nissen, J. "Community and Ethics in the Gospel of John." Pages 194–212 in *New Readings in John: Literary and Theological Perspectives from the Scandinavian Conference on the Fourth Gospel, Arhus, 1997.* Edited by J. Nissen and S. Pedersen. Journal for the Study of the New Testament: Supplement Series 182. Sheffield, Eng.: Sheffield Academic Press, 1999.

———. "Mission in the Fourth Gospel: Historical and Hermeneutical Perspectives." Pages 213–31 in *New Readings in John: Literary and Theological Perspectives from the Scandinavian Conference on the Fourth Gospel, Arhus, 1997.* Edited by J. Nissen and S. Pedersen. Journal for the Study of the New Testament: Supplement Series 182. Sheffield, Eng.: Sheffield Academic Press, 1999.

Nissen, J., and S. Pedersen, eds. *New Readings in John: Literary and Theological Perspectives from the Scandinavian Conference on the Fourth Gospel, Arhus, 1997.* Journal for the Study of the New Testament: Supplement Series 182. Sheffield, Eng.: Sheffield Academic Press, 1999.

O'Day, G. "The Gospel of John." Pages 491–865 in vol. 9 of *The New Interpreter's Bible.* Edited by L. Keck. 12 vols. Nashville: Abingdon, 1994–2004.

———. "'I Have Said These Things to You . . .': The Unsettled Place of Jesus' Discourses in Literary Approaches to the Fourth Gospel." Pages 143–54 in *Word, Theology, and Community in John.* Edited by J. Painter, R. A. Culpepper, and F. F. Segovia. St. Louis: Chalice, 2002.

———. "Johannine Theology as Sectarian Theology." Pages 199–203 in *Readers and Readings of the Fourth Gospel.* Vol. 1 of *What Is John?* Edited by F. F. Segovia. Society of Biblical Literature Symposium Series 3. Atlanta: Scholars Press, 1996.

———. "John." Pages 381–93 in *Women's Bible Commentary: Expanded Edition with Apocrypha.* Edited by C. Newsom and S. Ringe. Louisville: Westminster John Knox, 1998.

———. "John's Voice and the Church's Preaching." *Word and World* 21 (2001): 394–403.

————. *Revelation in the Fourth Gospel: Narrative Mode and Theological Claim*. Philadelphia: Fortress, 1986.

Okure, T. *The Johannine Approach to Mission: A Contextual Study of John 4:1–42*. Wissenschaftliche Untersuchungen zum Neuen Testament 31. Tübingen: J. C. B. Mohr [Paul Siebeck], 1988.

O'Rourke, J. "Asides in the Gospel of John." *Novum Testamentum* 21 (1979): 210–19.

Pagels, E. *The Johannine Gospel in Gnostic Exegesis: Heracleon's Commentary on John*. Nashville: Abingdon, 1973.

Painter, J. "Earth Made Whole: John's Rereading of Genesis." Pages 65–84 in *Word, Theology, and Community in John*. Edited by J. Painter, R. A. Culpepper, and F. F. Segovia. St. Louis: Chalice, 2002.

————. *The Quest for the Messiah: The History, Literature, and Theology of the Johannine Community*. Nashville: Abingdon, 1993.

Painter, J., A. Culpepper, and F. Segovia, eds. *Word, Theology, and Community in John*. St. Louis: Chalice, 2002.

Parker, P. "John and John Mark." *Journal of Biblical Literature* 79 (1960): 97–110.

————. "John the Son of Zebedee and the Fourth Gospel." *Journal of Biblical Literature* 81 (1962): 35–43.

Pelling, C. R., ed. *Character and Individuality in Greek Literature*. Oxford: Oxford University Press, 1990.

Petersen, N. R. *The Gospel of John and the Sociology of Light: Language and Characterization in the Fourth Gospel*. Valley Forge, Pa.: Trinity Press International, 1993.

Pollard, T. "The Exegesis of John 10:30 in the Early Trinitarian Controversies." *New Testament Studies* 3 (1956–57): 334–49.

————. "The Father-Son and God-Believer Relationships according to St. John: A Brief Study of John's Use of Prepositions." Pages 363–69 in *L'Évangile de Jean: Sources, Rédaction, Théologie*. Edited by M. de Jonge et al. Bibliotheca ephemeridum theologicarum lovaniensium 44. Gembloux, Belgium: J. Duculot, 1977.

Polman, G. H. "Chronological Biography and AKME in Plutarch." *Classical Philology* 69 (1974): 169–77.

Potterie, I. de la. *La vérité dans saint Jean*. 2 vols. Analecta biblica 73–74. Rome: Biblical Institute Press, 1977.

Reinhartz, A. *Befriending the Beloved Disciple: A Jewish Reading of the Gospel of John*. New York: Continuum, 2001.

Rensberger, D. "Anti-Judaism and the Gospel of John." Pages 120–57 in *Anti-Judaism and the Gospels*. Edited by W. R. Farmer. Harrisburg, Pa.: Trinity Press International, 1999.

————. *Johannine Faith and Liberating Community.* Philadelphia: Westminster, 1988.

————. "The Messiah Who Has Come into the World: The Message of the Gospel of John." Pages 15–23 in *Jesus and the Johannine Tradition.* Edited by R. Fortna and T. Thatcher. Louisville: Westminster John Knox, 2001.

————. "Spirituality and Christology in Johannine Sectarianism." Pages 173–88 in *Word, Theology, and Community in John.* Edited by J. Painter, R. A. Culpepper, and F. F. Segovia. St. Louis: Chalice, 2002.

Rhoads, D., and K. Syreeni, eds. *Characterization in the Gospels: Reconceiving Narrative Criticism.* Journal for the Study of the New Testament: Supplement Series 184. Sheffield, Eng.: Sheffield Academic Press, 1999.

Ringe, S. *Wisdom's Friends: Community and Christology in the Fourth Gospel.* Louisville: Westminster John Knox, 1999.

Robinson, J. A. T. *The Priority of John.* Oak Park, Ill.: Meyer-Stone, 1985.

————. *Redating the New Testament.* London: SCM, 1976.

Rohrbaugh, R. "The Gospel of John in the Twenty-First Century." Pages 257–63 in *Literary and Social Readings of the Fourth Gospel.* Vol. 2 of *What Is John?* Edited by F. F. Segovia. Society of Biblical Literature Symposium Series 7. Atlanta: Scholars Press, 1998.

Ruckstuhl, E. "Johannine Language and Style." Pages 125–47 in *L'Évangile de Jean: Sources, Rédaction, Théologie.* Edited by M. de Jonge et al. Bibliotheca ephemeridum theologicarum lovaniensium 44. Gembloux, Belgium: J. Duculot, 1977.

————. *Die literarische Einheit des Johannesevangelium: Der gegenwärtige Stand der einschlägigen Erforschung.* Freiburg, Switz.: Paulusverlag, 1951.

Saldarini, A. J. *Pharisees, Scribes, and Sadducees in Palestinian Society.* Wilmington, Del.: Michael Glazier, 1988.

Sanders, J. N. *The Fourth Gospel in the Early Church.* Cambridge: Cambridge University Press, 1943.

Schiffman, L. "At the Crossroads: Tannaitic Perspectives on the Jewish-Christian Schism." Pages 115–56 in vol. 2 of *Jewish and Christian Self-Definition.* Edited by E. P. Sanders, A. I. Baumgarten, and A. Mendelson. 3 vols. Philadelphia: Fortress, 1980–1982.

Schnackenburg, R. *The Gospel according to St. John.* 3 vols. New York: Seabury, 1980–1982.

Schneiders, S. "'Because of the Woman's Testimony . . .': Reexamining the Issue of Authorship in the Fourth Gospel." *New Testament Studies* 44 (1998): 513–35.

———. "John 20:11–18: The Encounter of the Easter Jesus with Mary Magdalene—A Transformative Feminist Reading." Pages 155–68 in *Readers and Readings of the Fourth Gospel*. Vol. 1 of *What Is John?* Edited by F. F. Segovia. Society of Biblical Literature Symposium Series 3. Atlanta: Scholars Press, 1996.

———. "Women in the Fourth Gospel and the Role of Women in the Contemporary Church." *Biblical Theology Bulletin* 12 (1982): 35–45.

———. *Written That You May Believe: Encountering Jesus in the Fourth Gospel*. New York: Crossroad, 1999.

Schnelle, U. "Recent Views of John's Gospel." *Word and World* 21 (2001): 352–59.

Schottroff, L. "Important Aspects of the Gospel for the Future." Pages 205–10 in *Readers and Readings of the Fourth Gospel*. Vol. 1 of *What Is John?* Edited by F. F. Segovia. Society of Biblical Literature Symposium Series 3. Atlanta: Scholars Press, 1996.

Schuchard, B. *Scripture within Scripture: The Interrelationship of Form and Function in the Explicit Old Testament Citations in the Gospel of John*. Society of Biblical Literature Dissertation Series 133. Atlanta: Scholars Press, 1992.

Schürer, E. *The History of the Jewish People in the Age of Jesus Christ (175 B.C.–A. D. 135)*. Revised and Edited by G. Vermes, F. Millar, and M. Goodman. 3 vols. in 4. Edinburgh: T&T Clark, 1973–1987. Vol. 3, part 1.

Schweizer, E. *Ego eimi: Die religionsgeschichtliche Herkunft und theologische Bedeutung der johanneischen Bildreden, zugleich ein Beitrag zur Quellenfrage des vierten Evangeliums*. Forschungen zur Religion und Literatur des Alten und Neuen Testaments 38. Göttingen: Vandenhoeck & Ruprecht, 1939.

Scott, M. *Sophia and the Johannine Jesus*. Journal for the Study of the New Testament: Supplement Series 71. Sheffield, Eng.: Sheffield Academic Press, 1992.

Segovia, F. F. *The Farewell of the Word: The Johannine Call to Abide*. Minneapolis: Fortress, 1991.

———. "The Gospel at the Close of the Century: Engagement from the Diaspora." Pages 211–16 in *Readers and Readings of the Fourth Gospel*. Vol. 1 of *What Is John?* Edited by F. F. Segovia. Society of Biblical Literature Symposium Series 3. Atlanta: Scholars Press, 1996.

———. "John 1:1–18 as Entrée into Johannine Reality: Representation and Ramifications," Pages 33–64 in *Word, Theology, and Community in John*. Edited by J. Painter, R. A. Culpepper, and F. F. Segovia. St. Louis: Chalice, 2002.

————. "The Journey(s) of the Word of God: A Reading of the Plot of the Fourth Gospel." *Semeia* 53 (1991): 23–54.

Segovia, F. F., ed. *Literary and Social Readings of the Fourth Gospel.* Vol. 2 of *What Is John?* Society of Biblical Literature Symposium Series 7. Atlanta: Scholars Press, 1998.

————. *Readers and Readings of the Fourth Gospel.* Vol. 1 of *What Is John?* Society of Biblical Literature Symposium Series 3. Atlanta: Scholars Press, 1996.

Senior, D. *The Passion of Jesus in the Gospel of John.* Collegeville, Minn.: Liturgical, 1991.

Shepherd, W. H. *The Narrative Function of the Holy Spirit as a Character in Luke-Acts.* Society of Biblical Literature Dissertation Series 147. Atlanta: Scholars Press, 1994.

Siker, J. *Disinheriting the Jews: Abraham in Early Christian Literature.* Louisville: Westminster John Knox, 1991.

Sloyan, G. *John.* Interpretation. Atlanta: John Knox, 1988.

————. *What Are They Saying about John?* New York: Paulist, 1991.

Smith, D. M. *The Composition and Order of the Fourth Gospel: Bultmann's Literary Theory.* New Haven, Conn.: Yale University Press, 1965.

————. "The Contribution of J. Louis Martyn to the Understanding of the Gospel of John." Pages 275–94 in *The Conversation Continues: Studies in Paul and John in Honor of J. Louis Martyn.* Edited by R. Fortna and B. R. Gaventa. Nashville: Abingdon, 1990.

————. "Ethics and the Interpretation of the Gospel." Pages 109–22 in *Word, Theology, and Community in John.* Edited by J. Painter, R. A. Culpepper, and F. F. Segovia. St. Louis: Chalice, 2002.

————. "Johannine Studies since Bultmann." *Word and World* 21 (2001): 343–51.

————. *John.* Abingdon New Testament Commentaries. Nashville: Abingdon, 1999.

————. *John among the Gospels: The Relationship in Twentieth Century Research.* Minneapolis: Fortress, 1992.

————. *The Theology of the Gospel of John.* Cambridge: Cambridge University Press, 1995.

Smith, R. H. "Exodus Typology in the Fourth Gospel," *Journal of Biblical Literature* 81 (1962): 329–42.

Staley, J. "What Can a Postmodern Approach to the Fourth Gospel Add?" Pages 47–57 in *Jesus in Johannine Tradition.* Edited by R. T. Fortna and T. Thatcher. Louisville: Westminster John Knox, 2001.

Stibbe, M. W. G. *John as Storyteller.* Cambridge: Cambridge University Press, 1992.

————. *John's Gospel.* London: Routledge, 1994.

Talbert, C. H. *Reading John.* New York: Crossroad, 1992.

Tenney, M. C. "The Footnotes of John's Gospel." *Bibliotheca sacra* 117 (1960): 350–63.

Thatcher, T. "A New Look at Asides in the Fourth Gospel," *Bibliotheca sacra* 151 (1994): 428–39.

————. *The Riddles of Jesus in John: A Study in Tradition and Folklore.* Society of Biblical Literature Monograph Series 53. Atlanta: Society of Biblical Literature, 2000.

————. "The Riddles of Jesus in the Johannine Dialogues." Pages 263–77 in *Jesus in Johannine Tradition.* Edited by R. Fortna and T. Thatcher. Louisville: Westminster John Knox, 2001.

Thielman, F. "The Style of the Fourth Gospel and Ancient Literary Critical Concepts of Religious Discourse." Pages 169–83 in *Persuasive Artistry: Studies in New Testament Rhetoric in Honor of George A. Kennedy.* Edited by D. F. Watson. Journal for the Study of the New Testament: Supplement Series 50. Sheffield, Eng.: JSOT Press, 1991.

Thomas, J. C. *Footwashing in John 13 and the Johannine Community.* Journal for the Study of the New Testament: Supplement Series 61. Sheffield, Eng.: JSOT Press, 1991.

Thompson, M. M. *The God of the Gospel of John.* Grand Rapids: Eerdmans, 2001.

Tilborg, S. van. *Imaginative Love in John.* Leiden: Brill, 1993.

————. *Reading John in Ephesus.* Leiden: Brill, 1996.

Tobin, T. H. "The Prologue of John and the Hellenistic Jewish Speculation." *Catholic Biblical Quarterly* 52 (1990): 253–69.

Tolmie, D. F. "The Characterization of God in the Fourth Gospel." *Journal for the Study of the New Testament* 69 (1998): 57–75.

————. *Jesus' Farewell to the Disciples: John 13:1–17:26 in Narratological Perspective.* Biblical Interpretation Series 12. Leiden: Brill, 1995.

Van den Heever, G. "Finding Data in Unexpected Places (or: From Text Linguistics to Socio-rhetoric): Towards a Socio-rhetorical Reading of John's Gospel." *Neotestimentica* 33 (1999): 343–64.

Vaughan, B. N. Y. "Sermons in John and the Problem of Justice." *Theology* 102 (1999): 186–94.

Von Wahlde, U. C. *The Earliest Version of John's Gospel: Recovering the Gospel of Signs.* Wilmington, Del.: Michael Glazier, 1989.

————. " 'The Jews' in the Gospel of John: Fifteen Years of Research." *Ephemerides theologicae lovanienses* 76 (2000): 30–55.

————. "The Johannine 'Jews': A Critical Survey." *New Testament Studies* 28 (1982): 33–60.

Weiss, K. "πυρέσσω, πυρετός." Pages 956–58 in vol. 6 of *Theological Dictionary of the New Testament*. Edited by G. Kittel and G. Friedrich. Translated by G. W. Bromiley. 10 vols. Grand Rapids, 1964–1976.

Wenham, D. "A Historical View of John's Gospel." *Themelios* 23 (1998): 5–21.

Westermann, C. *The Gospel of John in the Light of the Old Testament*. Peabody, Mass.: Hendrickson, 1998.

Whittaker, C. R. "The Poor." Pages 272–99 in *The Romans*. Edited by A. Giardini. Chicago: University of Chicago Press, 1993.

Wilson, R. McL. "Philo and the Fourth Gospel." *Expository Times* 65 (1953–1954): 47–49.

Windisch, H. "John's Narrative Style." Pages 25–64 in *The Gospel of John as Literature: An Anthology of Twentieth-Century Perspectives*. Edited by M. Stibbe. Leiden: Brill, 1993.

Witherington, B. *John's Wisdom: A Commentary on the Fourth Gospel*. Louisville: Westminster John Knox, 1995.

Yee, G. *Jewish Feasts and the Gospel of John*. Wilmington, Del.: Michael Glazier, 1989.

Index of Modern Authors

Index of Ancient Sources

8:48   7, 69, 70, 96, 119,
    163, 166
8:48–52   72
8:49   99
8:50   138
8:51   30, 118, 127, 138
8:51–52   99, 105
8:51–53   114
8:52   69, 70
8:53   120
8:54   53, 138
8:54–55   54
8:55   54, 165
8:56   127, 200
8:56–58   114
8:56–59   71
8:57   69, 120
8:58   66, 123, 128, 203
8:59   28, 40, 72, 204
9   11, 14, 17, 19, 32, 33,
    40, 54, 72, 73, 78, 81,
    83, 85, 93, 94, 96, 97,
    101, 107, 111, 159,
    166, 167, 168, 189
9–10:21   31
9:1–3a   147
9:1–7   28, 40, 62, 192
9:1–8   83, 172, 189
9:1–12   72
9:1–18   172
9:1–41   32
9:2   58, 127
9:3   64, 65
9:4   64, 202
9:5   66, 92, 102, 122,
    138
9:6–7   147
9:7   6, 109, 161, 196
9:8   33, 147, 192
9:8–10   40
9:8–12   82
9:11   40, 82
9:12   28
9:13–17   82
9:13–18   68
9:13–41   40, 82
9:14   109
9:16   40, 43, 72, 82, 120
9:17   40, 82
9:18–21   33
9:18–23   40, 82
9:20–23   167
9:22   69, 82, 158, 162,
    165, 166, 168, 170,
    187, 216
9:22–34   189

9:24   40, 70, 82, 119
9:24–34   82
9:27   82
9:28   158, 167
9:28–29   51, 54, 71, 83
9:29   70, 82, 119
9:33   40, 65, 82, 202
9:34   33, 82, 94, 96,
    167, 192
9:35   59, 65, 83, 128
9:35–38   82
9:35–39   202
9:37–38   40
9:38   82, 94, 167
9:38–39   96
9:39   92, 118, 127
9:39–41   71
9:39–10:21   82
9:40   116
9:41   70, 165
10   25, 29, 40, 44, 77,
    83, 86, 124, 219
10:1   72
10:1–3   142
10:1–3a   125
10:1–5   6, 116, 127, 153
10:1–6   118
10:1–16   143
10:1–21   40
10:3   209
10:3–4   81
10:3–5   209
10:3b–5   125
10:4–5   84
10:5   125
10:6   109, 116, 118
10:6–7a   125
10:7   66, 122, 125
10:7–8   142
10:7b–10   125
10:8   72, 125
10:9   66, 122, 125, 138
10:10   43, 53, 58, 73,
    86, 99, 125, 136, 138,
    203
10:11   66, 122, 125
10:11–15   125
10:12   72, 125
10:14   66, 122, 125
10:15   53, 113
10:15–18   205
10:16   125, 142, 151,
    160
10:17   52, 102
10:17–18   28, 62, 120,
    121, 125

10:18   65
10:19   69
10:20   70
10:22   32, 36, 109
10:22–23   30
10:22–38   40
10:22–39   189
10:23   109
10:24   69, 70, 117, 216
10:24–26   16
10:26   96
10:27   30
10:28   52, 138
10:29   52
10:30   53, 60, 200, 201
10:30–33   71
10:31   31
10:31–33   69, 70, 72
10:31–39   204
10:32   65, 119
10:33   120, 163, 199
10:34   151
10:34–35   132
10:34–36   127
10:35   151
10:36   52, 64, 66, 201,
    202
10:37–38   60
10:38   53, 96
10:39   31, 69
10:40   30
10:40–41   152
10:41   43
11   11, 17, 27, 43, 73,
    75, 80, 83, 97, 111,
    136, 138, 143, 182,
    192, 203
11–12   27, 36, 40, 81,
    107, 161, 166
11–12:8   34
11:1   30, 44
11:1–3   147
11:1–44   40
11:1–46   28, 62
11:1–12:50   22
11:1–17:26   22
11:2   80, 81, 110, 141
11:2–3   80
11:3   80, 182, 186
11:4   66, 105, 138
11:5   80, 182, 183, 186,
    187
11:7   27, 75, 147
11:8   58, 72
11:9–10   138, 153
11:11   80, 127, 147